"If you've ever wanted to go to Israel—or want to go again—*Rediscovering Israel* will transport you there. Seeing Israel through Middle Eastern eyes, through the cultural lens of Jesus' world and His life, is absolutely transformative. I traveled to Israel with Kristi in 2019, and traveled again with her while reading this book. The pictures, descriptions, and details place you right there in the Land. People say that, after a pilgrimage to Israel, you never read the Bible in the same way again, and they're right. But reading this book did that for me too. It brought the Living Word of God even more alive, and I'm forever grateful."

—**Tamera Alexander**, *USA Today* bestselling author of *A Million Little Choices*

"My wife and I have had the privilege and honor of walking with Kristi McLelland for years. Since the beginning, we have been moved by her teaching and ability to break down God's Word so that we can begin to grasp and understand the depth of God's truth and love. A few years ago, we took the opportunity to go to Israel with Kristi, and we were truly stirred by how God used Kristi and the land of Israel to bring us into a deeper walk with Jesus. Kristi is a sincere servant of God who seeks to encourage believers in their pursuit of Christ. Gratefully, the teaching we received freely from Kristi is available to us all in written form. What a treasure."

—**TobyMac**, contemporary Christian artist

"Kristi McLelland has an exceptional ability to make sense of the Scriptures from a Middle Eastern perspective. *Rediscovering Israel* is a user-friendly gem, tracing God's redemptive plan, within the Land, from start to finish, never overlooking the primary plot of the story when she says, '…so that the world will bear witness to Him [Jesus].' This is why our students crave Kristi's teaching. I predict you will as well."

—**Edward M. Smith**, president, Williamson College, Franklin, TN

"I have been waiting for a book from Kristi McLelland since the day I first heard her speak. This has surpassed anything I hoped for. Kristi's ability to serve a complex meal in bite-sized morsels invites you into a most beautiful feast. From Genesis to Revelation, this book shows us Jesus in a way that can only leave us loving Him more."

—**Melinda Doolittle**, recording artist

"This book provides priceless insights that will enhance, broaden, and deepen your appreciation of the Bible. Having traveled to the Holy Land on a team led by Kristi, I can confidently say that *Rediscovering Israel* is as close to that experience as I could have hoped for."

—**Curtis Zackery**, pastor, author of *Soul Rest*

"Are you ready to have your mind explode and your heart expand at the same time? Beyond *education*, in reading *Rediscovering Israel* you will have an *encounter*. I cannot herald enough Kristi McLelland's deep, contagious passion for the Scriptures and her rich Middle Eastern lens into the treasure of God's Word from beginning to end. She has unearthed and strung together a gorgeous antique necklace of appetizing pearls (to use her metaphor) for us to feast upon. Weaving stories and history alongside archaeology, Kristi disciples us from anthropocentrism to Theocentrism: the world, the Plan, does not revolve around *me*, but around *God*. *Rediscovering Israel* will not leave you a *spectator*. It will *stretch* you to leave your preconceived intellectual borders, and it will *shift* you. 'Jesus came to save us from our sins in order to send us into the world.' A wholesome education through a Hebraic prism, yes; and even greater, a refreshing encounter with the Living God."

—**Ken Alpren**, Sr. Rabbi, founder of Kol Dodi, Nashville, TN

"A few years ago, I was fortunate to go on a trip to Israel with Kristi McLelland. Right off the bat, I was blown away by her ability to teach and clarify the Scriptures. They came to life in a way that resonated deep within my soul, which only the Word of God can do. Kristi has a way of breaking down historical and cultural barriers of context to help us discover the deeper meanings of Bible texts."

—**Michael Tait**, lead singer of Newsboys

"From Kristi's teaching, I have learned so much about the world in which Jesus walked. Having lived my whole life in America, I read the Bible through a Western worldview. But when I was introduced to Kristi's teaching, I began understanding the Word of God with a new lens. I can't think of anyone better from whom to learn about Israel."

—**Mandisa Lundley**, recording artist

REDISCOVERING
ISRAEL

KRISTI McLELLAND

HARVEST HOUSE PUBLISHERS
EUGENE, OREGON

Cover design by Faceout Studio, Molly von Borstel
Cover image © by vvvita / Shutterstock
Interior design by Aesthetic Soup

For bulk, special sales, or ministry purchases, please call 1-800-547-8979.
Email: Customerservice@hhpbooks.com

This logo is a federally registered trademark of the Hawkins Children's LLC. Harvest House Publishers, Inc., is the exclusive licensee of this trademark.

Rediscovering Israel
Copyright © 2023 by Kristi McLelland
Published by Harvest House Publishers
Eugene, Oregon 97408
www.harvesthousepublishers.com

ISBN 978-0-7369-8770-7 (Hardcover)
ISBN 978-0-7369-8771-4 (eBook)

Library of Congress Control Number: 2023934124

Printed in Colombia

23 24 25 26 27 28 29 30 31 /NI/ 10 9 8 7 6 5 4 3

To my parents James and Carolyn McLelland
for instilling within me a deep love
for the Word and for the Land.
Though neither of you ever made it to Israel,
a McLelland can surely be found in the Land.
My love to you both.

ACKNOWLEDGMENTS

Taking adventures is an important part of living life, and the best adventures are the ones that find us—as *Rediscovering Israel* found me.

The best adventures are also those taken in community—in the fellowship of journeying together. It has been so meaningful to partner in this work with two people who love the Text in context as much as I do and who, too, have spent extensive time in the land of Israel. I am deeply grateful to Rebekah Joy for crafting years of my lectures, teachings, and experiences into an engaging and compelling narrative form that is the book you are now holding. This work has also been greatly enhanced and refined through Geoff Carroll's invaluable perspective and scholarly research.

The pictures in *Rediscovering Israel* are a combination of my and Rebekah Joy's experiences in the lands of the Bible, as well as the work of Killian Rose, a gifted photographer who beautifully captured locations in Israel. A picture is indeed worth a thousand words.

Thank you to Kathleen Kerr for opening this door and extending the initial invitation…as well as for loving The Chronicles of Narnia as much as I do!

I am appreciative of the Harvest House family who has so warmly received me. Bob Hawkins, thank you for your leadership at Harvest House and for welcoming me to the table. Steve Miller, it has been an honor to work alongside you. Your expertise as senior editor coupled with your patience and kindness have been such a gift. Thanks to Sherrie Slopianka and Lindsay Lewis for paving the way for this book to be launched into the world. Special gratitude goes to Brad Moses, Kim Moore, Becky Miller, and Beth Hawkins for the roles each of you has had in bringing this work to life.

Finally, I am grateful beyond words for every person who has gone to Israel with me over the last fifteen years. Experiencing pilgrimage together will travel inside us for the rest of our lives. We can never unsee what we have seen. Thank you for praying this book into existence and for me in this process. I hope *Rediscovering Israel* inspires you to remember and relive your pilgrimage journey again and again.

CONTENTS

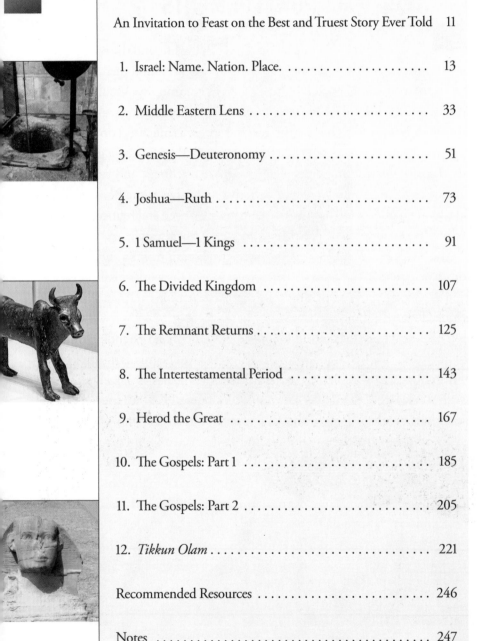

Kristi on a camel
her first time in
Egypt, with the Giza
pyramids in background

Kristi's first time praying at the Western Wall in Jerusalem

AN INVITATION TO FEAST ON THE BEST AND TRUEST STORY EVER TOLD

Hello, friend!

Life has a way of bringing opportunities for adventure; the best adventures are the ones that find us. An adventure found me in 2007 when a door opened for me to go study the Bible in Egypt and Israel. Little did I know that this adventure would change my life forever...that it would change *me* forever. I went to Israel and discovered that God is *better* than I ever knew.

Learning the biblical story in its original cultural context introduced me to an entirely different way of seeing, processing, and interpreting the Bible.

Kristi's first boat ride on the Sea of Galilee

Teaching at a sheepfold

In the copper mines at Timna Park in the southern wilderness of modern Israel

It's something I call the "Middle Eastern lens." For Westerners, taking off our Western cultural lens and putting on a Middle Eastern lens *adds* greatly to our understanding of what the biblical authors and characters—Middle Easterners living in a Middle Eastern cultural framework—meant by what they said and did. In the words of author, professor, and New Testament scholar

Looking out from Maktesh Ramon in the Wilderness of Paran

Gary M. Burge, "We have forgotten that we read the Bible as foreigners, as visitors who have traveled not only to a new geography, but to a new century. We are literary tourists who are deeply in need of a guide."[1]

I have the privilege of teaching the Bible in its historical, cultural, linguistic, and geographic context. It is my honor to serve you in this way through the following pages. I pray the living God will meet you at this biblical table and feed you to the full. We are not orphans, and we are not fatherless. We do not have to scrounge through the Word of God to feed ourselves. We are sons and daughters with a good Father. We are invited to pull up our chairs to this biblical table and posture ourselves to receive the feast the Lord has prepared for each of us.

The Bible is not only the best Story that's ever been written, it is also the truest! Every story within the Bible is like a pearl. What's more beautiful than a single pearl is a *string* of pearls. As we journey through the Bible from Genesis to Revelation, we will do so through the Middle Eastern lens of Scripture, stringing together the pearls of this timeless, transformational Story!

All the best,
Kristi McLelland

Chapter 1

ISRAEL: NAME. NATION. PLACE.

A s we begin our journey through the biblical narrative, let's do so with the understanding that the first step in studying the Bible is not reading; the first step is prayer. Similar to how we pray before we eat food at our dinner tables, we want to pray before we eat the Word of God. The Jewish people primarily pray *after* they eat their meal, not before it.[1] When they say the blessing, they are not blessing the food; there is no such thing as a holy hot dog or sanctified salami![2] Rather, they pray and *bless God* for providing the food. In that same spirit and posture, we want to bless God for providing the written Word for us. For giving us the Story of the Bible and inviting us to locate ourselves in it.

Two thousand years ago, Jesus gave the New Testament church what has become known as the Lord's Prayer, which has been a unifying agent for the Christian church, whether Catholic or Protestant. There is a Jewish prayer that is more than 1,000 years older than the Lord's Prayer. This Jewish prayer goes all the way back to Deuteronomy 6 and is called the Shema. *Shema* is the Hebrew word for "you hear." The Shema is a prayer of unification for the Jewish people. Then and now, Jews learn the Shema and pray this prayer at fixed times during the day. This is the first prayer Jesus would have learned growing up as a child; He would have recited it daily throughout His life. In

English, the Shema says, "Hear, O Israel: The LORD our God, the LORD is one. Love the LORD your God with all your heart and with all your soul and with all your strength" (Deuteronomy 6:4-5).

The Jewish people believe that anytime we do the smallest thing to love God or love our neighbor, we cause the kingdom of God to come down to the ground. It is this prayer that reminds them of that. As you read the Shema in Hebrew, imagine Jesus walking down a road 2,000 years ago praying this with His disciples: *Sh'ma Yisra'el Adonai Eloheinu Adonai echad. V'ahav'ta et Adonai Elohekha b'khol l'vav'kha, uv'khol naf'sh'kha, uv'khol m'odekha* (*D'varim* 6:4-5).

Jesus would recognize this in His language! We want to be a people who hear from the Lord, who lean in to who He is and what He is like. We want to be participants, not just spectators.

Receiving the Word of God

Pondering how we approach the Word of God, or our posture toward Scripture, is vital at the outset of our journey. This includes understanding distinctives between the West and the Middle East,[3] which we will explore in depth in the next chapter. Every culture has nuances and values that set it apart from others. For example, in the West, we are more Greco-Roman than Hebraic. As a culture, we tend to be more like Aristotle, Socrates, and Plato than Jesus, Peter, or Paul in that we are more philosophical: Faith is what we *think* rather than what we *do*. Faith is a set of beliefs we cognitively know, more than a lifestyle we walk out—as it is for the Jews.

Let's look at our posture through the lens of Psalm 19, a psalm about the Word of God:

> The law of the LORD is perfect,
>   refreshing the soul.
> The statutes of the LORD are trustworthy,
>   making wise the *simple*.
> The precepts of the LORD are right,
>   giving joy to the heart.

> The commands of the LORD are radiant,
>> giving light to the eyes…
> They are more precious than gold,
>> than much pure gold;
> they are sweeter than honey,
>> than honey from the honeycomb.[4]

Notice the word "simple." Oftentimes we as Westerners define terms differently than the biblical world defined them. Don't you want to know how God defines a word? I sure do! I also want to understand the meaning the biblical authors intended to convey in the words they wrote under the inspiration of the Spirit.

The word "simple" is a great example because in Western culture, someone who is simple is childish or not very smart. This same word sometimes carries a different meaning in the Hebrew, where "simple" can also mean "being open." As it relates to our posture toward Scripture, to be simple is to be open or receptive when we come to the Word of God.[5]

Psalm 19 describes the Scriptures as being sweeter than honey from the comb.[6] The Jewish people are visual, and they take God at His Word. When they read the Scriptures, they don't passively philosophize about them; rather, they set out to do what they read. For instance, in Jewish preschools where Torah—the first five books of the Hebrew Bible or Christian Old Testament—is being taught to children, rabbis come to visit and, upon reading in Psalm 19 that the Scriptures are sweeter than honey, they pass around a small vat of honey, inviting the children to dip their pinkie finger into it and taste it. Then the rabbis will tell the children, "This is what the Word of God tastes like. You take it in, and it is good for you. You let it do its work."[7]

Jewish people don't so much view it as *reading* the Word of God; rather, they view it as *eating* the Word of God. They consume it.[8] They let it do what it wants to do. The weekly Bible reading for Jewish people is called a *parashah*—translated as "portion" in English. Each day, Jews eat their *parashah*, their portion of the Word of God, by taking it in and allowing it to do whatever is necessary inside of them. This posture is fundamentally different than approaching the Scriptures with a mindset that says we must dig something out to feed ourselves. That's the posture of an orphan, the fatherless, the one who has to contend for self.[9] When we come to the Scriptures as sons and daughters, we recognize that God is inviting us to come ready to receive, to be fed.

I believe the best meals we can eat are the ones we don't have to cook! The Bible is a meal—a table of fellowship—prepared for us. We come postured to receive, to hear from the Lord, to *shema*, to take in everything God wants to say and then act upon it. There is a difference between leaning inward and going down compared to looking up and out. The latter keeps us buoyant, giving us vision and a gaze set upon the Lord. After all, if we stare at ourselves long enough, we'll get depressed!

The Bible was given for us to first eat communally, and to then let that inform us individually. We are hungry for the Word of God. We reject the scarcity mentality of an orphan. We posture ourselves to receive. We lean back. We look up. We open our mouths and our hearts wide to the living God. We want to be simple in the way Psalm 19:7 defines it: *open*. We want the cares of the world to fall away so we can be all in as we eat the Word. We want God to say and do as He desires.

A Journey of Discovery

Western and Middle Eastern educational systems and learning methods differ in many respects. Again, Westerners are more Greco-Roman than Hebraic. Western students tend to rely on a set of notes from their instructors, thus allowing them to have advanced ideas as to where lectures are headed. In comparison, rabbis teach through discovery. They take their *talmidim*, Hebrew for disciples, on a journey by opening the Text in such a way that its meanings become self-evident and settle into the heart.

We want to be a people on a journey of discovery rather than seeking only to acquire more knowledge. We want to receive revelation that comes from the Lord and is powerful enough to transform our lives from the inside out.

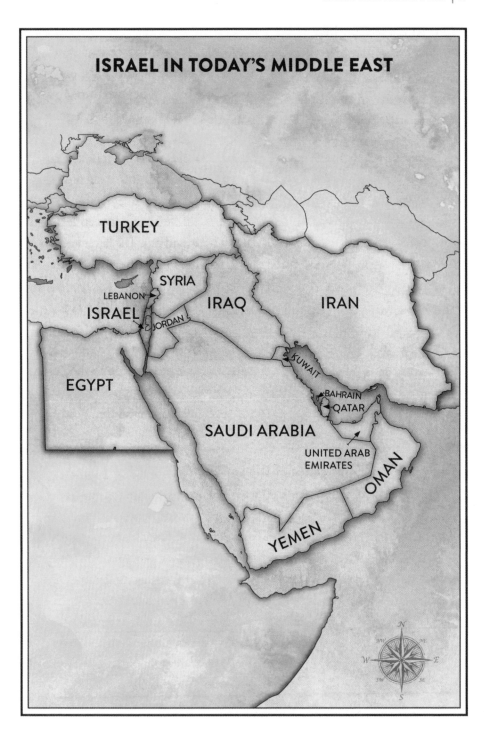

Questions to Consider

Perhaps the most important phase in building a house is that of constructing a solid foundation.[10] As we set out on our journey through the metanarrative of the Bible, we will do so by answering a couple of key questions to anchor us and provide points of orientation and understanding.

Our first question: *Why that land?* When we think of Israel, when we consider the relatively small area known as the Holy Land, within the greater context of the entire globe, why did God choose for Jesus to be born in this piece of real estate? Why wasn't He born in the Far East? Why was wasn't He born in the Western Hemisphere? Why wasn't He born in some region of South America?

The modern State of Israel is quite small in comparison to her neighbors. When we locate this strip of land on a map both in ancient times and presently, we see that she is surrounded by other countries. Why did God see to it for Jesus to be born here? *Why that land?*

Our second foundational question is this: *Why that name?* Where does *Israel* come from? What does it mean? What are its implications? And how does it grow and mature throughout the Story of the Bible?

As we lay this foundation, we are going to discover the *geographical* and *spiritual* significance of the land in antiquity.

Geographical Significance of the Land

In Genesis 12, the Bible introduces us to a man known as Abram or Abraham in the West. In the Middle East, he is called Avram or Avraham, as *v* and *b* are the same letter in the Hebrew language.

To help us begin to recognize the geographical importance of the land in the days of the Bible, let's look at Genesis 12:1-3:

> The Lord had said to Abram, "Go from your country, your people and your father's household to the land I will show you. I will make you into a great nation, and I will bless you; I will make your name great, and you will be a blessing. I will bless those who bless you, and whoever curses you I will curse; and all peoples on earth will be blessed through you."

Avram comes from a place called Ur of the Chaldeans. We will see throughout Scripture that geographic locations—*where* events happen—are key to understanding the Text. *Where* an incident occurs is just as important as *what happens* in the story line. With that in mind, we need to answer this question: Why does God move Avram from Ur of the Chaldeans to the land of Canaan?

If you are a Middle Easterner hearing this story, bells and whistles are going off because, in antiquity, your family—your clan, your tribe—is everything.[11] You never move away from them. You are born in a village. You grow up in that village. You eventually marry the boy or girl two tents down. Your families join. You have as many kids as you can because your kids are your social security. They farm your land and herd your livestock. You continue to join families within the village. Moving away is not a consideration.

Already in the biblical story, just twelve chapters in, God is revealing Himself to be a living God who does things in very unusual ways. He's writing a story that is quite different from what Avram knew. Which brings us back to our question. If moving away from one's family and tribe is so abnormal, why does God move Avram out of Ur of the Chaldeans and into the land of Canaan? Remember, we are discovering the *geographical* significance of the land.

In Avram's day, there was an important public road—referred to by today's scholars as the International Trunk Road or International Coastal Highway—that passed directly through the land of Canaan. God moves Avram from Ur of the Chaldeans to Canaan because He is placing him in the mix of humanity in this multicultural part of the world. Canaan serves as a land bridge connecting three different continents: Africa to the south, Europe to the northwest, and Asia to the east. The nations bring their commerce and trade through the International Coastal Highway. This provides insight as to why there were so many wars in this region in antiquity. It was not so much about control of the land; rather, whoever controlled the International Coastal Highway controlled worldwide trade. The Egyptians, Assyrians, Babylonians, Persians, Greeks, and Romans were constantly fighting for this region; they wanted the highway.

This context helps us understand some biblical dynamics. Israel is a nation that starts out as a theocracy. *Theos* is Greek for "God." God is Israel's king, until the Israelites come to the prophet Samuel expressing their desire for a human king, like all the other nations around them.[12] Saul becomes the first monarch or king of Israel. David is the second; Solomon is the third.

Solomon achieves extraordinary wealth by controlling the International Coastal Highway. According to 1 Kings 9:15, Solomon built up three cities—Hazor, Megiddo, and Gezer—which served as tax stations along this trade route. Solomon could then implement shrewd taxation tactics. For example, if the Africans came through with 5,000 sheep, Solomon could allow them to pass via the highway, but they had to pay the tax—leaving 200 sheep with the king. When the Europeans brought their textiles and fabrics, Solomon allowed them to use the route as well, but required they leave twenty pounds of fabric as a tax. The same would have been true for the Asians coming through with their products; passage was permitted if they paid the tax.

Throughout the New Testament period, the Roman Empire is in power and has control of the International Coastal Highway. We see, for instance, Romans residing in an Israelite city called Capernaum, located along this key roadway. Matthew 8:5-13 details Jesus' interaction with a Roman centurion in this city.

We are beginning to recognize a significant factor in understanding the Bible through a Middle Eastern lens. Oftentimes as Westerners, we are taught to read the Bible and ask, "What does it teach me about *me*?" We seek understanding and look for application. The Middle Eastern way is first and foremost to read the Bible and ask, "What does this teach me about *God*?" It is a completely different approach to the Scriptures. When reading the Bible with Middle Eastern eyes, we want to look for what each story shows us about who God is, what He is like, and what it means to know Him and walk with Him.

Perhaps you've heard it said that the number one rule in real estate is location, location, location. Throughout the biblical narrative, *where* something occurs is never happenstance. Location matters. Setting provides clues to the overall story. We learn much about God's heart through His decision to move Avram out of Ur of the Chaldeans and into Canaan, positioning him right alongside the International Coastal Highway.

Spiritual Significance of the Land

Now that we better understand the geographical significance of the land, we're going to discover the *spiritual* implications of the land in Avram's day. An important cultural consideration is that names in the Middle East carry weight.[13] Names indicate destiny—what a person is going to do, be, or embody. This is true about Avram, which means "exalted father." *Av* means "father" and *ram* means "exalted/held high." In Genesis 17, God changes Avram's name to Avraham or Abraham, meaning "father of many." Over time, Avraham's name becomes a reality.

I heard a statement years ago in Israel that burned into my soul. It goes like this: "God meets His people exactly where they are; He never leaves them there." So many of the biblical stories are about God coming and finding us, not about us having to go find God.[14] Our role is to allow ourselves to be found and brought home by the living God. God comes to Avram and moves him out of all that is familiar, miles and miles away to a place called Canaan. God positions Avram along the land of the International Coastal Highway, and the question becomes, *Why?* What are we learning about the heart of God in this move in Genesis 12?

Our answer lies in Acts 17:24-27, some of the most poetic language in the New Testament and part of Paul's famous sermon on Mars Hill in Athens:

> The God who made the world and everything in it is the Lord of heaven and earth and does not live in temples built by human hands. And he is not served by human hands, as if he needed anything. Rather, he himself gives everyone life and breath and everything else. From one man he made all the nations, that they should inhabit the whole earth; and he marked out their appointed times in history and the boundaries of their lands. God did this so that they would seek him and perhaps reach out for him and find him, though he is not far from any one of us.

Paul's Areopagus/Mars Hill sermon at the Acropolis of Athens

I love when the Bible provides information and then tells us why it is doing so! Through this portion of Scripture, we discover that God has predetermined the exact times and places we will inhabit the earth. We are meant to live where we live and to know the people we know. Why? So that mankind might seek and find Him, though He is not far from us.

God moves Avram out of Ur into the land of Canaan. What is the *spiritual* significance of him being positioned next to the International Coastal Highway? While Abraham is known as the father of Judaism, Christianity, and Islam, he is also known as the first missionary. In the New Testament, missions involves being sent out, *going to* a place. I love to travel; I am built for it! Years ago, I worked for an organization in which my job was to take teams on international missions trips. As New Testament Christians, when we think of missions, we typically think of *going*. The Latin word *missio* means "sent/mission." The Greek term is *apostolos* and the Hebrew *shalach*. All of these mean "sent/sent ones."

We want to hang on to that while also understanding how missions works with Avram in the Old Testament. Rather than sending Avram to the nations, God positions Avram—a monotheist, or follower of one God—along the International Coastal Highway. Then He sends the nations to Avram. This is missions in reverse. Avram stays, and he and his descendants fill the land of Canaan. These descendants go on to demonstrate to the world what it looks like to be a tribe committed to justice and righteousness.[15] They leave the corners of their fields unharvested so the poor and the stranger, the fatherless and the widow can find something to eat.[16] They welcome the alien, the foreigner among them, because they remember what it was like being slaves in Egypt.[17] They are meant to inhabit the land and display the kingdom of God ethic to the nations as they pass through the International Coastal Highway for commerce. Foreign nations are bearing witness to a holy people living under the rule and reign of a holy God. They demonstrate to the world what it is to know and walk with the living God.

Avram is called to inhabit space in proximity to the International Coastal Highway. He goes about his everyday life, routines, and responsibilities. As the Africans, Europeans, and Asians come through, they trade their goods while also hearing about the God of the Israelites. These polytheistic cultures are being exposed to the monotheistic idea that there is one God, not many. That's not a bad road trip, is it? Making some money and going home with a revelation of the living God. This is missions in reverse: Instead of God sending people to the nations, God sends the nations to a people.

We need to continue traveling and serving international communities, offering support in ways they deem to be most beneficial. But understand this: The Bible is contending from the book of Genesis that God moves Avram out of Ur and positions him close to the International Coastal Highway because God's heart has been missional from the beginning. And He's not just coming for some; He's coming for all. He wants all to know Him—through Avram, through his descendants, through the twelve tribes of Israel. God was and is reaching for the entire world.[18]

What Is Your Space?

Several years ago, a man from England moved into the house next to me. I wanted to be a good neighbor, so the day he was moving in, I went over and introduced myself. Here in the West, when we meet someone new, we tend to ask two questions: "What is your name?" And, "What do you do?" We often define each other by the latter. In the Middle East, when you strike up a conversation with a stranger, they don't ask what you do until well into the conversation. They want to know your name and your family—who you are of, your tribe and people.

I introduced myself to my new neighbor, and of course he asked the two questions: "What is your name? What do you do?" At the time, I was on staff at a church and teaching Bible at a Christian college. To this day, I cannot be a covert Christian because my vocations are indicative of my faith! When I answered him, his response was visceral, as though I had told him I had leprosy. He was clearly not okay with my choice of professions.

I found out he was a self-professed atheist, had never been to church, and had a lot of opinions about Christians, God, and the Bible. We started living life as neighbors, and when you're that close to a person, though you cannot know their story unless they tell you, you can observe patterns. I could see his striving and straining as he embraced a lifestyle of trying to find *shalom*—peace, wholeness, flourishing, and harmony—outside of God. Every once in a while we would talk, though he didn't have a lot to say to me.

One night, he pulled in as I was sitting on my front patio. I will never forget his slumped posture as he got out of his car—he looked like the weight of the world was on his shoulders. He saw me outside and—much to my surprise—came over and sat beside me. I looked at him and kindly asked, "Is it working for you? Are you about done? You look tired." We sat there for the next hour as he told me his story, pouring out everything that was going on in his life. Nothing appeared to happen as we talked, but I knew he was listening. That encounter occurred years ago, but I'll never forget it. He moved away about three months afterward, and I've not seen him since. I have no idea what his life is like or if he has come to faith in Jesus. But I do know that he heard—and I didn't have to get on a plane and go to England. God brought England to me.

Sometime after that a family from India moved in across the street. One day I saw the father walk to their mailbox, so I suddenly felt the need to walk to my mailbox! I headed out to meet him. Sure enough, he asked me the two questions. I told him my name, and that I was on staff at a church and taught Bible at a Bible college. He replied to the latter by exclaiming, "Oh, you're a monotheist!" I said, "Yes, I'm a Christian, a follower of Jesus! I am monotheistic in my faith and in my frame."

He told me his family was from India. I asked if they were Hindu or Muslim, and he said they were practicing Hindus. "So, you're polytheistic in your frame," I acknowledged. He emphatically agreed: "That's right! My whole family, we practice Hinduism." Now I'm a little crazy sometimes, but he was friendly, and I felt like I could get away with this. "May I ask you a question?" I inquired, just to be safe. "Sure," he replied. So, I went for it: "Do you get tired of keeping up with all of your gods?" I was thinking about the numerous gods in the Hindu Pantheon! My new neighbor didn't miss a beat. He looked right back at me and said, "Isn't it boring having just one?"

That fired me up! He could give it and take it, which intrigued me even more. I told him we needed to have dinner so we could talk further, which we did soon after. He and his wife invited me over and shared a lot about Hinduism. I love to learn; after all, a teacher is fundamentally a learner. I took notes as they talked. When I spoke, I didn't discuss church history or the Nicene Creed. I didn't talk about denominations or the difference between a Baptist and a Pentecostal. I shared with them about the person of Jesus, because we don't just follow a creed, we follow a man! He is the heart and essence of our faith. A few years later, that family moved away. I didn't have to get on a plane and go to India; God brought India to me.

The space I inhabit is my life. It's my daily interactions. It's the grocery store I frequent. God gave Avram specific space—his everyday life, lived along the International Coastal Highway. How about you? What is *your* space?

As the world watches us, as they witness the way we live our everyday lives, it should raise a curiosity in them about who the living God is and what He is like. One of my favorite seminary professors used to say, "Curiosity may kill the cat, but it leads men to Christ!"

Hovering. Down. Toward. In.

God is reaching for the nations, and we see it so beautifully as we track the Story of the Bible. From the very beginning, God has been systematically coming closer and closer. He has been moving toward us. In Genesis 1, the Spirit of God hovers over the waters.[19] Next, God comes down and lives among His people in the desert; God had His own tent, called the Tabernacle.[20] Then, at the beginning of the New Testament, God moves toward us and takes on flesh; God incarnate lives among us.[21] At Pentecost, when the church is birthed, the Holy Spirit comes and dwells within us.[22] Notice the movement as God has been coming closer and closer: Hovering. Down. Toward. In.

The Bible doesn't say that we have to go find God. From beginning to end, the biblical narrative communicates that God is coming for us! The question is, Will we allow ourselves to be found and brought home? When we love someone who is struggling, we often pray desperate prayers like, "Lord, help them see the light! Please, let them come home! Help them know the truth!" I encourage us all to set aside those prayers. Rather than praying that they will come home, let's ask God to *go get them*! My mentor of twenty-five years often said, "It's a maybe prayer when you pray for someone to come home, because maybe they will and maybe they won't. But a prayer you can pray all day every day, that you can rest assured God will answer, is a prayer for God to go get the lost!"

This shifts us from offering prayers of desperation to prayers anchored in expectancy. God is a God who comes and gets us when we are lost. That is who He is! God meets His people exactly where they are, but He refuses to leave them there. God brings us home. God is coming for everybody! Not just for the Jew, but for the Gentile as well. He has been missional since the beginning of the Story. I hope it comforts you to know that the living God is pursuing you!

Why That Name?

The next question we're going to answer is, Why that name? Throughout Scripture, the term *Israel* travels. Initially, *Israel* is a name. Then, *Israel* is a nation. Finally, *Israel* becomes a place. Where is Israel first mentioned in the narrative of the Bible? As we discover the answer to this question, let's remember that we are looking for the heart of God—that's the Bible with a Middle Eastern lens.

When you introduce yourself to someone, you give them your name. As previously mentioned, in the Middle East, your name is your destiny, what you will embody. Jewish parents typically wait eight days after their son is born to name him.[23] They need to spend some time with their baby boy to discern his name. On the eighth day—the day the boy is to be circumcised— they have a naming ceremony with family and friends. If they are conservative, a rabbi usually comes and, along with the father, holds up the baby and declares his name. Everyone gets excited and they celebrate by eating a lot of food and sweets! I've had the chance to experience one of these ceremonies in Israel. Bestowing a name casts vision and sets direction; it offers clues as to who a person is and what he is going to be like.

God is referred to by many names throughout the Bible. What is interesting are the moments when God names Himself, as portrayed in Exodus 3. Moses, having fled from Egypt to Midian years prior, is on the far side of the wilderness tending his father-in-law's flock. Scripture does not indicate that Moses knows the living God at this point. It is striking that Moses is not out in the desert looking for God; rather, God is out in the desert looking for Moses. Moses reaches Horeb, the mountain of God, and notices a bush that is on fire, but not burning up. When he moves toward the bush to take a closer look, the living God calls out to him and introduces Himself: "I am the God of your father, the God of Abraham, the God of Isaac and the God of Jacob."[24] This phrase occurs more than once in the Bible.[25] Because names are so significant in the Middle East, we should be curious about the meanings of these names.

Avraham means "father of many"—he had a good name.[26] *Isaac* means "laughter" or "one who laughs"—another good name![27] Jacob means "follower, heel snatcher"—an idiom for supplanter or deceiver.[28] In Hebrew, his name is *Ya'akov*, as the *J* and the *Y* are the same letter. We say Jesus, Hebrews say *Yeshua*. Ya'akov is *not* a good name.

Remember, a name is symbolic of one's destiny. How did Ya'akov get his name? What did he do at birth? Ya'akov was a twin. As his older brother Esau was being delivered, Ya'akov grabbed Esau's heel. He was greedy from birth. He wanted to be first. This is how Genesis introduces him. As his parents waited eight days to name him, they may have been saying, "He's a heel snatcher; he wants to be first."

Years later, when Isaac is aging and going blind, Ya'akov one day disguises himself to be Esau. Remember, Ya'akov's name also means "deceiver." When Ya'akov approaches his father, Isaac asks, "Who is it?" or "Who are you?"— ways of asking, "What is your name?" Ya'akov replies: "I am Esau, your first-born." He tricks his father into giving him his older brother's birthright.[29] Ya'akov is living up to his name as a deceiver, heel snatcher, and supplanter.

With that context in mind, let's return to Exodus 3. The living God pursues Moses in the desert and can introduce Himself to Moses using any name He desires. It is critical for us to perceive this the way Moses would have. God knows that for Moses' culture, names are weighty. God meets Moses in his framework and introduces Himself in this way: "Moses, I am the God of your fathers! I am the God of the *father of many.* I am the God of the *one who laughs.* And I am also the God of the *deceiver*—the swindler, the heel snatcher, the supplanter. I am coming for everyone."

We are prone to watch our affiliations closely. If you or I were introducing ourselves to Moses, we would likely say, "I am the God of Abraham and Isaac," while omitting Ya'akov. We would not want to be associated with that name. Yet God is unafraid to affiliate His name with Ya'akov because He knows He can change Ya'akov's name. The first books of the Bible teach us that God is a name changer. This is key, because if your name is your destiny, when God changes your name, He is changing your destiny!

The questions then become, Will Ya'akov always be Ya'akov? Will he always be the deceiver? Is the script already written for him? Does he have hope of a better name, of a better life?

From Ya'akov to Israel

As we journey together, we will discover that biblical stories are like pearls. What's more beautiful than an individual pearl is a strand of pearls strung together into a necklace. As we close out this first chapter, we are going to string some biblical pearls together, like a thread woven through a tapestry. Sometimes we view these stories as isolated and disconnected from one another, but we're about to see how they are linked.

Let's take another look at Ya'akov—this time in Genesis 32. Ya'akov wrestles with a man through the night. The man recognizes he cannot overpower Ya'akov, so he touches the socket of Ya'akov's hip in such a way that Ya'akov walks with a limp from then on. The man tells Ya'akov to let him go, but Ya'akov replies, "I will not let you go unless you bless me."[30]

The last time Ya'akov was seeking out a blessing, it was from his father, Isaac.[31] To get that blessing, Ya'akov lied about his name, claiming to be Esau. He used deception to take his older brother's birthright. Genesis 32 is Ya'akov's redo. The same scenario resurfaces for him as Ya'akov is once again in a moment where he is asking to be blessed. This helps us to better understand why the man asks Ya'akov, "What is your name?" The last time

Ya'akov requested a blessing and was asked to identify himself, he lied! This is Ya'akov's do-over, and this time, he answers with the truth.

We tend to read right over that. But if your name is your destiny, when Ya'akov tells the truth, he is, in essence, saying, "I'm a deceiver. I'm a heel snatcher. I'm a supplanter—that is who and what I am." Through a Middle Eastern ear, this sounds like a confession. Jacob is telling the truth about who he is.

If you ever need to know how God will deal with you in a moment, take note of what is happening here. Ya'akov has just told the truth. God is not afraid to affiliate with him because He knows He can change Ya'akov's name and give him a much better one. This interaction is where the biblical story introduces us to the word *Israel*, which began as the new name given to Ya'akov. The man Ya'akov has been wrestling with declares, "Your name will no longer be Ya'akov, but Israel." The literal meaning of *Israel* is "one who struggles with God." The deceiver becomes the overcomer in this moment. God takes Ya'akov's name and gives him a better one; transformation is underway.

There are only seven times in the entire Bible when God calls a person's name twice.[32] Each time, He is about to radically change their life. One of these occasions happens in Exodus 3, when God calls out, "Moses, Moses!" I want God to call my name twice. Whatever your name is, whatever the truth is about who you are, whatever is going on in your life, God is not afraid to affiliate with you...to join His name with yours. He has the power to change your life. God always meets His people where they are; He absolutely refuses to leave them there. He meets Ya'akov right where he is; He refuses to leave him there. Ya'akov becomes Israel; the deceiver becomes the overcomer. He goes on to have twelve sons, known as the twelve tribes of Israel. Eventually, Israel becomes a place. Geography takes on the name of its inhabitants when the Israelites take over the land.

Jacob's Well is located in modern-day Nablus, a city known as Shechem or Sychar in biblical days. In the New Testament,[33] Jesus has a conversation with a Samaritan woman at this well named after a patriarch from the days of

Jacob's Well near the ancient city of Shechem (modern-day Nablus)

Genesis. Jacob's Well is very deep and has never run dry. The Bible is not only the best Story that has ever been written, but also the truest. These things happened!

God Comes Close

The living God has been missional from the very beginning. He meets us where we are, while refusing to leave us there. The Story of the Bible is God coming closer and closer to us. Hovering, down, toward, and in! The question is, Will we allow ourselves to be found by Him?

Before moving on, take a few minutes to consider this: What is your space? How has God planted and positioned you with where you live, with who you know, and with what you do?

In the next chapter, we are going to learn how to take off our Western lens and put on our Middle Eastern lens so we can approach the biblical text on its terms. If you've ever read the Bible and wondered what in the world it was talking about, there was likely some cultural nuance in motion.

God is better than we know; He is not afraid to affiliate with us. God is a name-changer; He changes our essence, our nature, who and what we are. Because of who God is, the redemption, restoration, and renewal of all things is underway. This is good news!

Chapter 2

MIDDLE EASTERN LENS

As we continue to journey through the biblical narrative, we are going to acquire some new glasses. These new frames and lenses will help us better understand what the biblical authors and characters meant by what they said, wrote, and did. As our vision is enhanced, it may feel like the Bible is shifting from black and white to color!

I grew up attending church and was active in church-related activities. A few years after completing my undergraduate degree, I went to seminary. With this as my background, I had ample knowledge of the Bible prior to first studying in Egypt and Israel in late 2007 and early 2008. But by studying Scripture within its cultural context, my understanding was—and continues to be—enhanced and sharpened. As we view Scripture through a new lens, we are not doing away with all we have previously learned. Rather, we are *adding to*—which is an important distinction to keep in mind.

I've been a professor in the Biblical Studies Department at Williamson College since 2004 and have been taking teams to Israel since 2008. I specialize in teaching the Bible in its original historical, cultural, linguistic, and geographic context. This Middle Eastern framework will be our emphasis as we seek to better perceive what is happening throughout the biblical narrative.

The Heart of God

When it comes to reading the Bible, we must first determine what we are looking for with our new frames. I teach a college course called Hermeneutics, which focuses on biblical interpretation. As Westerners, we have been taught certain questions to ask of the Bible when we read it. It shouldn't come as a surprise, then, that we ask different questions of the Text than those who are from a Middle Eastern background. In the West, we have been conditioned to read the Bible and ask, "What does this teach me about me?" Because we want the application, we strive to discover how we should live in light of what we are reading.

When I was on my school basketball team in ninth grade, we would do a form of conditioning known as suicides. As I sprinted up and down the court in practice one day, I got winded—so much so that when I finished, I bent over because I couldn't catch my breath. A senior on the team came over to me, leaned down, and said, "Hey, there's no air down there. Stand up! Open up your diaphragm and breath in. The air is up here, not down there!" From then on, when I would run suicides and feel out of breath, rather than bending and going low, I would lift my head and open myself up so I could take in the air.

Anytime we read the Bible, Old Testament or New, we want to adjust our gaze to be looking for *the heart of God*. The psalmist describes the Lord as being the lifter of our heads.[1] I believe we are ever being invited to experience the Lord lifting our heads as we approach His Word. We don't want to go in and down like I did while gasping for air after running suicides. We want to look up and out. We want to behold the living God, to know who He is and what it is like to walk with Him.

When interacting with the Bible, we are learning to ask several questions: What does this passage teach me about God? Why is God doing this here? Who is He in this text of Scripture?

God is the point of every biblical story! The narrative of Scripture reveals who He is as He interacts with humankind. We are seeking to discover the heart of God. Doing so will drastically change our interaction with the Bible. Instead of reading it and immediately trying to find our application, let us instead choose to look up, gaze at God, and let Him breathe on us.[2] Doesn't that sound like a more life-giving posture as we approach the Scriptures?

A Holistic, Big Picture

Next, our new frames invite us to approach the Bible in a holistic, big-picture fashion. The Bible is one Story, meant to be understood from beginning to end. The rabbis say every biblical story is like a pearl: beautiful and of great price. But what is more beautiful than one pearl? Many pearls strung together to make a necklace.[3] If you've ever looked out an airplane window while flying, you've experienced the enhanced perspective offered by seeing the land and water below while flying above it at 35,000 feet. That is what we are doing as we string the pearls of Scripture together while viewing them from a big-picture perspective. We are discovering how to place each pearl within the greater Story. As we do, we will find all the biblical stories coming together to tell one Story!

Every January, I start a new journal that I keep throughout the year. In December, I set aside several days to go back and read through my entries from that year. This is my attempt to get up above my life, look down at it from 35,000 feet, and remember what God has done. It also helps me approach the new year by tracking what the Lord is already doing and which direction He is taking me. Without fail, every December I am amazed at the things God has done in my life—much of which I've already forgotten!

Do you ever suffer from spiritual amnesia? Where you forget what God did three months ago in your life? There is something about getting up above ourselves that allows God to give us a vision for the entirety of our lives. As we hover above the Scriptures, seeing how the biblical stories are attached and married to one another, we are going to gain a better vision of the whole metanarrative of the Bible and be able to locate ourselves in the Story of Scripture.

Location, Location, Location

In the previous chapter, we mentioned the third factor of our new frame and will expand on it here. It is said that rule number one in real estate is location, location, location! This is similar throughout the biblical narrative: Where events occur is of great significance. When the Bible provides a geographic location, it is giving a cultural indicator. As Westerners, we have not been trained to pay attention to whether something happened in the capital city of Jerusalem, in the northern region of Galilee, in Nazareth where Jesus grew up, or in the Negev, a southern Israeli desert. We haven't been taught to notice sites and settings. But through a Middle Eastern lens, location, location, location is extremely important!

Think about it like this: There are vast differences between Los Angeles, California, and Cleveland, Mississippi. New York City is unique from Abilene, Texas. When you watch a news anchor reporting on something that is happening in Washington, DC, all sorts of cultural assumptions permeate your thoughts because of what you know about Washington, DC. Similarly, if you hear about events going on in rural Alabama, you have various cultural indicators informing you because you know the area.

The Bible is the same way. Location, location, location! Why did Jesus take His disciples all the way to a place called Caesarea Philippi in the northern part of Israel to have the conversation recorded in Matthew 16? It is there that He asks, "Who do people say the Son of Man is?"[4] Why doesn't Jesus have that conversation in Jerusalem? Why does He not have it in the south? Why Caesarea Philippi? Because of the historical and cultural significance of this region known as Gaulonitis.[5]

Throughout His earthly ministry, Jesus often healed people.[6] But when He raised a man named Lazarus from the dead in John 11, the Pharisees responded by plotting to take His life.[7] This was not Jesus' first miracle, nor was it the first time He had raised someone from the dead.[8] The issue wasn't just what Jesus had done, it was *where* he had done it—Bethany, and what that means in the greater Story.[9]

In Mark 11:23, Jesus makes this statement: "Truly I tell you, if anyone says to this mountain, *Go, throw yourself into the sea*, and does not doubt in their heart but believes that what they say will happen, it will be done for them." Jesus isn't making a philosophical statement; He is not Aristotle, Socrates, or Plato. Jewish teaching is visual, so the question becomes, What did "*this* mountain" and "*the* sea" mean in the first-century world? When you understand these two geographical landmarks, you understand what Jesus is saying. I take my biblical studies teams to the region where Jesus took His disciples when He made this statement. As we look out on the Israeli horizon, only one mountain and one sea are visible.

The living God has entered down into the dust and ruin with us! I don't know about you, but I don't need a philosophical Jesus. I need a real Jesus who enters in with me. These things happened! Location provides clues regarding what the Bible is actually saying.

Imagine the apostle Paul still being alive today. If he were to visit the United States in the same way he visited the Mediterranean cities of Ephesus, Philippi, Corinth, Thessalonica, and Rome, and he wrote letters to the cities of San Francisco, Miami, and Seattle, what issues would he mention? What topics would he address? What matters would he prioritize?

When we read the Bible understanding who the biblical authors were writing to, as well as the culture of the places, cities, and regions, it transforms the Bible from black and white to color. They were speaking into a specific time, a specific place, and a specific people.

God's Photo Album

Last, but not least, our new frame includes understanding how the Bible functions like God's photo album. The Scriptures are not exhaustive. They don't tell us every detail about every moment that happened. *The Bible is not an all-inclusive record.*

Today, we typically store our pictures in digital spaces like cell phones and laptops. I'm old enough that I still have actual photo albums, with pages I can turn as I look through the pictures. When we choose what pictures to place in our photo albums, the events and instances we capture often involve birthdays, weddings, vacations, and holiday celebrations—important moments we want to remember. We're not likely to include a picture of us shopping at the local grocery store on a Monday night. Our photo albums contain the most significant people and moments of our lives, some light-hearted and joy filled, others perhaps more serious and tear eliciting.

The Bible functions similarly—like God's photo album. What we have is exactly what He wants us to have. When you read Scripture, have you ever considered that you are reading the stories, the pearls, God chose for you to have? In this we again see glimpses of the heart of God. While we acknowl-edge that there are some difficult passages throughout the biblical narrative, we also see the living God consistently working to bring about restoration, renewal, and redemption.

When I was in seminary, one of my professors often made a statement that has stuck with me. He told us, "God did not give you the Bible for you to read it," which caught all of us off guard. As seminary students, reading and studying the Bible was primarily how we spent our time! He reiterated: "God did not give you the Bible for you to read it; *He gave you the Bible so it could read you.*"

What if this is true? That God has given us the Bible so that, as we read it, it is simultaneously reading us?

The Gospel of John was written approximately thirty years later than Matthew, Mark, and Luke. The latter three are known as the Synoptic Gospels because they record Jesus' story similarly. Matthew, Mark, and Luke were already in circulation when the apostle John penned the fourth Gospel, which reads differently and has a unique emphasis. John would have known that Matthew, Mark, and Luke had been available for a while. I think it is so interesting that the last thought he gave us, in John 21:25, is this assertion: "Jesus did many other things as well. If every one of them were written down, I suppose that even the whole world would not have room for the books that would be written."

We have a story of Jesus healing a leper,[10] but He could have healed 10,000 others we don't know about! We aren't privy to all the miracles and

Kristi's Dad's Bible

other acts Jesus did, but I love that John says He did *many* other things! John seems to have understood the Spirit was guiding him to write down the very accounts God wanted us to have. This encourages me greatly every time I open my Bible, giving me the confidence that I am reading what the living God purposed for me to read. He meets us in the Scriptures. God shows us His photo album—

Kristi's Dad's Bible

who He is, what He is like, and what it's like to walk with Him.

As a 21-year-old senior in college, I experienced the devastating loss of my dad. My father had many attributes I loved. He was a good man who spoke identity and purpose into me. My father gave me a gift that has traveled with me throughout my life. When I was a little girl, my earliest memories of my father included waking up and walking into our kitchen, where I would see him sitting at our kitchen table with a cup of coffee and his Bible. Every morning, that's what I woke up to. Before I could even read, I remember looking around a corner, watching my dad reading his Bible and wondering, *What is it in that book, that every morning of his life, he's reading it?* One morning, I ran into the kitchen, climbed in his lap, and asked him, "Why do you read your Bible every morning?" He looked down at me and said, "I read it because it makes me better for you and your mom!" So much of my love for the Scriptures comes from my dad. He taught me to love them by loving them. He didn't *tell* me to love the Scriptures; rather, he loved them, and I came to love them because he did. I loved my dad. I was a daddy's girl and wanted to do whatever my dad was doing.

As parents and grandparents, what heritage are we are passing down? When our children and grandchildren bear witness to our lives, do they see us touching the Scriptures and allowing them to read us? God has given us His photo album—the stories He wants us to have. Jesus did many other things beyond what is recorded in the Scriptures. I imagine that at the wedding supper of the Lamb we are going to hear some of the stories that didn't get included in the Bible!

I pray that we will always be known as a people of the book, as those in the early church were known—even before the biblical canon was finished. My mentor of twenty-five years shared some wisdom with me that I've never forgotten. She said, "Kristi, you are going to spend your life professionally teaching the Bible. You're going to touch it a lot. If you want to stay healthy, you need to commit to always be studying a portion of Scripture that has nothing to do with your profession. Not prep for a sermon, teaching, or class. Make sure that you are simultaneously touching another part of the Word of God that's just you and the Lord." This is our opportunity to meet the living God through the Scriptures and be changed by Him.

Middle Eastern Frame

Let's do a quick review of the four components that make up our frame. First, we want to approach Scripture looking for the heart of God. We're not bending down; we're looking up. We want to be buoyant in our posture. Next, the Bible is one Story. It is a holistic, big-picture 35,000-foot view.

Third, location, location, location! When the Bible gives us a geographical location, it's providing a cultural indicator. We can know a lot about a story simply by where it happens in the Bible. Last, but not least, the Bible is not exhaustive; it is exactly what God wanted us to have. It functions like His photo album.

A New Lens

Now that we have our frame, we're going to get our new lens by taking off our Western lens and putting on our Middle Eastern lens. The Bible, from Genesis to Revelation, was primarily written by Middle Easterners in a Middle Eastern context. These writers were from a different time and world.

In Genesis 15, God came to Avram and told him to bring a heifer, goat, and ram, as well as a pigeon and a dove. If God came to you today and instructed you to go get these animals and birds, you would be confused. But when we read the story, it is clear that Avram knows exactly what to do and why. God was inviting him into typical everyday covenant activity in antiquity. In our day, when a guy gets down on one knee and pulls out a ring, we know he is about to ask a covenant question: "Will you marry me?" When God comes to Avram, He is meeting him exactly where he is, in his culture and time. God always meets His people exactly where they are, yet He refuses to leave them there. The living God journeys with us.

As we get our Middle Eastern lens to go along with our Middle Eastern frame, we are adding to our current understanding of the Scriptures. We're not throwing anything away; rather, we are enhancing our understanding of what the biblical authors meant by what they said, wrote, and did.

Foundational to our new lens is recognizing that every culture has cultural idioms—sayings and phrases indigenous to a place and a people. As a part of your specific culture, you know its idioms. Some American idioms include, "It takes one to know one." "You can't teach an old dog new tricks." "What happens in Vegas stays in Vegas." Imagine a people living 2,000 years from now, where Asia is currently located. They speak a different language, but they are reading some of our literature. They come across this phrase: "What happens in Vegas stays in Vegas." How would they perceive that? What kinds of questions would they ask? They'll probably wonder what was going on in Vegas! Or, if they read, "You can't teach an old dog new tricks," they may say, "In that civilization, they had old dogs and they tried to teach them new tricks!"

The Bible is full of Semitic idioms. Those living in the biblical period would have known exactly what the writers meant by what they were saying. We're being invited to learn some of these idioms to gain a better understanding of the Bible. For example, throughout rabbinic language, we see the phrases *abolish the law* and *fulfill the law*. To abolish the law is to wrongly interpret the Scriptures, while fulfilling the law is to rightly interpret the Scriptures.[11] Jesus used this cultural idiom in Matthew 5:17 when He said that He did not come to abolish the law, but to fulfill it.

I learned how different our Western culture is from Middle Eastern culture in dramatic fashion when I took my first biblical studies team to Israel. There's nothing quite like personal experience to help you understand a new concept! After studying in the land in late 2007 and early 2008, I was back in Jerusalem with my first team. We were only three days into our trip when a woman on the team approached me and told me her tooth was hurting so badly that she felt like she needed to go to a dentist. Of course, I had no idea where a dentist was. So, I told Kamal, our bus driver, what was going on, and asked if he could take us to a dentist. Demonstrating typical Middle Eastern hospitality, Kamal said, "No problem, no problem. Come with me!"

The team stayed in the Old City of Jerusalem enjoying an extended lunch while Kamal, the woman with the toothache, and I headed off to find a dentist. As we were walking along, Kamal suddenly turned down a dirty, foul-smelling alleyway. I assumed we were taking a shortcut to the dentist. Then Kamal turned again and entered a doorway. I couldn't believe it! I was thinking, *Oh, no, no, no—the dentist can't be in the alleyway!* Much to my dismay, we walked into a room about eight feet by six feet, with no art on the walls. The only window was a slit near the ceiling, where a naked, electrical cable was hanging down, along with a fixture-less light bulb. Two white plastic lawn chairs that looked like somebody had tied them to the back of a truck and dragged them through the Sahara rounded out the decor. I stared at Kamal, stunned. Casually, he said, "This is the dentist office." It was unlike anything I had ever seen!

I was still wide-eyed and in shock when a man walked through a screen door similar to the latched kind at my grandmother's house in rural Mississippi. He began to speak to Kamal in Arabic, which I couldn't understand. As they talked, I looked back and forth between them. Abruptly, Kamal looked at me and declared, "This is the dentist, and he says he will see her now." I was thinking, *Oh, no way*, but deferred to the team member and asked what she wanted to do. She said, "Kristi, I'm hurting so badly, I'm just going to let him take a look."

We walked through the door into another room. There were no medical credentials on the walls. Instead, there were all sorts of sticky notes filled with Arabic writing. In the corner was a dental chair with a light that shines down in your face. I started to feel a little better—at least this man had a dental chair, which the team member sat in. Now, personal space is different in the West and Middle East. In the West, we wait in the waiting room with our friends and family, and occasionally go back with them to see the doctor. But in the Middle East, people live and work in closer proximity. Thus, Kamal and I were only about six feet away from the team member and dentist.

When I get nervous, I talk. So, as the dentist examined her mouth, I was chattering incessantly to Kamal. "Come on, this is the dirtiest office I've ever seen! There's no way this man is a dentist! How do you know him? There aren't any credentials on the walls. Did you see the chairs out in the lobby? Did you see the naked electrical wire attached to the lightbulb? Why are we here? Is he going to take good care of her? He's got to take care of this lady on my team!" Kamal calmly reassured me, "It's okay! It's okay! It's okay!"

A few minutes later, the dentist turned to Kamal and said something in Arabic. Kamal looked at me and translated: "Kristi, he says she has a fully abscessed tooth. She is going to need a root canal." I asked the woman what she wanted to do. We were three days into our trip, with nine more days to go. She said, "I am really hurting; I'm going to let him do it." For the next hour and fifteen minutes, this dentist gave a woman on my first-ever biblical studies team a root canal! I was six feet away, sitting in a chair and nervously questioning Kamal: "How do you know this man? I don't feel good about this! What is he doing to her? Would you bring *your daughter* to this dentist?"

We finally made it to the end of the procedure. As the lady got up from the chair, much to my surprise, the dentist looked over at me and began to address me in perfect English! In that moment I thought, *There's an idiot in the room, and it is most definitely me!* I will never forget what came next. He asked, "Can I teach you a lesson about Western healthcare versus Middle Eastern healthcare?" I was so embarrassed. I replied, "Yes sir, please teach me a lesson about Western healthcare versus Middle Eastern healthcare."

He continued, "You people in the West care about form; you care about what something looks like. Here in the Middle East," he said, "we don't care about form, we care about function. We want to know what a thing does." He certainly had my attention, and he wasn't finished. "You spend $1,500 in America to get a root canal. You're not paying for the quality of your dentist. You're paying for the very nice waiting room that you sit in, which gives the office the right form and tells you that you are at a reputable dentist. Here in the Middle East, we don't care about that."

As if all that wasn't enough, he then added, "I studied at Oxford." I wanted to reply, "Well, I went to college in Mississippi!" Sometimes you're just beat!

The team member paid around $150 for that root canal. When we got home from the trip, I encouraged her to go see her dentist and get her tooth checked. She did so and was told that her tooth looked great. Ten years later, I ran into her at a store. The first question I asked was, "How's that tooth?" She said it has never given her a problem.

Here's the point: The dentist had been educated at Oxford and was one of the best in Jerusalem, but I didn't have eyes to see it! I come from a culture where dentists' offices look much more sophisticated. Kamal had been honorable and taken us to the best dentist he knew, but because the setup was different than what I was accustomed to, I didn't know how to make sense of the moment.

Often when we read the Bible, this is what happens! We read it with our Western eyes, sensibilities, and cultural biases, all of which affect how we view Scripture and what it means. But the Bible is a Middle Eastern text. This is why we are getting our Middle Eastern lens—to help us ask the same questions of the Text that the ancients asked. Again, it's back to our posture. We should never simply read the Bible. We should always interact with it. It's alive, and so are we. And we want to be sure we approach the Scriptures through the appropriate cultural lens.

West	Middle East
Form	Function
How did that happen?	**Why** would God do that?
Understand → Believe	Believe → Understand
Law // Rule // Principle	Story // Narrative
What does it teach me about **me**?	What does it teach me about **God**?
Dig deep, get down in it... Analysis—pick it apart	Read through it... Synthesis—bring it together
Study to acquire **knowledge**	Posture to receive **revelation**

Form Versus Function

As the dentist in Jerusalem told me, in the West, we are a people who care about form. In this, we are more Greco-Roman than Hebraic. When we read the Bible, we want to know *how something happened* or *what it looked like*. In the story of Moses, have you ever wondered what the bush aflame yet not consumed looked like?[12] Or how about seeing Creation being spoken into existence—going from nothing to everything! We are a people of form.

Those who are in the Middle East are primarily concerned with function or what a thing does.[13] When Middle Easterners read Scripture, they don't ask, How did that happen? or What did it look like? They ask what I believe is a better question—that, when answered, reveals the heart of God: Why would God do that?

Let's go back to Exodus 3 and ask, Why would God do that? Why would God reveal Himself to Moses? The answer is found in what God says to Moses: "I have indeed seen the misery of my people in Egypt. I have heard them crying out because of their slave drivers, and I am concerned about their suffering."[14] Here, Scripture reveals the heart of God to us. He not only sees our pain but feels it. He empathizes and enters in with us. Oftentimes when we are hurting, we wonder where God is because He feels distant. Yet Exodus 3 illustrates that He is watching over us. He feels what we feel.[15]

Understanding Versus Believing

This next one is a biggie I often encounter with my college students. As Westerners, we are much more like Aristotle, Socrates, and Plato. That means we come from a Grecian perspective, where man is the measure of all things.[16] The Age of Enlightenment yielded for us a tendency to believe something only if we can understand it. We have an inherent need to understand *before* we will believe.

In the Middle East, people approach the Scriptures by saying, "God, I believe You; I take You at Your word. Out of my belief, provide me with understanding." Abraham believed God, and it was credited to him as righteousness.[17] What if the degree to which we first believe determines how much revelation we get? What if the amount of revelation God bestows upon us is predicated on how open we are to receiving it?

Many years ago, I started a rhythm where each time I open my Bible, I say to God, "Lord, I take You at Your word. Help me to understand whatever I'm about to read, but I already believe You." This has changed my interaction with the living God as I approach Him through His Word.

Me-Focused Versus God-Focused

As Westerners, we often read the Bible and ask, "What does this teach me about myself?" In the Middle East, they ask a better question: "What does this teach me about God?" I like to say that if we stare at ourselves for too long, we'll get depressed. The Bible was not given to us for us to stare at ourselves as we interact with the Text. The Bible was given that we might stare at God. As we gaze at Him, we will be changed from the inside out.

There is a book in the Bible called Jonah. Interestingly, when you ask people what the book of Jonah is about, they typically give a strange answer. They say it is about Jonah. But it's *not*! God is the purpose and point of every biblical story. The miracle of the book of Jonah is not that a large fish swallowed a man for three days and nights. Rather, the miracle is that God loves evil people and sends His prophets to proclaim the truth about Him to them.

Jonah got sent to Nineveh.[18] Remember, location, location, location! Nineveh was the capital of the Assyrian Empire. The Assyrians were bad news—they invented crucifixion.[19] The Romans later perfected this form of execution, but the Assyrians predated them in conquering and torturing their enemies. The Assyrians would come in like a flood, abusing and enslaving their captives. They were known for running hooks of strings through slaves' noses and pulling them.[20] God came to Jonah and said, "I want you to go to Nineveh." That would be like God coming to us today and saying He wants to plant us in the middle of ISIS territory.

Jonah didn't go to Nineveh right away; he went the opposite direction. He was not afraid of proclaiming the one true God to the Assyrians. Rather, Jonah didn't want to go to Nineveh because he was fully aware of how gracious and compassionate God was. He knew that if he went to Nineveh and preached, the Assyrians would repent, and God would save them. Jonah didn't want the evil Ninevites rescued.[21] The miracle of the book of Jonah is that God comes to save evil people.

The Ninevites repented, and Jonah went up on a mountain and pouted!

Can you imagine a preacher or evangelist getting angry about people responding to their altar call? Jonah preached, an entire city responded, and he was upset about it! In the very last verse of Jonah, God says to the prophet, "Should I not have concern for the great city of Nineveh, in which there are more than a hundred and twenty thousand people who cannot tell their right hand from their left?"[22] The book of Jonah is not about Jonah. Rather, it is about the living God, who is the point and purpose of everything we read and encounter in the Scriptures. God was willing to send one of His prophets to the cruelest, most evil people on the planet. That is who He is.

Looking at Scripture through a different cultural lens invites us to ask different questions.

Knowledge Versus Revelation

As a Western people, we study to acquire knowledge. In this way we are also more Greco-Roman than Hebraic. Often when we read the Bible, we do so with the goal of enhancing our overall knowledge of the Scriptures. There is nothing wrong with that. Remember, we're adding to, not taking away. But Middle Easterners don't study primarily to acquire knowledge; they study to revere God. They posture themselves to receive. They understand that they cannot open the living Word and mine things out to feed themselves in an eternal way. If they're going to be fed, God has to do the feeding. We find a beautiful phrase repeated throughout the Old Testament that illustrates this: "The word of the LORD came to…"[23]

How differently would you study the Scriptures if you approached them not to *learn something*, but to *encounter someone*? Not to gain more knowledge about the Text, but to posture yourself to be fed, giving time for the Word of the Lord to come upon you? No prophet of Israel ever went and got their word from the Lord. From beginning to end, the word of the Lord always found the prophets as they lived lives postured to receive. When the word of the Lord came to them, they were open and ready—at times even with great resistance—to take it in.

Because of the living God, we can afford to lay down our striving and straining. We are not orphans; we are sons and daughters, and God fully intends to feed us the manna of His Word every time we approach Him through the Scriptures. Whatever it is that we need to hear, whatever it is that God needs to impress upon us, as we posture ourselves to receive the Word, we will be ready to inherit it when it comes—to take it in, eat it, and let it do its work.

———■———

Whatever it is in your life right now that feels like dust and ruin, whatever is going wrong, the Bible promises the everyday presence of the real and living God. Let's ask Him to give us eyes to see Him in His Word, in the Story He's given us known as the Bible. As we feast on the Scriptures, may the word of the Lord find us and come upon us. May the Lord be the lifter of our heads, the strength in our gaze, the fixture in our frame. We take hope in knowing that the Bible is not just the best Story that's ever been told, it is also the truest!

GENESIS—DEUTERONOMY

In chapters 1 and 2, we addressed the importance of approaching Scripture on its cultural terms, through a Middle Eastern lens. This means flying over the Scriptures at 35,000 feet, looking for the heart of God in everything we read and encounter. We notice location and discover the significance of where events happen. We revere Scripture, seeing it as God's photo album—the best of what He wanted us to have so we can know and understand who He is and what He is like.

In this chapter, we're going to eat the first five books of the Bible: Genesis, Exodus, Leviticus, Numbers, and Deuteronomy. These books are known in Hebrew as *Torah*, or Instruction—the Five Books of Moses. In Greek, they are called the *Pentateuch*: *penta* means "five," and *teuchos* means "books."

The Bible is one Story, best read and understood from beginning to end. If you are at the beach with a new novel, you don't open it to page 276 and read a chapter, then go back to page 111 and read a couple lines, then fast-forward to page 309 and read three paragraphs. No, you read a story from beginning to end, from start to finish. As we journey through the biblical narrative, we will feast on Genesis through Revelation.

Genesis-Deuteronomy

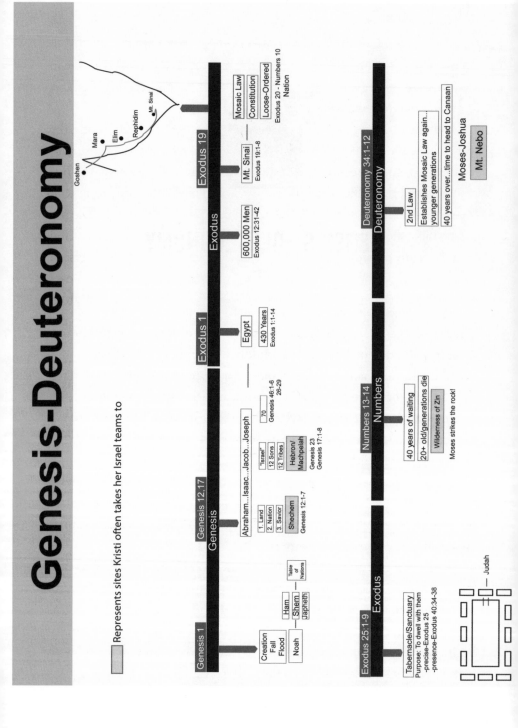

Represents sites Kristi often takes her Israel teams to

Genesis 1

Genesis

Creation
Fall
Flood
Noah

Ham
Shem
Japheth

Table of Nations

Genesis 12,17

Genesis

Abraham...Isaac...Jacob...Joseph

1. Land
2. Nation
3. Savior

Shechem
Genesis 12:1-7

"Israel"
12 Sons
12 Tribes

70
Genesis 46:1-6
26-29

Hebron/Machpelah
Genesis 23
Genesis 17:1-8

Exodus 1

Exodus

Egypt
430 Years
Exodus 1:1-14

600,000 Men
Exodus 12:31-42

Exodus 19

Exodus

Mt. Sinai
Exodus 19:1-8

Mosaic Law
Constitution
Loose-Ordered Nation
Exodus 20 - Numbers 10

Goshen
Mara
Elim
Rephidim
Mt. Sinai

Exodus 25:1-9

Exodus

Tabernacle/Sanctuary
Purpose: To dwell with them
-precise-Exodus 25
-presence-Exodus 40:34-38

Judah

Numbers 13-14

Numbers

40 years of waiting
20+ old/generations die
Wilderness of Zin
Moses strikes the rock!

Deuteronomy 34:1-12

Deuteronomy

2nd Law
Establishes Mosaic Law again... younger generations
40 years over...time to head to Canaan

Moses-Joshua

Mt. Nebo

Promise Maker and Promise Keeper

The first book of the Bible is called Genesis, which means "origin" or "beginnings." The first eleven chapters of the Story play out like a movie in fast-forward mode, with events happening quickly. It is here that God lays a foundation from which the rest of the Story is told.

Genesis 1:1-2 says, "In the beginning God created the heavens and the earth. Now the earth was formless and empty, darkness was over the surface of the deep, and the Spirit of God was hovering over the waters." The first two verses of the Bible reveal the living God to us. We learn that He is all-powerful—so much so that He created the heavens and the earth. The rest of the Bible shows us that He is also good. Throughout the Scriptures, God is consistently coming closer and closer to humanity. In the second verse of the Story, the Spirit of God is hovering over the surface of the deep, or over the waters. As we continue onward, we are going to see the Spirit move from hovering in Genesis to coming down, toward, and ultimately, in. From the beginning, God has been bridging the gap.

As we trace the first eleven chapters of the Bible, everything is presented from a macro perspective. In Genesis 1 and 2, God creates. In Genesis 3, Adam and Eve eat the fruit, realize they are naked, and cover themselves. In Genesis 4, the word "sin" is mentioned in the Bible for the first time,[1] leading up to Cain killing Abel.

Fast-forward to Genesis 6 and 7. By this time, humanity is so given over to depravity that God floods the earth. If you are a parent, you know how disruptive it feels when your children are at odds with each other. You want them to live in harmony and be at peace. In these days in Genesis, corruption was rampant. Humanity was set against humanity, with much blood being shed. God instructs a man named Noah to build an ark. Immediately before the flood comes, Noah gets on the ark with many animals, as well as his wife and three sons, and their three wives. They are the only people who survive the flood and carry on the line of humanity. There's redemption in this flood story. The rabbis say that the flood was not so much an act of judgment as it was an act of mercy. We see this line of thinking in the Tree of

Life Version, which gives Genesis 7 the beautiful title "Deliverance Through the Flood." The living God presses the reset button.

Humankind is diverse. We look different from each other. Have you ever wondered about how all the distinct humans populated the earth? Genesis 10:32 says, "These are the clans of Noah's sons, according to their lines of descent, within their nations. From these the nations spread out over the earth after the flood." Genesis 10 is known as the Table of Nations. Rich and beautiful cultural and racial diversity came from one family line. Early in the Story, different related people groups spread throughout the earth.

The first eleven chapters of the Bible take us on a wild journey from creation to sin entering the Story, a worldwide flood, the redemption of humanity through one family, and the tower of Babel. That's a lot! These chapters move quickly; through them, God sets the stage for the rest of the Story.

As we continue to Genesis 12, we are going to start stringing the biblical pearls together. Remember, the Bible is one Story. After eleven chapters of events happening in fast-forward mode and on a big scale, in Genesis 12, the movie slows down. It's like we watched a "previously on…" overview before the movie begins. The earth is inhabited with different people groups. God then puts His finger on one man, Avram, whose name God later changed to Avraham. Avram was a Shem-ite or Semite, a descendant of Shem, the father of Semitic people.

We soon encounter one of the most important and beautiful sequences of moments in the entire Story of the Bible. In Genesis 12, God reveals Himself as a promise maker; the rest of the biblical narrative reveals that He is also a promise keeper. God comes to Avram in a place called Ur and makes some significant promises to him, sometimes referred to as the Abrahamic covenant.

First, God tells Avram that he is going to make him into a great nation. That's a big promise! Second, God says that through Avram, all the nations of the earth will be blessed. Though debated, some consider this to be one of the earliest messianic prophecies or promises given in the Bible, foretelling the coming of Jesus, who would bless the entire world. And third, God appears to Avram at Shechem and says He is going to give his offspring that land—often referred to as the Promised Land—known then as Canaan because the Canaanites were inhabiting it.[2]

As a reminder, God moved Avram from Ur of the Chaldeans to this land because of the International Coastal Highway. Avram was like a missionary. God has been coming and reaching for the nations since the very beginning. His plan was that Avram and his descendants would multiply and fill the land. God was raising up a new tribe such as the world had never seen. They would live like sons and daughters of a living God who was benevolent, providing the sun and rain without requiring harmful worship.[3]

The first two verses of the Bible show that God is very powerful; He created everything. The rest of the Bible demonstrates that God is also very good. In Genesis 12, God reveals Himself as a promise maker. The rest of the biblical narrative displays how He is also a promise keeper.

Here is where the story gets gospel gorgeous! Throughout Genesis 12, God repeatedly tells Avram, "I will. I will. I will." This was entirely different language than would have been customary from other gods. In antiquity, people understood that when they planted their seeds in the ground, their crops needed sun and rain to grow so they could live in abundance and have enough food to survive. They also figured out that they did not control the sun or the rain. If their crops didn't grow, they would die. The question then became, Who provided the sun and the rain? If not humanity, it must be the gods.

The gods of antiquity were rooted in scarcity and provision. If you needed to appease them so they would provide sun and rain, you planted your seed in the ground and then offered sacrifices to them in the hopes that they would respond favorably. If water didn't come, even though you had sacrificed, you offered more sacrifices. When there was still no rain, you offered further sacrifices—all the way up to your children. Avram lived in a day of child sacrifice.[4] The gods of antiquity were capricious, animalistic, and scary. The ancient world knew the gods as demanding. You were uncertain as to what they were going to do to you or require from you. Thus, you worshipped to appease them, in the hopes that they would provide sun and rain for your crops.

In contrast, in Genesis 12, the living God showed up with what would have been radical language. He did not come to Avram saying, "I'm going to take and demand from you." Rather, He told Avram what *He* was going to do, repeatedly saying, "I will. I will. I will." This God, unlike the other gods of antiquity, was a covenant maker; He would also prove to be a covenant keeper.

God Will See to It

As we move on to Genesis 22, we'll string some pearls from another famous biblical story. Avram's name has been changed to Avraham. He is living in a day of escalated sacrifice to the capricious gods. But the living God comes to him and says, "You don't have to do all these things because I will, I will, I will." God meets Avraham exactly where he is, in his day and time, with what he knows of worship and the gods of antiquity.

The text tells us that sometime later—after Genesis 12, and after God made the three promises to Avram—God tested him by telling him to take his "only son Isaac" and to go to the region of Moriah. There, he was to sacrifice Isaac on the mountain God would guide him to. When we read this, we are appalled. How could a kind, loving God ask Avraham to do such a thing? But when Avraham heard this directive within his cultural framework, he would have been thinking, *Yes, this is exactly what the gods require. If I'm going to enter a covenant relationship with this God, of course He is going to ask for my firstborn son.* Avraham and Isaac set off for Mount Moriah. Avraham knew how the story was going to end because this was how they did things in his day.

But the story didn't end as expected! The living God acts by providing a ram in the thicket for Avraham to sacrifice. For the first time, a god is interacting with humanity in a way that communicates, "Avraham, we are going to live together in a covenant relationship, but you are not going to have to sacrifice your son. I am going to do the heavy lifting here. I am a covenant maker, and I am also going to be a keeper of the covenant." This is beautiful. In Hebrew, it doesn't say God provides. Rather, it says, "God will see [to it]"—meaning that when God sees, He is motivated to act. Avraham did not have to sacrifice his son because God intervened. In Avraham's day, this was something the world had not experienced. Remember, God was at the beginning stages of raising up a tribe who would interact with Him in a way the world did not yet know. They were accustomed to doing all the work to appease the gods. The living God came on the scene saying, "I will. I will. I will."[5]

In the narrative of Scripture, these are some of the first attributes we see about who God is and what He is like. In the West, we often refer to this event as the sacrifice of Isaac, but Isaac doesn't get sacrificed! In Judaism, this story is known as the *Akedah*, or "the binding [of Isaac]." Kind of makes you love God, doesn't it?

Isaac has a son named Jacob, or Ya'akov, whom we read about in chapter 1. God was not afraid to affiliate Himself with Ya'akov because He knew He could change Ya'akov's name and give him a better one. At the river Jabbok, the angel of the Lord changed Ya'akov's name to Israel, meaning "one who struggles with God." He went on to have twelve sons who became known as the twelve tribes of Israel.

Participating with God

Genesis 23 is often overlooked, but it details some of the most important moments in the Story. Something major happens in the metanarrative of Scripture as we fly over it at 35,000 feet.

God has promised Avraham that *He* will do the work. Avraham is walking around the land carrying three promises. At this point in the story, the Israelites don't yet own the land, so Avraham is a foreigner there. Sarah dies, and Avraham wants to bury her. The problem is, because he is a foreigner, none of the land has been deeded to him. Yet he is holding on to a promise that God is going to give him not only a burial plot, but also the entire land.

In antiquity, official business was done at the city gates.[6] Avraham goes

City gate at Dan, in northern Israel

to meet the elders of the city, who are gathered here and serve as communal judges. People bring their cases to the elders, who then offer a ruling. Avraham wants to *buy* a piece of the land; he doesn't want to rent. In Genesis 23, Avraham is seeking to participate with God by becoming a landowner, thus seeing the first part of the promise of land come to fulfillment. He is getting involved with what God said He will do.

In this story, the Hittite people own the real estate at a place in Hebron called Machpelah, where Avraham, Isaac, and Ya'akov were all buried. To this day, you can visit the tombs of the patriarchs and each of their wives, who are also buried there (with the exception of Rachel). Avraham goes to the city gates because he wants to purchase the fields of Machpelah in Hebron so he can bury Sarah. He approaches the landowner, Ephron the Hittite. To better understand the cultural significance of what is about to happen, we need to keep in mind that the Middle East is an honor/shame culture. People do not speak in terms of right and wrong; rather, they speak in terms of what is honorable and shameful. Lying is one of the most shameful things you can do in the Middle East. Telling the truth and being a person of your word is honorable.

Cave of Machpelah/Tomb of the Patriarchs in Hebron

Avraham is at the city gate with Ephron and the city officials. In this public moment, they start negotiating, a custom of Middle Easterners and many other cultures around the world. Avraham says, "I want to buy the cave at Machpelah so I can bury Sarah." Ephron says, "No, my Lord, just use it temporarily."[7]

But Avraham doesn't want to borrow the cave; he wants to own it. He presses further: "No, my Lord. I want to buy it. Give me a fair price for the field." They are engaged in typical back-and-forth bargaining. "No, my Lord, bury your dead." "No, my Lord, I want to buy it." "No, my Lord, please just bury your dead."

In front of the city officials, Avraham insists that Ephron give him a price; Ephron finally relents. He says the field, the cave at Machpelah, is worth 400 shekels of silver.[8] Now, this does not mean much to us until we consider that David pays Araunah just fifty shekels of silver for his threshing floor, which later becomes the Temple Mount.[9] Ephron quotes a price of 400 shekels, thinking Avraham will say no because it's too much. But in this public moment at the city gate, Avraham says, "I will pay it."

I don't know anyone who is willing to pay millions of dollars for a house worth $200,000! But Avraham knows that in an honor/shame culture, as soon as he says, "I'll take it," Ephron cannot renege on his public offer. In essence, Avraham is saying, "I'll take it for four hundred shekels of silver because I want to participate with what God is doing no matter what it costs me. I don't want to rent the land, nor do I want to borrow it. I want to own it."

Avraham then counts out 400 shekels of silver, indicating he is a wealthy man. In this beautiful moment, the living God works in harmony with Avraham to bring the first part of the promise to pass. One of the most important verses in the story is Genesis 23:20, which says, "The field and the cave in it were deeded to Abraham by the Hittites as a burial site." Avraham now owns the first portion of the promise! This pearl in the greater narrative reveals that God's promises aren't always realized all at once. Fulfillment often happens over time, through a process. Long before the Israelites inherit the land, they have this story of their father Avraham negotiating with Ephron the Hittite to purchase the first piece of real estate in the Promised Land.

This story is both beautiful and convicting. Every time I read it, I take a hard look at myself and ask, "Am I going to partner with God like this? Am I going to say yes, no matter what it costs me, no matter if it costs me more than I think it should?" Are we like Avraham in our responses to the promises God has spoken to us? Are we willing to hand over our 400 shekels of silver to get involved with what God is doing in our life and world? Avraham's actions in Genesis 23 anchor his honor among the Jewish people.

Out of Egypt, into the Desert

Ya'akov's favorite son, Joseph, is what we call a transitional figure in the Story. As a young man, Joseph's brothers throw him into a cistern, then sell him to a band of traders who take him to Egypt. He is then sold to Potiphar, one of Pharaoh's top officials. After being falsely accused by Potiphar's wife, Joseph is thrown into prison. Years later, Joseph interprets Pharaoh's dream and is swiftly promoted from prison to second-in-command of Egypt. At the end of Genesis, in the midst of a drought, Joseph's father, Ya'akov, along

The lower panel depicts foreigners making bricks. They would fetch water, mix it with mud, shape the mixture into bricks using a mold, and allow the bricks to dry before measuring and moving the finished product onward.

(cont.) Slightly to the right of center, a taskmaster with a whip sits and watches, while another is standing to the right with a whip. This wall painting is located in the tomb of Rekhmire, in Egypt's Theban Necropolis. Rekhmire was an Egyptian vizier under Thutmose III; his position was similar to that of biblical Joseph in Egypt.

with other family members—seventy in all—move from the land of Canaan to Egypt. They settle in Goshen, a choice area where they can count on water, a vital resource then and now in that region of the world.

In Exodus 1, a new pharaoh comes to power who is no longer favorable to the Israelite people.

Mud bricks at the Ramesseum, located in the Theban Necropolis in Upper Egypt

While in Egypt, the Israelites take literally God's command to be fruitful and multiply! They increase in numbers so much that the new pharaoh feels threatened by them and thus enslaves them. Their ancestor Joseph held a place of prominence, power, and influence, but now, the Israelites are in bondage to the Egyptians.

They remain slaves in Egypt for many generations; at this time, a generation is forty years.

In Exodus 12–14, God miraculously delivers His people out of Egypt, then parts the Red Sea so they can walk through *on dry ground.* The living God knows how to do a thing well! After years of slavery, in one night, the Israelites are set free from their captors. Let's try to envision what this would have looked like. Having existed for years under impossible expectations while their humanity is ruth-

At Medinet Habu, this relief depicts Pharaoh Ramesses III as lord or possessor of a strong arm. This language is congruent with the Exodus narrative, as well as other biblical passages that describe the Hebrew God rescuing His people (see Exodus 3:19-20; 6:6; 15:16; Deuteronomy 26:8; Psalm 89:10; Isaiah 59:1).

lessly worked out of them, the Israelites who walk through the Red Sea don't embody strength and courage. Rather, they are desperate and afraid. They enter the desert systemically and generationally broken. But remember, God's vision and promise is that this people will inhabit the land and rightly represent Him so the world will know what it is like to walk with Him.

If God had taken the Israelites out of Egypt and planted them directly in the Promised Land, they would have burned it to the ground. They were not yet ready to inherit and inhabit the land, or to live in wellness. There was a deep work God needed to do in them before He could place them along the International Coastal Highway for the nations passing through to observe. I don't know about you, but it can be tempting for me to question where God is after three consecutive bad days. It was generations for the Israelites! They had lost their ability to perceive the living God at work on their behalf, perhaps even losing their faith in Him. God knew His people needed to be healed and restored so they could experience renewal and mending where they had been torn.

As the people head into the desert in this condition, the first place they come to is Marah, which means "bitter."[10] In the desert, one of the primary resources people need is water. The Israelites quickly become thirsty. If you recall, the gods of antiquity were worshipped in the hopes that they would provide sun and rain, or water. The water at Marah is bitter, and the Israelites are thirsty. Moses takes a piece of wood and throws it down into the water, which turns from bitter to sweet. The water is described using the Hebrew word *matoq*, which carries not just the connotation of sweet water, but pleasant water. This is who God is; He provides His people with choice water in the desert.

Next, the Israelites come to a place called Elim. When I studied in Egypt, we traced the physical exodus by going down the Nile River and stopping at various locations. The day we studied at Elim, the temperature was 127 degrees! We got off the bus and immediately began sweating. We experienced the extremely hot weather for eight hours while studying, but these conditions were ongoing for the Israelites.

Nile River

It is after Elim that they feel hunger.[11] In a world of scarcity, where the gods provide sun and rain, the Israelites face provisionary uncertainty. Will the Egyptian gods they have known for generations supply food? Or will it be the living God who delivered them from Egypt? After all, what good was it for Him to deliver them if He can't spare them in the desert?

In the Wilderness of Sin, the living God provides food for the Israelites. *Manna*, as this daily bread from heaven is called, tasted like coriander seed with honey.[12] God supplies preferred water in the desert at Mara, and then, in the Wilderness of Sin, He begins providing daily bread and meat, which continues for forty years. Day after day, God shows the Israelites it is Him who provides the sun, rain, food, and water. Simultaneously, He is restoring, renewing, repairing, and ministering to the Israelites, giving them back their humanity, their identity, and their sense of relationship with Him that had been lost in Egypt through years of slavery.

Next, the people come to a place called Rephidim. For the first time in the desert, the Israelites have to fight. They face the Amalekites, who attack them from the rear, where the most vulnerable individuals travel.[13] The newly freed Israelites do not yet know how to wage war. This is a lopsided battle with unequal foes. The Amalekites are supposed to annihilate the Israelites. When the skirmish begins, Moses goes up on a mountain with two friends, Aaron and Hur. As long as Moses' arms are raised, the Israelites are winning. But if Moses puts his arms down, the Israelites start losing. Aaron and Hur hold Moses' arms up all day, until the Israelites defeat the Amalekites.[14]

Put yourself in an Israelite's sandals. You have experienced generations of brutal slavery. You are miraculously delivered in one night through the Red Sea. Now the living God, who is shepherding you through the desert, provides pleasant water, great-tasting bread, and your first military victory. You're starting to feel a bit more confident, aren't you? You're beginning to realize *this* God might actually guide, protect, and provide for you all the way through the desert!

After Rephidim, the Israelites arrive at a famous place known as Mount

Sinai.[15] God had promised Avram that He would give him descendants as numerous as the sand on the seashore,[16] that he would become a nation. For a people group to become a nation, they need a land or space to inhabit, as well as a governing body of laws. For example, in America, we have the Constitution. At Sinai, this loose federation of ex-slaves are forged and formed into an official nation with their own constitution or governing body of laws to canopy them. They receive instructions for how to live under the rule and reign of God, for the glory of God. The constitution given at Sinai is known as the Mosaic law, or Torah.

Let's break this down culturally. In antiquity, two tablets were typically used for covenantal activity between a king and a leader. When we watch artistic renditions such as Charlton Heston portraying Moses in the 1956 classic *The Ten Commandments*, we often see one tablet with the first five commandments on it, and another inscribed with commandments six through ten. That is not likely how the tablets looked. Rather, each tablet would have had all Ten Words—as they are called in Hebrew—on it. In that day, the two tablets functioned like wedding rings. Again, this was covenantal activity between a king and his governor. The king would keep one tablet, reminding him of the governing body of laws, and the governor would have a duplicate tablet reminding him of those same laws. All the laws were given to both parties.

Reflecting on the events of Mount Sinai, God says this about the Israelite nation: "Therefore I am now going to allure her; I will lead her into the wilderness and speak tenderly to her... 'In that day,' declares the LORD, 'you will call me "*my husband*"; you will no longer call me "*my master*."...I will betroth you to me forever...and you will acknowledge the LORD.'"[17] Jewish people perceive the events at Mount Sinai as a wedding.[18] God brings His people to the desert to marry them, to enter into covenant faithfulness with them. The two tablets, inscribed by the very finger of God, serve as rings, similar to how we exchange wedding rings. The night God gives the tablets to Moses is like the wedding night of God with His people.

Moses is gone forty days and forty nights, and the Israelites question whether he is going to come back. Let's again put ourselves in their sandals. We're stuck in the desert. We've lost our leader, Moses, and the God who has been shepherding us. So, what do we do? We act like orphans. We strive and strain. We make our own golden calf and start worshipping it. While Moses is up on the mountain getting the tablets, the Israelites are at the base of the mountain, cheating on their wedding night by reentering the practice of worshipping the Egyptian pantheon. The Israelites return to what they know.[19]

Moses eventually descends the mountain with the tablets and, upon seeing what the Israelites are up to, gets angry and throws the tablets down, smashing them and signifying that the covenant is no more. The Israelites can't even hold the covenant for one night. The living God has miraculously brought them out of Egypt, parted the Red Sea so they could walk through on dry ground, provided pleasant water and great-tasting daily bread, defeated the Amalekites, and brought them to Sinai to marry them— but they are cheating on their wedding night!

What's so beautiful is how God responds to their unfaithfulness, in stark contrast to the gods of antiquity, who were impulsive and ever ready to exact vengeance when angered. God sees what is going on and instructs Moses to return to the mountaintop so He can write a new set of tablets or provide two new rings. One of the first actions God takes after the Israelites are unfaithful on their wedding night is to atone for and cover their sin!

There are a couple significant pearls we want to string together here. Prior to going back up the mountain, Moses directs the people who are for the Lord to come to him. The Levites quickly gather with Moses. Then, following instructions, they strap on their swords and kill 3,000 Israelites who do not choose to stand with the living God.[20] Sinai in the Old Testament and Pentecost in the New Testament are seen as connectors in the biblical narrative. At Sinai, 3,000 lose their lives. At Pentecost, 3,000 are saved.[21] God is bringing restoration and renewal within these stories.

At Sinai, God gives the Israelites their constitution; they are formed into a nation. Already in the story, the first promise to Avraham has been fulfilled.

The Israelites have become a nation with their own governing body of laws. The living God is demonstrating that He is not just a promise maker, He is also a promise keeper.

For a people who had generations of slavery in their recent history, it is understandable that the Israelites start doubting God. As they journey through the desert, they need to see and experience God moving on their behalf. This loose federation of ex-slaves is now consolidated, brought together under the canopy of God's laws. He marries His people at Sinai and is about to do something the world has not yet seen.

In Exodus 25, God chooses to dwell among the Israelites. As His people prepare to journey toward Canaan, He says, "I no longer want to be above you. Build a tabernacle for Me. Build a sanctuary for Me." *Tabernacle* means "dwelling place." The Israelites live in tents in the desert; the Tabernacle is a tent. God is saying, "Build Me a tent and put it beside your tent, because I'm coming down to live with and among you." Remember, the narrative of Scripture shows us that God moves from hovering to down, toward, and in!

Tabernacle replica at Timna Park in the Negev desert of southern Israel

In the Negev desert of southern Israel is a place called Timna Park; it has a one-to-one replica of the Tabernacle, built according to the specifications given in Exodus. Visitors can see the size and scale of the Tabernacle and its furnishings, including the altar, brazen laver, and Holy of Holies. The first time I saw this replica, I was amazed by how small and ordinary everything looked.

The Tabernacle was God meeting the Israelites exactly where they were at. After years of slavery, all throughout their desert journey God was parenting, healing, restoring, and renewing His people. He provided them with pleasant water and bread that tasted like honey. He helped them defeat the mighty Amalekites. He gave them a constitution and turned them into a nation at Sinai. He married them and then atoned for them after they cheated on their wedding night. His faithfulness carried them through.

Through the Tabernacle, God was coming down to live among His people. In Numbers 2, He tells them to put His tent—the Tabernacle—in the middle of the camp, with the twelve tribes placed around it in specific fashion. The tribes surround God; He is central to them. In other words, God is to be the epicenter of the Jewish people. He is making sure that every Israelite tribe can see Him.

In Exodus 40, the Israelites finish setting up God's tent, and the glory of the Lord fills the Tabernacle. They can "see" Him. He starts guiding them through the desert as a pillar of fire by night and a pillar of a cloud by day. Wherever He goes, they all pack up and follow. He is moving them through the desert, restoring and renewing them. Years ago, I came across this rabbinic statement that I've never forgotten: "It took God one night to get the Israelites out of Egypt, but it would take forty years to get Egypt out of the Israelites."[22] As it was for the Israelites, so our time in and through the desert is also a process.

During this journey, God is with and among His people, living in a tent at the center of all twelve tribes, with Judah serving as the gatekeepers to the eastern entrance of God's tent. He is restoring what had been lost in them. He's doing this because they are moving toward the Promised Land. He is

According to Numbers 13, the Wilderness of Zin was part of the area the twelve spies explored. Later, the Israelites are in the Wilderness of Zin when Moses strikes the rock with his staff instead of speaking to it as the Lord instructed (see Numbers 20).

getting them ready to steward the land, to rightly represent the living God as the nations come through the International Coastal Highway.

Forty Years of Waiting

In Numbers 13–14, the Israelites are still in the desert, but they're getting closer to Canaan, the Promised Land. Moses sends out twelve spies or surveyors, one leader from each tribe. They are instructed to go into the land, scout it out, and return with a report. Ten spies come back and say, "There are giants in the land. We look like grasshoppers in their eyes. We cannot take the land." The other two spies, Joshua and Caleb, offer a different report: "We *can* take the land." The Israelites have to choose which of these conflicting reports they will believe. Ultimately, they side with the ten and rebel against Moses, as well as against God's plan. They've already defeated the Amalekites at Rephidim, thus experiencing victory with the odds against them. So even if there are giants in the land, they have faced—and conquered—giants in the desert. Yet this doesn't convince them to believe the report from Joshua and Caleb.

We are about to witness a difficult parenting moment. After the scouts return and the people choose the advice of the ten rather than the two, God responds to their rebellion with severity. He says, "Because of your disobedience and unfaithfulness, you are going to stay in the desert one year for every day that the spies explored the land."[23] God specifically says that the Israelites will remain in the desert until every one of them 20 years old and older has died. Can you imagine being 19 years, 11 months, and 27 days old—and realizing you barely made the cut?

The Israelites will continue in the desert for forty years, a period often referred to as the wilderness wandering. But they know where they are; they've been headed toward Canaan the entire time—they're not lost! They're not *wandering* in the desert for forty years, they're *waiting*. For forty years they will wait for everyone twenty years and older to perish in the desert. Now, where my mind goes when I think about this is, *What about the last man standing?* Years and years have passed, and everybody knows he's the last one. When he goes, they can get out of the desert. I have no idea what happened to that last guy, but I would not have wanted to be him…always sleeping with one eye open!

It took God one night to get the Israelites out of Egypt, but it took Him forty years in the desert to get Egypt out of the Israelites. To give back what had been taken, to marry them, to prepare them to steward the Promised Land and demonstrate how to live under the canopy of the living God, under His rule and reign. To show a watching world what it looks like to interact with a God who does not require you to throw your children in the fire, who benevolently provides sun and rain, who is a covenant maker and covenant keeper, who covers and atones when you cheat on your wedding night.

The Second Law

Now we come to Deuteronomy, the last book of Torah. All the Israelites twenty years old and older have died in the desert. As a nation about to enter the Promised Land, the people are young. Only those under twenty at the start of the wilderness waiting experienced Sinai. Many were not yet born, and thus didn't experience the miraculous crossing of the Red Sea—or were too young to remember it. There is a new generation preparing to inherit the land. The word *Deuteronomy* means "second law." *Deuteros* means "two," and *nomy* (or *nomos*) means "law." God does not give a new law to this new generation. Rather, He gives the old law—the same Mosaic law—to the younger generation so that as they head into the land, they will be a formidable nation with their constitution, their governing body of laws. This is why Deuteronomy seems repetitive. It is a reiteration of so much that has already happened.

In Your Desert Seasons, Write

As we close out the Pentateuch, let's consider a thought. God gave *words* to the Israelites while they were in the desert. The Hebrew phrase *davar bamidbar* means "word in the wilderness." The words of the Lord came to Moses on Mount Sinai in the form of the Ten Words or Ten Commandments, along with the other *mitzvot* or "commandments"—totaling 613 in all. These words received in the wilderness were later recorded in what became the Torah.

I once heard a rabbi talk about how important it is for us to write during our desert seasons. All too often, when we are in a difficult time, we focus primarily on getting out of it. But this rabbi said, "The question when you are in the desert is not 'God, how do I get out of this desert?' The question is 'God, how do I carry the lessons of the desert with me? How do I not lose these things?'" God used the desert to forge and form His people as they were preparing to enter the land.

If you're in a desert season, make it a priority to write! You don't want to forget the things God is showing you, the ways He is forming you, and the deposits He is forging in you. You want to remember your *davar bamidbar*, your word in the wilderness. So write! We can be so quick to rush out of the desert, but sometimes we need God to faithfully walk with us for forty, fifty, even sixty years. Instead of asking, "How do I get out of this?," let's practice asking, "How do I carry the lessons of the desert with me?"

A Faithful God

From the very beginning, God has been a covenantal God who says, "I will do it. I will do it. I will do it. You don't have to throw your children into the fire. I'm a covenant maker and a covenant keeper. I'm going to see you through to the end." Ask the living God to meet you exactly where you are. You may feel like you're in a desert, coming out of one, or heading into one. God is astonishing in the care He provides to His people as He journeys with them.

God is faithful. Left to ourselves, we are faithless—we would have been at the bottom of Mount Sinai with the golden calf. But God is a God who saves, atones, renews, and restores. He tabernacles with us. In this portion of the redemptive narrative of Scripture, the first five books amaze us as we see that God is not just all-powerful, He is also all-good. When He enters into a covenant with us, He emphasizes what *He* will do. God is so much better than we ever knew!

Chapter 4

JOSHUA—RUTH

We continue to reiterate that the Bible is one Story, best read and understood from beginning to end. God serves as the purpose and point of every biblical account. Each story functions like a pearl. We are about to string some pearls together as we eat the next three books in the biblical narrative.

In the previous chapter, we started in Genesis and concluded with Deuteronomy. Now we pick up the story line with Moses' successor, Joshua. The Israelites have reached the end of their forty years of wilderness waiting; it is time for them to move into the land. The book of Joshua is known as the book of conquest, in which the promise of land is fulfilled. Remember, it took God one night to get the Israelites out of Egypt, but it took forty years in the desert to get Egypt out of the Israelites. God served as their shepherd and rebuilt their faith in Him after years of slavery.

Crossing Over

In Joshua 1:2-3, God instructs Joshua to prepare the Israelites to cross the Jordan River into the land. He says, "I will give you every place where you set your foot, as I promised Moses." Canaan, the land God gave the Israelites, was not empty at this time in history. Seven people groups, whom I refer to as the "ites"—the Canaanites, Hittites, Hivites, Perizzites, Girgashites, Amorites, and Jebusites—inhabited it.[1] The "ites" occupied the land, yet God continued to assure Joshua and the Israelites, "I am giving you *this* land."[2]

This was continued fulfillment of God's promise to Avram, but the Israelites had to take the land through war. From the very beginning to the present day, God has been looking for a people who will participate with Him in seeing the promises come to pass. The Israelites were not going to cross the Jordan into a spacious, empty land where they could simply set up their homes and start their new lives. God would do His part, but they had to do theirs as well.

Now we better understand the "be strong and courageous"[3] charge that God repeatedly speaks to Joshua as he prepares to lead the people into the land of inheritance. And Joshua would not be alone; the living God promises to be with him wherever he goes.[4] Joshua and the officers communicate to the people that they are to get ready, because they will be crossing the Jordan River in three days. From there, it will be one against seven, an unenviable matchup in most any scenario. The Israelites will be vastly outnumbered, a reality that makes the "do not fear" admonition even more relevant.

At this time in Israel's history, the people are in possession of an important object: the Ark of the Covenant. They followed it through the desert for forty years, and it is vital that they do not lose it. When the Ark sat in the Tabernacle, or in God's tent, the glory of the Lord showed itself above the Ark. Where the Ark of the Covenant was, God was enthroned between the cherubim. The Israelites followed the Ark through the desert—a beautiful picture illustrative of the way that valiant kings of old always led their people into battle. Alexander the Great was known for this; his men loved him because he was the first one to the fight. He didn't hide behind his soldiers; rather, he served as the tip of the sword. The Ark of the Covenant leading the Israelites symbolizes God functioning as king over all Israel. Moses never wore a crown, and he never carried a scepter. He was not Israel's king and ruler; he was Israel's prophet and leader. God was her king in a form of government known as a theocracy.[5] God, as king, prepares to lead His people across the Jordan and into the Promised Land, where one nation will come up against seven.

As we come to Joshua 3, I want to anchor us in the greater metanarrative. The new generation born in the desert did not experience the miraculous crossing of the Red Sea. God profoundly showed up on behalf of their predecessors, but as these younger Israelites prepare to go into the land, most of them do not have a water story. God is about to give them their very own water miracle and show up for them in the way He did for the prior generation.

Let's get into the mindset of an Israelite man for a moment. You know that in three days you will cross the Jordan River, but you are not crossing it alone. Your wife and children are with you. You also know that there are seven "ites" on the other side of the river; when they figure out you are in the land, they will come for *all* of you. How do you feel? What's going on inside of you? You're likely wondering how you will be able to fight the "ites" and protect your family at the same time!

As an Israelite woman, you know that you will soon be crossing over with your husband and children. You've heard about the seven "ites" in the land and you see your husband preparing to fight. You ponder how he can fight while simultaneously defending you and your kids.

Now we better understand what the Israelites faced in one of the most beautiful stories in the Bible. I love that God has a way of giving every generation their God-stories! If you have children or grandchildren, nieces or nephews, you want God to show Himself to them as He did to this new generation of Israelites.

If you are preparing to cross the Jordan River and fight seven "ites," wouldn't you like a boost from God showing up and demonstrating His presence with you? I know I would need assurance that He is not going to leave or forsake me. This generation has grown up hearing the stories about the miraculous crossing of the Red Sea. Now they're staring at the Jordan River, wondering, *Will God do it for us? Is He with us the way He was with*

Moses? Is He with our new leader Joshua *the same way He was with Moses?* God is about to answer their concerns definitively and extraordinarily.

Let's take a quick look back at Moses and the crossing of the Red Sea. Remember, *Moshe* means "drawn out." After the Israelites depart from Egypt, the Egyptians pursue and trap the people from behind as the Red Sea traps them in front. We have the privilege of knowing how this story turns out. But can you imagine being in that moment with the Red Sea in front of you, and the Egyptians closing in? When Moses follows God's instructions and stretches out his hand, the Red Sea splits.[6]

Sometimes we have to stretch out our hands and trust, by faith, that God will not only part the waters, so to speak, but also hold them back while we cross—even when everything in us is screaming that the walls of water could come crashing in at any time. The living God gives instructions and is faithful to do His part, while often inviting us to be *active* participants in the story. We are about to see the same rhythm with Joshua and the new generation of Israelites.

A faith-filled Joshua tells the Israelites to consecrate themselves because the Lord "will do" amazing things among them. He then instructs the priests who are carrying the Ark of the Covenant to step into the Jordan River—when they do, the waters will part. This story takes place during harvest season, *when the river is at flood stage.* This higher-than-normal water flow was the precise time when God invited these Israelites to experience their own water story.

The priests do as directed and carry the Ark of the Covenant, the presence of the Lord, out to the middle of the Jordan River. The entire nation of Israel crosses over opposite of Jericho, *on dry ground.* I love this imagery of God in the middle of the Jordan River holding back the waters! Joshua 3 says the Jordan stopped flowing and piled up in the town of Adam, which was a considerable distance away.[7] What a sight that must have been for the residents! God is functioning like a faithful king who goes before the Israelites in their scariest moments. When we're afraid, we often ask, "God, where are You?" Scripture shows us that the living God goes in first. When we get into our hardest, most devastating moments, God is already there.

Joshua-Ruth

Represents sites Kristi often takes her Israel teams to

The Ark of the Covenant was the most important object to Israel! Why? It represented the presence of God; He dwelled there.
Exodus 25:10-22

© 2023 New Lens Biblical Studies

Joshua

Joshua 1:1-11
Moses — Joshua
Conquest — Land
2nd of 3 promises to Abraham fulfilled
Give — War
Jordan River

Joshua 3:1-17
Ark of the Covenant
Crossing the Jordan
Joshua 5:1-3
Missions/witness
God *through* Israel

Joshua 6:1-7
Jericho
Casement walls
Rahab lives *in* the wall
-First of many...Ai, etc.
-Land allotments, the twelve tribes

Joshua 8:30-35
Mosaic Law/National Constitution Renewed
Mt. Ebal, Mt. Gerizim
-Shechem is at the base of these two mounts!
-They go to the place where God first gave the promise to Abraham.

Joshua 23:1-16
Prohibition
1. Don't intermingle
2. Don't intermarry
Joshua 24:1 — Shechem
Land

Judges

Judges 2:6-19
Judges Rule Israel
"Dark Ages of Israel" ~300 Years
Sin Cycles

Judges 3:7-11; 6:1; 7:1-8
Spring of Harod
Samson — Prototype
Boaz — Remnant

SIN
SLAVERY BONDAGE
JUDGE FREEDOM

Ruth

Ruth 1:1
Remnant
Light in the Darkness
Boaz — Kinsman Redeemer
★ This story is the light during the 300 years of Dark Ages.

THERE IS ALWAYS A REMNANT!

Divine Protection at Gilgal

This generation of Israelites now has its own miraculous dry-ground crossing, mirroring that of Moses and their ancestors. But still there remains a problem. As soon as they step foot on the other side of the Jordan, the seven "ites" are waiting! The people may be feeling a bit more confident having watched the Jordan River part before their eyes, yet their posture is still vigilant, watching for which "ite" is coming first. Will it be the Perizzites or the Canaanites? Maybe the Hivites? Or will all three advance at once? Either way, war is coming! God has promised to give them the land and be with them in battle, but receiving their inheritance still requires them to fight.

Now we encounter another extraordinary moment in the Bible. God often chooses ways and methods other than what we would choose if we were writing the story. After the Jordan River crossing, the Israelites have tangible evidence that God stands with Joshua just as He did with Moses, and with them as He did in and through the desert. In Joshua 5, God requires something unexpected of the Israelites as they prepare for war: Joshua is to make flint knives and circumcise all the males. It's like the Lord says, "Wait! There's a little something we need to take care of before we go any further." The Israelite men of military age—who had been circumcised while in Egypt—all died in the desert. Those born during the wilderness years are the ones God instructs Joshua to circumcise upon entering the land. This place of mass circumcision is called Gibeath Haaraloth, which literally means "hill of the foreskins." I think we can all agree that there's not enough Neosporin in the whole world to see this story through!

As the Israelite women consider this directive, they realize that if all their men get circumcised, it renders the fighters incapacitated and thus unable to protect their families. Isn't it interesting that the first thing the living God does after they cross the Jordan and head into the land with the seven "ites" is disable every Israelite man? At this point, if the Israelites' safekeeping is up to them, they are in big trouble!

God is teaching the Israelites a new kind of trust. We would expect God to arm the Israelites, maybe equip them with special weaponry the world has not yet seen, that the seven "ites" can't conquer. Instead, God chooses to immobilize every Israelite male—and let's be clear: This type of procedure doesn't heal overnight! The first day, the Israelites are scared that the "ites" will attack while the men are debilitated. The next day, they're still nervous, but the "ites" don't come. They experience the same on day three. By day nine, the Israelites start figuring out there's divine protection in motion; the living God is watching over them.

The story continues as the Israelites celebrate Passover. The next day, they eat the fruit of the land. One of my favorite verses in the entire Bible describes what happens next: "The manna stopped the day after they ate this food from the land; there was no longer any manna for the Israelites, but that year they ate the produce of Canaan."[8] For forty years in the desert, God provided daily bread for the Israelites—without them having to sacrifice their children or worship through extreme, harmful practices. When they crossed over and could eat the fruit of the Promised Land, the manna ceased. Incredible!

Just like the Israelites have a new water story, they also have a new Sinai story—a recommitment-to-the-Lord story. They now have a new food story and will soon have a new victory story. It's the Exodus 2.0.

Divine Intervention at Jericho

This new generation has embodied its own water story. The Israelite males have experienced mass circumcision. They've healed up, celebrated Passover, and now it's time to go.

The first city they have to fight against is Jericho. In antiquity, people considered a city to be prominent if it had a wall. Jericho was not only walled, but she was also one of the most formidable, fortified cities in the entire land of Canaan.[9] We would have written this script differently, but God requires the Israelites to take Jericho first!

Let's look at this story with a Middle Eastern eye. If a city is going to take the time to build a wall, they're also going to equip it with soldiers on top of the wall, watching day and night for advancing enemies. These sentries are armed with spears as well as bows and arrows. This describes the prominent city of Jericho, with its wall and watchmen looking out across the Plains of Jericho, ready to defend when an invading force approaches.

Remember: Back in Joshua 1, God repeatedly tells Joshua not to be afraid, but to be courageous. If you are an Israelite on the Plains of Jericho, looking at the walls of the city with sentries on top, how do you feel? You're looking at your brother and asking, "Can we do this? Can we take them?" He responds, "Are you kidding me? We've got to start with Jericho; why couldn't we take on a small village first?" It's amazing that God instructs His people to begin in this way.

The Israelites approach the walls of Jericho, and God tells all the armed men to march quietly around the city one time each day for six days. What's going through the minds of the scouts on the walls as they watch this unusual sight day after day? As the Israelite men march around the city, they expect to be attacked any minute! They may even feel embarrassed. By this point they're wanting to renegotiate the plan with God, who is asking them to intentionally put themselves in harm's way. This is yet another pearl of God with His people, another miraculous display of His protection of them.

We can envision the Israelite men returning to their tents at night, in awe that they are still alive, and astonished that this marching order continues day after day. As they sit around their campfires, they say, "Okay, the God of our fathers is about to do it again. We've got our own water story. We had that amazing—but painful—mass circumcision, and God protected us as we healed. He gave us our own Sinai story. Now we're getting ready to take Jericho. Could He be giving us a new victory-over-the-Amalekites story?"

Joshua 6 describes how, on the seventh day, the Israelites march around the city in the same manner as before, but seven times instead of one. On their final lap, the priests sound the trumpets, the men shout, and the walls of Jericho fall. The Israelites rush in and take their first city in Canaan—one of the most important and most fortified, located close to the center of the country. By nightfall, they miraculously have possession of one of the strongest cities they'll face in the Promised Land.

In the end, not one Israelite male had to raise his sword, spear, javelin, or shield. God is keeping His word to His man Joshua and to the Israelites: "I will never leave you, nor will I forsake you. I go before you into battle as your king." The living God always goes first!

The ruins of Old Testament Jericho are about one mile from New Testament Jericho. These ruins are now called *tell es-Sultan*.[10] It's amazing to see the scale and size of the city in the middle of the day, in the Middle Eastern sun, and to imagine Israelite men quietly walking around it for six days before seeing the walls fall on the seventh. One step at a time, God is fulfilling all three of His promises to Avram!

Renewal of the Covenant

As we continue to eat the biblical narrative, by way of reminder, we are traveling over it at 35,000 feet. We are noticing location, location, location. We are looking for the heart of God in everything. We understand that the Bible functions like God's photo album; He has given us the stories He wants us to have in Holy Writ.

A lot has gone down for the Israelites. They've crossed over the Jordan. All the adult males have been circumcised. They have taken Jericho without raising a weapon. The Israelites need to catch their breath. They do so by going back to a place that's important in their story.

As we fast-forward to Joshua 8, the people move onward in Canaan, ready to conquer another king and acquire more land. In antiquity, when you go to war and win, you absorb the people group you defeated. You get their land, crops, sheep, cattle, and population, who usually become your servants or slaves. After conquering the city of Ai, Joshua takes the Israelites to Mount Ebal and Mount Gerizim.[11] The ancient city of Shechem, where God reiterated His promise of descendants and land to Avram,[12] is located at the base between these mountains—which is why Joshua and the people come here to renew the covenant. Six tribes stand facing Mount Ebal, while the other six stand facing Mount Gerizim. Joshua builds an altar and copies the law of Moses onto stones. We have seen this covenantal activity before!

These stones are rings for the new generation. Joshua and the Israelites get a copy, and God gets the other copy. This is a beautiful moment; it reminds us that the Bible is one Story with location playing a significant role in stringing the biblical pearls together.

While still at Shechem, at the base of Mount Ebal and Mount Gerizim, Joshua reads the *entire* law in the presence of the Israelites, including the women and children, as well as the foreigners living in their midst. In the Torah, God gave the Hebrew people 613 laws, or *mitzvot*, to help them live under His shalom.[13] Tell the truth: Would you be able to stand in the hot sun for hours while Joshua read the entire Book of the Law? The Hebrews are an oral people. They retell their stories to their children and their children's children at their annual feasts and festivals. We see this modeled as Joshua reads the law word for word; he is speaking to them, washing all Israel with the instructions of God.

Now that the Israelites are filling and inhabiting the land, they are positioned to rightly represent the living God to all the nations that will travel on the International Coastal Highway. By the end of the book of Joshua, two of God's three promises to Avram have been fulfilled.

Blessings and Curses

When Joshua read the words of the law, it included "the blessings and the curses."[14] It is important for us to understand what this passage means, not only with regard to ancient Israelite theology, but for us today. When the Bible talks about blessings and curses, it is not referring to divination or sorcery. What God was saying to the Israelites, and what remains true today, is that if we live under His rule and reign, if we live under His instructions, we are better positioned to experience shalom—a sense of harmony and wholeness. There's a simple joy in choosing life by being where you're supposed to be, doing what you should be doing.

As for curses, when we step out from under God's canopy and do things our own way, when we lay hold of the illicit that is not meant for us, it is our own sin that devastates us by fracturing shalom. To paraphrase British author G.K. Chesterton, "Man cannot break the laws of God, he can only break himself against them."[15]

Living in the way of shalom—which is the blessed life—may not always look or feel the way modern culture often defines "blessed." But if we choose to *not* live under the rule and reign of God, we may lose our sense of peace, experience shame and separation, and want to hide—all factors contributing to a life that *feels* cursed.

Joshua's Farewell

Just as Moses passed away at the close of Deuteronomy, Joshua prepares to, in his language, go the way of the earth.[16] Joshua 23 is his farewell speech, overflowing with evidence of God's faithfulness. Joshua's words throughout this chapter express the shalom that results from living under the canopy of God versus not.

Joshua reminds the Israelites that God has been moving on their behalf, fighting for them and driving out the other nations in the land. Using beautiful poetic language, he says, "One of you routs a thousand, because the LORD your God fights for you, just as he promised."[17] This valiant leader exhorts the Israelites to obey everything in the Book of the Law of Moses and hold fast to the Lord their God. He gives them two prohibitions: They are not to intermingle nor intermarry with the remaining people groups in the land. Joshua knows that if they do so, their hearts will be led astray, toward other gods. The very next book in the Bible is Judges, which details how the Israelites do in upholding these mandates.

Sin-Slavery-Liberation

The book of Judges is known as the dark ages of Israel. By this point in the Story, God has fulfilled two of the three promises made to Avram and his descendants. They are a nation. They are now inhabiting and filling the land. They are the new tribe God raises to display His glory to the watching world. The time of Joshua's successors, the judges, lasts around 300 years.

Throughout the book of Judges, the Israelites descend into a downward spiral of sinning by forsaking the living God and following other gods. Two primary foreign gods become a temptation for the Israelites: Baal, the god of rain or storm, and Asherah, a mother goddess. This takes us back to worshipping the gods for provision versus scarcity. You worship Baal when you need crops; you worship Asherah when you need babies.

Because of their sin, God allows the Israelites to be enslaved to a foreign people group. They cry out, and God raises up a judge who leads the Israelites in battle against the people group who suppresses them. The Israelites overthrow that people and live for the Lord all the days of that judge's life. But when that judge dies, the Israelites sin again by forsaking the living God and serving other gods. Again, God allows them to be enslaved. They cry out. God raises up a judge who liberates them. They live for God all the days of that judge. The judge dies, and the Israelites sin again. This is the sin-slavery-liberation cycle of the book of Judges.

Judges 3 details the accounts of Israel's first three rescuer judges. The Israelites do evil by worshipping the Baals and Asherahs. The Lord is angry with them, and turns them over to Cushan-Rishathaim, the king of Aram Naharaim. The Israelites are subjugated to this king for eight years. They cry out to the Lord, and He raises up Othniel to be their deliverer. Here we see the cycle: The Israelites sin, are subjected to slavery, then cry out to God; He sends a judge to liberate them. The Spirit of the Lord comes on Othniel, and he goes to war against Cushan-Rishathaim. God delivers the king of Aram into the hands of Othniel, and the land has peace for forty years until Othniel dies. Then the Israelites again do evil in the eyes of the Lord. He gives them over to Eglon, king of Moab, while raising up a deliver named Ehud. And on and on it goes.

Here is where it's important to understand how we define terms differently than people did in antiquity. When we think of a judge, the image that typically comes to our minds is that of a man or woman wearing a black robe, sitting at the front of a courtroom and holding a gavel. While it is true that during the biblical period judges decided matters of law, they were also *warriors*. When the Israelites cried out for help, God raised up a judge—a warrior—who would lead them into battle against the people group who suppressed them. The Israelites would then overthrow their oppressors.

Delicate Darkness Put Out the Sun

The time of the judges is known as a time when every man did as he saw fit. Israel had no king; she had no visible, chosen leader.[18] The Israelites followed Moses and the *mishkan*—or Tabernacle—through the wilderness, then Joshua and the Ark after they were in the Promised Land. Joshua succeeded Moses, but no one leader succeeded Joshua.[19]

One of the judges God raises up is Samson. Whatever Samson is instructed to do, he does the opposite. If he had been given a list of what *not* to do, he would have done everything on it. We've established that names are extremely significant in the Bible. Samson's name, in Hebrew, is *Shimshon*, which means "sun ray."[20] The function of Samson's life—his destiny—is to be an agent of light like a ray of sun. Does Shimshon live up to his name?

Samson is a Nazirite, living under a Nazirite vow.[21] According to Numbers 6, a man or woman taking the Nazirite vow has three prohibitions: abstain from wine and other fermented drinks, as well as anything from the grapevine; refrain from cutting their hair; and avoid touching a dead corpse.

In Judges 14, Samson kills a lion with his bare hands. Later, as he is headed back to Timnah, he stops to look at the lion's carcass and sees a swarm of bees and honey in it. Disregarding his Nazirite vow, Samson uses his hands to scoop honey out of the carcass. Upon arriving at Timnah, he holds a seven-day feast. Though the text doesn't explicitly say Samson drinks wine at this feast, it would have been highly unusual that he did not.[22] This type of feast was like a drinking party; weddings in antiquity were often seven-day celebrations that included an abundance of wine. Jesus performed a miracle at one such feast, known as the wedding at Cana.[23]

Sometime later, Samson notices a Philistine woman named Delilah and intermingles with her. Remember, *Shimshon* means "sun ray" or "sun-man." When Shimshon comes on the scene, he should be like a ray of light. This was God's purpose for him. Interestingly, Delilah sounds like *laiy'lah*, the

Hebrew word for "night." It is as though the sun ray is hanging out with the night. I've even heard Delilah transliterated as "delicate darkness." In 2 Corinthians 6:14, the apostle Paul asks, "What fellowship can light have with darkness?" As this story goes, delicate darkness wears down the sun ray; Samson eventually tells Delilah the source of his strength. She puts him to sleep and cuts his hair. Then the Philistines rush in and capture Samson, this great man of strength who suddenly has no strength.[24] A powerful way to describe what happens here is *delicate darkness put out the sun.* Night overcame the sun ray! The first thing the Philistines do is put out Samson's light—his eyes—because the eyes are the light in the human body.[25] After the light of the sun ray is put out, Samson is taken back to Gaza and put in prison.

Here, we see God do something beautiful for Samson that He also does for us. *God goes with us into our self-imposed exile!* When we get out there, He comes with us, like a shepherd that leaves the ninety-nine to search for the one until he finds it. When he finds it, he joyfully puts it on his shoulders and carries it home—that's what Jesus teaches in Luke 15. Samson's eyes have been removed; his light put out. His hair has been cut; his strength is gone. He's in prison in Philistia, but God is with him in his exile!

Have you ever questioned whether you've gone too far or messed up too badly? Have you doubted whether even God could do something positive with your seemingly hopeless situation? Samson is a good example of getting it all wrong. What is God going to do with this man who has not lived up to his name, who has been overthrown by the delicate darkness?

While in the Philistine prison, Samson notices that his hair is growing back. Perhaps he wonders, *Is my strength going to return, or have I transgressed God so badly that I'm on my own? Is God with me in prison?*

This becomes an incredible redemption story! Samson is a wreck until the last moments of his life. The Philistines throw a party to celebrate their god Dagon delivering Samson into their hands. Thousands are present. They bring Samson out to make fun of him. This once-valiant warrior is now their entertainment. Samson asks a servant to help him rest against the temple pillars; he cannot see the pillars, but now he can feel them. He prays, asking

God to restore his strength, then pushes the pillars. The temple collapses, and Samson kills more Philistines at the time of his death than during his entire lifetime.[26]

Violence has never been God's ideal, yet in antiquity, might made right, and the strongest man or god won. For most of his life, Samson misrepresents the living God. At his death, he finally lives up to his name by toppling the temple of the Philistine god Dagon. We encounter more showdowns between the Hebrew God and Dagon in the next chapter, which provides further cultural understanding.

We may get it wrong 99 percent of the time, yet God can still show up magnificently in our last 1 percent and do more with it than with all we squandered. In the New Testament, Hebrews 11 is famously known as the Hall of Faith. This chapter lists the greats of Israel—including Samson.[27] Even if Samson didn't do right until the very end of his life, God was able to use even that moment for His purposes.

The Kinsman-Redeemer

Let's connect some pearls here. Samson gets involved with the delicate darkness, which overthrows the sun ray. In the end, God restores his life and his name. The next book in our Bibles is Ruth. After Judges, we all need some encouragement! The story of Ruth actually happens *during* the days of the judges. It is light in the darkness; evidence that there were some Israelites living honorably during the dark ages of Israel's history.

Early on, we are introduced to a man named Elimelek, his wife Naomi, and their sons, Mahlon and Kilion.[28] Remember, if you know the names, you have significant clues as to how the story will play out. In this case, *Mahlon* means "sick" or "disease," and *Kilion* means "annihilation" or "complete destruction." Upon hearing these names, a Hebrew knows exactly what is about to happen: They're both going to die! From Bethlehem in Judah, they go live in Moab because of the famine in their homeland. Elimelek dies, and Naomi is left with her two sons, who marry Moabite women named Orpah and Ruth. After living in Moab about ten years, Mahlon and Kilion also die, leaving Naomi with her Moabite daughters-in-law. Orpah stays in Moab with her people, while Naomi and Ruth return to Bethlehem. A determined Ruth tells Naomi, "Where you go I will go, and where you stay I will stay. Your people will be my people and your God my God."[29]

We fast-forward the story and are introduced to another Israelite male living in the days of the judges. His name is Boaz. Unlike Shimshon, Boaz is faithful. In this biblical story, Boaz shines as a faithful remnant of light. He is concerned with the rule and reign of God, with the ways of God. He wants to live well—what the Hebrews call upright and blameless.

In antiquity, men went off to war around springtime every year, as 2 Samuel 11:1 alludes to: "In the spring, at the time when kings go off to war…" War was cyclical; it was a way in which men provided for their tribe. A natural by-product of this was that, while all the men would go off to war, not all returned. This is where the Israelite practice of levirate marriage and the kinsman-redeemer comes into play.[30] The men who make it back home see what wives are now widowed and what children are left without an *av*—Hebrew for "patriarch" or "father." In this era, to be a female or a child without male covering and protection leaves you as good as dead. You need to be part of a house, a clan, a tribe. Remember, the Middle East is communal, not individualistic.

Upon returning to Bethlehem, Naomi and Ruth need a male covering. They need a man to perform a levirate marriage, a process that first requires finding the male relative most closely related to the now-deceased Elimelek. As an Israelite, it is this man's responsibility to marry Naomi and bring her under his covering, to sustain the family name and protect her and anyone in her household. This man is known as a kinsman-redeemer.

It's harvest season when Naomi and Ruth return to Bethlehem. Ruth goes out to glean and ends up in the fields of Boaz, a wealthy, influential man from Elimelek's clan. After seeing the generosity Boaz extends to Ruth, Naomi tells Ruth to go to Boaz at the threshing floor in the middle of the night and uncover his feet. When she does so, Boaz realizes he has an opportunity to be a kinsman-redeemer. Not to marry Naomi, as she is too old to have children, but to marry Ruth. Boaz knows there is a male relative closer to Naomi than he is. According to levirate law, that man is supposed to be the kinsman-redeemer. Notice the difference between Samson, who did life his way, and Boaz, who is meticulous to follow the Israelite laws of marriage and do things God's way.

Boaz goes to the city gates to do business, just as Avraham did with Ephron the Hittite when he purchased the cave at Machpelah for 400 shekels of silver. The man more closely related to Naomi approaches the gate and Boaz pulls him aside, along with ten elders. He describes the situation, asking the man if he wants to purchase Elimelek's land, which also means taking in Ruth the Moabite. In essence, Boaz asks if he wants to fulfill his obligation as kinsman-redeemer, which means becoming financially responsible for Ruth and Naomi. What this man ultimately says is that he doesn't want to endanger his own estate. He already has a wife and children to take care of. He has all he can handle. By law he is supposed to agree to be a kinsman-redeemer, but he says no. In front of the city elders and other witnesses, Boaz says, "I will be the kinsmen-redeemer. I will purchase the property of Elimelek, Mahlon, and Kilion. And I will marry Ruth."[31] This is such a beautiful story of light, of flourishing and shalom in the midst of the days of the judges. Ruth 4:14 aptly describes the mood: "The women said to Naomi: 'Praise be to the LORD, who this day has not left you without a guardian-redeemer. May he become famous throughout Israel!'"

God honors their prayer. Boaz becomes famous throughout Israel. He and Ruth have a son named Obed, who becomes the father of Jesse, who becomes the father of the future King David. The reward is always on the other side of obedience! Boaz assumes the cost and responsibility of bringing in not only Ruth, but also Naomi, to serve as their kinsman-redeemer. He has no way of knowing that he is going to end up in the lineage of the Messiah, as is stated in the closing verses of Ruth, as well as in the first chapter of Matthew.

God Is Faithful

God is faithful to His people. Two of the three promises to Avram have been fulfilled. The rest of the Story of the Bible is God fulfilling the remaining promise. He is better than we ever knew. He has never failed a person or group of people, and we will not be the first!

1 SAMUEL—1 KINGS

S o far, God has fulfilled two of the three promises made to Avram. As we continue journeying through the biblical narrative, we are well on our way to seeing Him be a perfect promise keeper. The Israelites have finished the conquest of the land that is detailed in the book of Joshua. In the book of Judges, the Israelites do what is right in their own eyes and experience the sin-slavery-liberation cycle. In the midst of the dark ages of the judges is the book of Ruth, a ray of light and hope.

Samuel and the Word of the Lord

The twelve tribes of Israel have been given their land allotments; they are now planted in the land. If all the tribes have a place to live, God does too! For the Israelite, God is located with the Ark of the Covenant. Wherever it is, God is. Wherever it goes, God goes. The first city in the Promised Land where the Ark of the Covenant rests, or where God lives, is a city called Shiloh.

In 1 Samuel 3, we are introduced to a transitional figure named Samuel. His name in Hebrew is *Shmuel* and means "one who hears God/one whom God hears."[1] Samuel lives up to his name; his ear is tuned to hear the voice of the Lord. Samuel has two primary roles or functions: he serves as the last judge of Israel, and he is also a prophet. His mother, Hannah, experiences years of barrenness prior to the Lord opening her womb. After weaning Samuel, Hannah takes him to the house of the Lord at Shiloh and dedicates him for a lifetime of service. Samuel is one of three in the Bible that take a Nazirite vow for life.

We pick up the story line with Samuel ministering under Eli the high priest. First Samuel 3:1-2 says, "In those days the word of the LORD was rare; there were not many visions. One night Eli, whose eyes were becoming so weak that he could barely see, was lying down in his usual place." I love this next part! Notice where it says Samuel is sleeping: "The lamp of God had not yet gone out, and Samuel was lying down in the house of the LORD, where the ark of God was."[2] Did you catch that? Samuel is near the Ark of the Covenant; he is sleeping positioned to hear from the living God. We see the power of proximity here as the Lord calls out to him.

The first time this happens, Samuel runs to Eli, thinking it is the priest who called him. Eli tells the boy to go lay back down. The Lord calls out to Samuel a second time, with him again thinking it is Eli. At this point, young Samuel does not know the Lord, nor has the word of the Lord been revealed to him.[3] The third time this happens, when Samuel again returns to Eli, the priest recognizes that it is the Lord calling the boy. He instructs Samuel to go back and lie down, and if the Lord calls yet again, to say, "Speak, LORD, for your servant is listening."[4]

This time, the Lord comes and stands near Samuel, then calls his name twice: "Samuel! Samuel!"—this is one of seven times in the Bible when God calls a person's name twice. Samuel responds as Eli instructed. What's so beautiful about this is that God calls out to Samuel first, before Samuel even realizes who is calling him! The Story of the Bible from Genesis to Revelation is not about how a lost people find their way home. The Story of the Bible is about how God perpetually looks for lost people to bring them home.

First Samuel 3 ends beautifully: "The LORD was with Samuel as he grew up, and he let none of Samuel's words fall to the ground. And all Israel from Dan [in the north] to Beersheba [in the south] recognized that Samuel was attested as a prophet of the LORD. The LORD continued to appear at Shiloh"—where the Ark of the Covenant was at this time—"and there He revealed himself to Samuel through his word."[5] Who is not letting whose words fall to the ground? Is God keeping Samuel's words from falling to the ground? Or is the prophet Samuel preventing the words of God from falling to the ground? This Hebraic phrase carries the idea of both! God and Samuel seem to have a relationship in which they esteem each other's words.

Imagine catching every word of the Lord that comes to you, taking those words in, and living from that place. And how about if God hears each of your words and doesn't allow any of them to go to waste? The living God catches our words. And when His words find us, we want to receive them and let them do their work. We see something similar in Isaiah 55:10-11:

> As the rain and the snow
> come down from heaven,
> and do not return to it
> without watering the earth
> and making it bud and flourish,
> so that it yields seed for the sower and bread for the eater,
> so is my word that goes out from my mouth:
> *It will not return to me empty,*
> but will accomplish what I desire
> and achieve the purpose for which I sent it (emphasis added).

Putting God in a Box

In the next chapter, 1 Samuel 4, the Israelites are about to go to war with their ancient nemesis, a people group known as the Philistines. It's important that we understand some historical and contextual nuances as we string these pearls together. The Hebrews are a desert or land people. Even in the modern State of Israel, it may be a beautiful sunny day, but the locals are typically not out on the Sea of Galilee. The boats on the water are usually tour boats carrying Westerners. The Hebrews are not a water people! Historically, water represented chaos or the abyss for them.[6] In contrast, the Philistines were a maritime or coastal people; they built ships and took them out on the water.[7] Their god, Dagon, represented this water-based people. The water people are about to battle the desert people: Dagon versus the living God.

In antiquity, when a nation went to war, it was believed that their god was fighting for them. The ten plagues experienced by Egypt were a showdown between the deified Egyptian pharaoh and the victorious God of Israel. In 1 Samuel 4, the Israelites go out to fight the Philistines and are routed, losing around 4,000 on the battlefield. The elders of Israel ask the returning soldiers why the Lord brought defeat upon them; they then suggest that the Ark of the Covenant be brought from Shiloh so the Lord will accompany them and save them from their enemies. The Israelites are starting to handle the Ark, their most important object, in an idolatrous way—like a lucky rabbit's foot. In this moment of defeat, God does not instruct them to bring out the Ark. But they remember how the waters of the Jordan split when the Ark of the Covenant was carried above the river.[8]

When the Ark arrives in their camp, the Israelites shout so loud that the ground shakes! The Philistines hear the noise and, upon learning the shouting is because of the Ark's presence, are afraid. "The gods have come into the camp," say the polytheistic water people. They recognize that the Ark is synonymous with the Israelites being empowered.

The Philistines and Israelites once again go to battle, with the desert people facing enormous loss; 30,000 Israelite foot soldiers die. On top of that, the Philistines capture the Ark of the Covenant and take it back to Philistia. At this point, if you're a Philistine, you're not thinking too highly of the Hebrew God. The Israelites were meant from the very beginning to rightly represent the living God, but they have misrepresented Him in the eyes of everyone around them. As we are about to see, when humans misrepresent God, He has a way of showing up and rightly representing Himself.

One of the commandments in the Decalogue, or Ten Words, says, "You shall not take the name of the LORD your God in vain."[9] We have often interpreted this in reference to our speech—that we are to abstain from cursing, and especially from using a curse word combined with God's name. Though this could be the meaning in the Hebraic language, it is not how the Jewish people understand and apply it. The two main Hebrew words in this commandment are *nasah* and *shaveh*. *Nasah* means "to carry, lift up, or utter." *Shaveh* means "vain, nothingness, or emptiness," having the idea of weightlessness. We are not to *nasah* the name of the Lord in *shaveh*. What the command is actually saying is, "You are not to carry the name of the Lord like it is nothing." This is much more pervasive than mere speech; it encompasses our entire lives!

Sometimes we just don't want to do the right thing. Have you ever been there? I often pray for God to give me the desire to want to do what's right. We need to be touched at the place of our want so we can rightly represent God with our lives, so we don't carry His name lightly, like it weighs nothing. The Israelites take the name of the Lord in vain by carrying it as if it were nothing and misrepresenting God in front of the Philistines. In response, God shows up and rightly represents Himself. This is one of my favorite passages in the Bible because God is about to go on tour!

God on Tour

At this time in history, the Philistines have five major cities that, together, are known as a pentapolis. Similar to how the United States has its own big five—New York City, Los Angeles, Houston, Chicago, and Philadelphia, the Philistine pentapolis includes Ashdod, Gaza, Ashkelon, Gath, and Ekron.[10] A high concentration of Philistines lives in every one of these five cities, in an area known as Philistia. The living God is about to tour among them, rightly representing Himself or carrying His own name with glory. The "glory" of God is *kavod* in Hebrew and *doxa* in Greek. In Hebrew, "glory" carries the idea of God's weight, heaviness, or honor. When God shows up in Philistia and carries His substance and weight, the Philistines see that He's not a lightweight; He's a heavyweight.

In antiquity, when you defeat a people group, they become your subjects. You absorb their land, cattle, agriculture, and sacred objects. The Philistines know that the Ark of the Covenant represents the God of the Israelites. After defeating them, per ancient practice, they take the Ark back to Philistia and put it in the temple of their god, Dagon. For them to put the Ark of the Covenant next to Dagon in his temple at Ashdod is like taking a victory lap. The Philistines see this as their god and the God of Israel spending the night together in the temple.

The next morning, they wake up and go into the temple of Dagon. Much to their surprise, Dagon has fallen face down, prostrate in a posture of worship, in front of the Ark of the Covenant. Seemingly unfazed, the Philistines *pick up their god who has fallen over.* Let's not overlook the irony of that! The story continues with night two of Dagon and the God of Israel in the temple. The next morning, they see that Dagon has again fallen face down, but this time it's worse; his head and hands have been broken off! During this era in antiquity, when one king defeated another, the victor would often cut off the head and hands of the conquered, symbolizing taking the other's authority and power.[11] Every Philistine who comes into the temple and sees Dagon prostrate, without his head and hands, understands exactly what the God of Israel has done.

The Philistines are getting nervous. After defeating the Israelites, they stopped thinking highly of the Hebrew God because they had captured the Ark of the Covenant. Now, this God is starting to represent Himself, as described in 1 Samuel 5: "*The LORD's hand was heavy* on the people of Ashdod and its vicinity; he brought devastation on them and afflicted them with tumors." In response to this, the people of Ashdod said, "The ark of the god of Israel must not stay here with us, because *His hand is heavy* on us and on Dagon our god."[12] The heavy hand of God carries the idea of glory, the opposite of vapor or nothingness. God is showing His weight, His substance. He is rightly representing Himself among the Philistines.

The Israelite God's first stop in the Philistine pentapolis is Ashdod. Because of the ruin that is happening, the residents send the Ark to the

Philistine city of Gath. It's like some dude said, "Hey, my mother-in-law lives in Gath…let's send the Ark to Gath!" The people there also break out in tumors, so they send the Ark to Ekron, another pentapolis city. The living God is on tour! At Ekron, the people realize the destruction they are experiencing is due to the Ark's presence amongst them. After all that has transpired, the Philistines finally get smart and say, "We need to send the Ark back to Israel. This is never going to stop!"

The Israelites feel like they have lost God—as the Ark has been gone for seven months—and are wondering if He is ever coming back. But God is about to return home! The Philistines get a new cart and hitch it up to two cows who have never been yoked. They put guilt offerings on the Ark, which was made of acacia wood and covered in gold. Now it is headed home on a cart pulled by two cows, with no human escort. Can you imagine being the Israelites at this town called Beth Shemesh as they look up one day and see the Ark entering the valley on a cart being pulled by two cows? They are witnessing God's homecoming, which is nothing short of miraculous because He is housed in a golden box traveling unattended. Through seven months in Philistia, the living God has rightly represented Himself. The Philistines now hold His name with weight, no longer treating it as nothing.

Israel Demands a King

As we continue flying over Scripture at 35,000 feet, we arrive at 1 Samuel 8—a chapter that is often overlooked yet is a key turning point in the story. Up to this time, Israel functions as a theocracy.[13] *Theos* is Greek for "God," and *krateo* means "to rule." God alone is Israel's king. Neither Moses nor Joshua, nor the judges nor Samuel, ever wore a crown or carried a scepter. They were prophets. They were priests. They were leaders. But God was Israel's king, leading His people into battle, splitting the abyss, and going first into the waters. God has repeatedly proven Himself faithful. Yet the Israelites approach Samuel, their prophet and final judge, and ask him to provide a human king for them. They want to be like all the other nations, who have a visible king to lead them into battle. Samuel tells the people,

1 Samuel-1 Kings

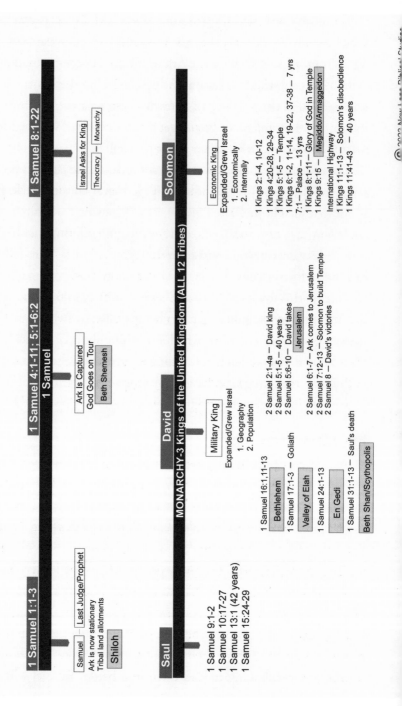

Represents sites Kristi often takes her Israel teams to

1 Samuel 1:1-3

Samuel — Last Judge/Prophet
Ark is now stationary
Tribal land allotments

Shiloh

1 Samuel 9:1-2
1 Samuel 10:17-27
1 Samuel 13:1 (42 years)
1 Samuel 15:24-29

Saul

1 Samuel 16:1, 11-13

Bethlehem
1 Samuel 17:1-3 — Goliath
Valley of Elah
1 Samuel 24:1-13
En Gedi
1 Samuel 31:1-13 — Saul's death
Beth Shan/Scythopolis

1 Samuel 4:1-11; 5:1-6:2
1 Samuel

Ark Is Captured
God Goes on Tour
Beth Shemesh

David
MONARCHY-3 Kings of the United Kingdom (ALL 12 Tribes)

Military King

Expanded/Grew Israel
1. Geography
2. Population

2 Samuel 2:1-4a — David king
2 Samuel 5:1-5 — 40 years
2 Samuel 5:6-10 — David takes Jerusalem
2 Samuel 6:1-7 — Ark comes to Jerusalem
2 Samuel 7:12-13 — Solomon to build Temple
2 Samuel 8 — David's victories

1 Samuel 8:1-22

Israel Asks for King
Theocracy — Monarchy

Solomon

Economic King
Expanded/Grew Israel
1. Economically
2. Internally

1 Kings 2:1-4, 10-12
1 Kings 4:20-28, 29-34
1 Kings 5:1-5 — Temple
1 Kings 6:1-2, 11-14, 19-22, 37-38 — 7 yrs
7:1 — Palace — 13 yrs
1 Kings 8:1-11 — Glory of God in Temple
1 Kings 9:15 — Megiddo/Armaggedon
International Highway
1 Kings 11:1-13 — Solomon's disobedience
1 Kings 11:41-43 — 40 years

© 2002 New Lens Biblical Studies

"This is not a good idea. What you're asking for is folly. This is not wisdom. No human will ever make a better king than the living God of Israel."

Let's pause and string some pearls together. Back in Genesis 12, when God makes His covenant with Avram, He repeatedly says, "I will. I will. I will." God's language was all about what He was going to do, not what Avram would have to do. When God is king, it's "I will, I will. I will." Samuel introduces new language to the Israelites. He cautions them, "Don't do this; a human king will *take* from you, and *take* from you, and *take* from you. It will be the opposite of how it has been with God as king. Don't do it!" Yet the Israelites persist.

In Samuel's response to the Israelites, he doesn't mince words describing what a human king will do and require of the people[14]—in stark contrast to God's generous posture with Avram. In a world where the gods are anchored in scarcity and provision, and sometimes require sacrificing firstborn sons, Samuel addresses the reality that a human king will take everything the Israelites prize most. In essence, Samuel is saying a human king will take everything from you. He will take your sons and daughters. He will take your crops, vineyards, and fields. He will take your servants.

In spite of all the warnings from their trusted prophet, the Israelites demand, "Give us a king." God gives them what they ask for and Israel shifts from a theocracy to a monarchy.[15] They transition from being a nation with God as king to a nation with a human as king.

The United Kingdom

Now we enter an era known as the United Kingdom, when all twelve tribes of Israel are unified as one nation. This period lasts throughout the reigns of Israel's first three kings or monarchs, beginning with Saul, who is followed by David, then Solomon. The United Kingdom lasts approximately 120 years.

Throughout the biblical narrative, the number forty carries significance. When we see forty, change is coming. In the Genesis flood, the rains fall for forty days and nights. When the Israelite spies go into the land of Canaan before the conquest, they are gone forty days and nights. After the spies return, the Israelites rebel, and God sentences them to forty years in the desert. Saul rules for forty years, as do David and Solomon. Jesus spends forty days in the desert. We are about to see the number forty in one of our stories, so we know change is coming.

Historically, David and Solomon are known as the two greatest kings of Israel. This has nothing to do with their spirituality; rather, Israel reached her zenith under their rule and reigns. Israel was never as geographically expansive, nor was she as wealthy and politically relevant as she was under the rule and reigns of David and Solomon. This is why we know them as the greats.

I teach a collegiate class on the canon of Scripture, or the history of how we got the Bible, which allows us to gain cultural and historical insight about Old Testament books. For example, ancient kingdoms were known for collecting the written compositions of or about their greatest kings. This is why Psalms, Proverbs, Ecclesiastes, and Song of Solomon are in the Masoretic text of the *Tanakh*, or Hebrew Bible—what is commonly known as the Old Testament. These texts are attributed primarily to David and Solomon, Israel's finest kings.

As we look at Saul, David, and Solomon, we're going to do so through a Middle Eastern lens. We want to perceive these accounts as the ancients would have seen, heard, interpreted, and applied them.

Israel's First King

First Samuel 9 introduces us to Saul, who would go on to become Israel's first human king. The Bible describes Saul as the most handsome man in Israel and a head taller than others. He is from the clan of Kish and the tribe of Benjamin. As we will soon see, Saul serves poorly as king; he is cowardly. The New Testament introduces us to another Saul, also from the clan of Kish and the tribe of Benjamin. New Testament Saul is a redo of Old Testament Saul. God reaches back to heal and restore, to renew and bring forward. Through New Testament Saul, God redeems a name and a life, bringing something better out of it.

Coronation day arrives for Old Testament Saul, detailed in 1 Samuel 10.

Israel prepares to take her first human king. Everyone shows up. Though Samuel had previously anointed Saul, when the Israelites look for him, he disappears! They inquire of the Lord as to where he is, and the Lord tells them that their soon-to-be king is hiding amid luggage! It's coronation day, with all of Israel gathered to watch Saul take the throne and scepter as first monarch of Israel. But he is hiding; he is cowardly. How are the Israelites feeling at this point? Are they remembering Samuel's warning about the folly of demanding a human king? Saul goes on to rule as king of Israel for forty years.

Slinger Versus Infantryman

Here, the Bible shifts from black and white into high-definition color. While Saul is still alive, the Lord commands Samuel to anoint the next king of Israel. Anointing a new king while the current king occupies the throne is certain to evoke jealousy. The Lord sends Samuel to the city of Bethlehem, to the home of a man named Jesse, who has eight sons. The Lord directs Samuel to anoint the youngest, David, as Israel's next monarch.[16]

Now we come to one of the most famous passages in the Bible. We are going to look at it in its historical and cultural contexts, the way the ancients would have understood it. In antiquity, some battles were fought by individuals instead of armies. This style of fighting was called representative warfare or single combat.[17] Instead of the mass carnage of thousands of men killing each other, each side selects a champion to fight the champion of the other side. With their champions facing each other, the armies line up on either side to watch man versus man. Whoever wins, their side wins. Whoever loses, their side loses.

Representative warfare is about to play out in our story as the water people (the Philistines) and the land people (the Israelites) go at it once again. This, however, is not just Goliath fighting David; it is the Philistine god Dagon fighting the living God of Israel. Each side's representative fights in the spirit and power of his tribe's deity. We will now experience the cultural clash of the titans.

Let's look at 1 Samuel 17 with Middle Eastern eyes. The Philistines, camped at Ephes Dammim, and the Israelites, camped in the Valley of Elah, prepare for war. Both sides occupy a hill, with a valley between them. The Philistine champion, Goliath, comes from Gath—one of the Philistine pentapolis cities. Goliath stands more than nine feet tall and is described as wearing a coat of scale armor. Does that sound familiar? Today's armed forces have men and women who serve in different capacities. Goliath is what we would call an infantryman, trained and equipped for hand-to-hand combat. His weaponry and size indicate his skill at killing his enemy up close.

For forty days, Goliath, the chosen champion of the Philistines, comes to the Valley of Elah and talks trash to the Israelites. He taunts and demands that they send out their champion to fight him. Keep in mind that King Saul stands a head taller than all other Israelites. He should be volunteering to fight Goliath. The king always goes first, but Saul is a coward. Here we discover cultural nuances that help us better understand the story.

In the West, we often think of David as a young boy when he fights Goliath because we find him at home tending his father's sheep while his older brothers are on the battlefield. But this isn't a characterization of his age. In the Middle East, then and now, it is the responsibility of the youngest child to take care of their parents. In taking teams to Israel, I worked for four years with a bus driver named Kamal, a Palestinian Christian. He is the fifth and final child in his family. One night as I was having dinner with Kamal and his wife, I asked him to tell me the story of how they met. Kamal said, "I chose my wife because I knew she would help me take care of my parents. It is my job as the last born or the youngest to take care of them."

David remains at home tending his father's sheep not necessarily because he is young, but because he is the youngest son. We read this story in 1 Samuel 17, but we discover relevant information in the chapter directly before. In 1 Samuel 16:18, one of Saul's servants says, "'I have seen a son of Jesse of Bethlehem who knows how to play the lyre. He is a brave man and a warrior. He speaks well and is a fine-looking man. And the LORD is with him." Did you catch that? David is a courageous man, a warrior. A boy would not be sent out as representative to fight against a grown man of another people group. That's a sure way to lose your nation! David is a man of war as well as a musician.

Armies in the Ancient Near East and throughout antiquity had whole divisions of soldiers called slingers who carried slingshots. Slingers maintained such accuracy they could shoot a bird out of the sky with a rock. Judges 20:16 describes "seven hundred select troops" who "could sling a stone at a hair and not miss." Their precision was remarkable!

Goliath is a grown man. David is a grown man. Goliath is an infantryman. David is a slinger.

David arrives at the Israelite camp on the fortieth day of Goliath's trash talking and taunting. There's that number forty! *Change is coming.* David hears Goliath and gives it right back to the Philistine champion. David cries out, "Who is this uncircumcised Philistine that he should defy the armies of the living God?" Now that's a shot below the belt! David is furious because Goliath carries the name of the Lord in vain; he's holding it too lightly. David overhears some soldiers talking about the perks King Saul provides to whoever fights and kills Goliath. Saul will pay the victor a nice sum of money and release him from any future tax obligation in Israel. Saul also promises to give the champion his daughter in marriage. David hears these incentives—which would not motivate a boy—and, as an adult man who is a seasoned warrior, says he will fight Goliath.

Keep in mind it should be King Saul who heads out to battle. Instead, he dresses David in his armor. Now, here, too, is where we have often assumed David was a boy—it's because Saul's armor does not fit him. But that is not what the text says. Rather, David puts on Saul's armor and says, "I can't go out in this because I'm not used to wearing it."[18] Slingers don't wear armor! They need to be free and agile, their arms unencumbered.

Now notice the story, a redo of what happened back in 1 Samuel 5. This makes me love the Bible! It's the fortieth day, and change is coming. David hears Goliath taunting and determines to go deal with him. David picks up his sling, goes over to the streambed, and gathers five stones. Historically and culturally, everyone present knows that David is going to win. Why?

Goliath must get to David in order to fight him! All David has to do is hit Goliath with a stone, which is like a bullet. Dagon and the living God are about to go at it in the Valley of Elah through a champion named Goliath and a champion named David.

David descends into the valley and Goliath starts walking toward him, planning to get close enough to fight. David takes off running toward Goliath, focused and on mission! While running, David reaches into his shepherd's bag, pulls out a stone, and puts it in his sling. He hurls the rock, hitting Goliath in the forehead right between his eyes. With a projectile coming that hard from a slinger, Goliath's body should have fallen backward! If you've ever been punched, you've likely experienced falling back from the impact. Yet Goliath falls face down! He never even gets close to David before David puts a stone in his forehead. Goliath's body falls forward, prostrate on the ground. Does this posture sound familiar?

You've got to love David because back when he was talking trash to Goliath, he said, "I'm going to kill you, and then I'm going to chop off your head with your own sword." What does a king do when he defeats another king? Remember Dagon and the living God in the temple? David takes out Goliath's sword and chops off his head. All who witness this moment know that the living God of Israel has again defeated Dagon. The Philistines run for their lives, with the Israelites in hot pursuit. The Israelites then plunder the Philistine camp. David takes Goliath's weapons, as well as the head of the Philistine champion. When Abner, commander of the Israelite army, brings David to Saul, David is still holding the Philistine's head!

In the pantheon of ancient gods, the living God of Israel shows up. He demonstrates His substance, weight, and glory in a temple in Philistia as well as in the Valley of Elah. A champion and a god lose their heads. The watching world comes to know and realize who the God of the Hebrews is. As David said to Goliath before killing him, "I'm going to chop off your head and the whole world will know that there is a God in Israel."[19] David does not fight for his own credit. He fights to carry the name of the Lord and give it the weight—the glory—it deserves. David rightly represents the Lord in the Valley of Elah.

Military King and Economic King

We know David as a military king. He's constantly going to war, increasing the size of Israel through geography and population. An entire chapter in the Bible lists the kings and kingdoms David defeated.[20] He is a hot-blooded man of war who will talk trash to you, chop off your head with your own sword, and then carry your head around. David is a military king, and this is how Israel expands while he is on the throne.

Solomon takes the throne next and is more of an economic king. He builds up the infrastructure of Israel, including three cities—Hazor, Gezer, and Megiddo—along the International Coastal Highway.[21] He sets up these three cities as tax stations, which helps him become extremely wealthy as he taxes the nations who travel through.

God tells David, "I will build *you* a house—a dynasty," and that David's son Solomon will build God's house.[22] As previously mentioned, God moves toward His people. He never intended to live in a permanent structure like a temple. Besides, the word we commonly translate as "temple" actually means "house." In the Bible, temples are pagan. Jesus said His Father's house should be called a house of prayer for all nations. God says, "Build me a tent. Build me a tabernacle." Solomon introduces the language of temple. What we're going to see in the next chapter is that Solomon builds many temples, but only one to the God of Israel. All the others are to the gods of the foreign women who enslave him.

God gives immense wisdom to Solomon, but the man rarely chooses to walk in it. The downfalls of Israel's economic king are wealth and women. We saw Shimshon get trapped by a Philistine woman; darkness put out the light. Solomon carries this same attraction to foreign women and experiences similar results. Throughout his life, Solomon is ruled. The governor gets governed. The king gets kinged. The ruler gets ruled. Wealth and women are ever his weaknesses, and this leads to the downward slide of a nation.

In our next chapter, the United Kingdom divides. In the Gospels, Jesus says, "If a kingdom is divided against itself, that kingdom cannot stand."[23]

Jesus is a Jewish man speaking to a Jewish audience. They know their history well. When He says that, everyone present is thinking about what we're going to look at next: Israel is about to be fractured and weakened. All because a king got kinged and a ruler got ruled by things other than the living God.

———— ▪ ————

How are you carrying the name of the Lord? In what ways are you taking the name of the Lord in vain? We want to be a kingdom-of-God people who are led by the Spirit of God, who are informed by the Word of God, and who rightly represent God. As a watching world observes us, may it bear witness to lives under the rule and reign of the living God. May we be a people who carry God's name as if it's *everything*, and not as if it's nothing.

Chapter 6

THE DIVIDED KINGDOM

I often tell my college students, "You have not learned a thing when you've seen it. You have not learned a thing when you've heard it. You have not learned a thing when you've seen *and* heard it. You have truly learned a thing when you can give it away."

We are meant to live like rivers, not lakes. The word of the Lord comes to us and is meant to flow through us to others. We become conduits and emissaries of the word of the Lord. At this point in your journey through the biblical narrative, what does it look like for you to live like a river with all that you are gleaning and beholding? In what ways are you allowing the word of the Lord to find you, enter you, and move through you to others?

In these next chapters, we are going to see how God responds when humanity does its worst. This speaks to some important questions many of us grapple with at some point: Is it possible for me to go too far? Can I get beyond even God's ability to save, restore, and bring me home? In spite of all that God intended for the Israelites, we are about to watch the lights go out completely. Then we will find out if God can turn them back on again.

Prophets and Priests

In the Old Testament, God sanctioned three different offices or roles within the kingdom of Israel. One was the kings, including Saul, David, and Solomon, the first three monarchs of Israel. The other two positions were prophets and priests. A prophet takes the words of God and gives them to the people. A priest takes the words of the people and gives them to God, primarily through the offering of sacrifices. A priest intercedes on behalf of the people. Essentially, the prophets and the priesthood are God's ways of communicating with His people. He wants us to be able to hear His words as He is hearing our words.

Israel Prospers Under Solomon

At this point in the narrative, Israel has shifted from a theocracy to a monarchy, from having God as her king to having a human as her king. Around 970 BC, Solomon comes to rule as Israel's third monarch. He is more of an economic king, focused on domestic and foreign policy. Solomon wants to build the wealth and strength of Israel from within. He does so by taxing the nations as they come through the International Coastal Highway. First Kings 9:15 lists three cities—Hazor, Megiddo, and Gezer—that served as tax cities or tax booths located on that main road.

At the end of the previous chapter, I mentioned that Solomon had two fundamental weaknesses that ruled him: wealth and women. We will soon see what happens when a king gets kinged, and when a ruler gets ruled. As we do, consider this: Who or what is governing you? Who or what is ruling you? Let's keep in mind God's original ideal for the Israelites, which was to fill the land and be a witness to the watching world, so the world could see what it looks like to walk with the living God.

As we work our way through an obscure part of the story, we'll string some pearls together. Solomon reigns over the United Kingdom, with all twelve tribes unified under his monarchy. First Kings 4 uses poetic language to describe the Israelites under Solomon's rule. They have plenty of food and drink. They are as numerous as the stars in the sky and the sand on the seashore. They are happy. Solomon's vast kingdom stretches from the Euphrates

River to the land of the Philistines, all the way to the border of Egypt. The people within Solomon's domain pay tribute and serve the king.

The text is specific in naming Solomon's vast *daily* provisions: thirty cors (approximately five metric tons) of the finest flour and sixty cors of meal; ten stall-fed cattle and twenty pasture-fed cattle; one hundred sheep and goats, along with deer, gazelles, roebucks, and fattened fowl. That's a lot of meals! Solomon's banquet table is overflowing. Everyone lives in peace and safety, "under their own vine and under their own fig tree."[1] This is a beautiful Jewish idiom for heaven. In other words, life under Solomon is heaven on earth. It is anchored in abundance. All is flourishing and there are plenty of provisions. The king's 40,000 stalls for chariot horses and 12,000 horsemen or charioteers offer a glimpse of his vast wealth. Designated officers keep provisions adequately stocked for the king and all those invited to his table. Life under Solomon is good!

First Kings 4 goes on to describe Solomon's unparalleled wisdom, insight, and understanding. His wisdom surpasses that of any other person in the East, even that of the mighty Egyptians. The Bible credits Solomon with speaking 3,000 proverbs and penning more than 1,000 songs. Solomon's acumen brings the nations to Israel. God's plan is for the nations to bear witness to something they had never seen. Kings send representatives to *shema* or listen to Solomon's wisdom. He is sought out for counsel by the nations, who don't come empty-handed. They bring tribute, making Solomon even wealthier.

In the Hebrew mind, a wise person is one skilled in the art of living life well. A wise person lives intentionally. Wisdom is not just being smart or intellectual; wisdom travels deeper. The nations are coming to Solomon—via the International Coastal Highway—because his wisdom surpasses that of all others. He is skilled in the art of living well. At this point in the story, life looks amazing for Israel. She is fulfilling her mandate to reach the nations with the message of the one true God, and she is revealing what it looks like to live under Him. But things are about to change.

God's House

Solomon builds God a house on Mount Moriah—known today as the Temple Mount—in Jerusalem, in the same location where Herod later added to the Temple rebuilt under Zerubbabel. In the Bible, temples were usually pagan, but from the beginning, God has wanted to live among His people. This is His heart! First Kings 6 details the specifications of God's house—the Temple, which took Solomon seven years to build. In contrast, it took Solomon *thirteen* years to complete his palace. Do not miss this: Israel's third king spent nearly twice the amount of time building his house as he spent building God's house.

The Cost of Intermingling and Intermarrying

What happens to this nation holding her space, ministering to a watching world, demonstrating what it looks like to be skilled in the art of living under the rule and governance of the living God? Solomon's greed takes over and, as his heart changes, the downward slide begins. *The lights go out.*

First Kings 11 is one of the hardest passages to read in the Bible. It is difficult to absorb because the story takes a turn. We pick it up in verses 1-2:

> King Solomon, however, loved many foreign women besides Pharaoh's daughter—Moabites, Ammonites, Edomites, Sidonians and Hittites. They were from nations about which the Lord had told the Israelites, "You must not intermarry with them, because they will surely turn your hearts after their gods." Nevertheless, Solomon held fast to them in love.

That phrase "held fast to them in love" is also used in Deuteronomy when the Israelites are instructed to "hold fast to [the Lord]."[2] Solomon is meant to be committed to the living God in fidelity, or *ahavah*, which is Hebrew for "love." Yet the king is not holding fast to the Lord; rather, he is holding fast to foreign women. And he will not let go.

The very reason God warned the Israelites not to intermingle or intermarry plays out with their king, whose heart is being turned toward the capricious, angry gods of other nations. As 1 Kings 11 continues, wealth and women capture Solomon, and he holds fast to them in love. Solomon's heart falters in devotion and commitment to the Lord, unlike that of his father, David.

The living God intended for Israel to display to a watching world what it looks like to live under His rule and reign. Yet two specific foreign gods are named in 1 Kings 11:5—one of the more sobering verses in Scripture— that Solomon follows and worships. The first is Ashtoreth, the fertility goddess of the Sidonians and precursor to Aphrodite. Worshipping at a temple of Ashtoreth involves sexual practice and immorality. The second foreign god is Molek, god of the Ammonites, one of the vilest gods in the Old Testament. Worship of Molek sometimes included parents throwing their children into a fire.[3]

When a king chooses a certain course of action, his people tend to follow. Solomon is supposed to be anchored in wisdom. He is meant to show the nations what it looks like to be skilled in the art of living and flourishing in wellness and harmony with the living God. But now as the nations come through Israel, they bear witness to the Israelites going to the temples of Ashtoreth and Molek. Do the Israelites look any different from the peoples of the other nations? Does Solomon stand out from the kings of the other nations?

In the previous chapter, we learned what one of the Ten Words (Commandments) means in the Hebrew language. "You shall not take the name of the Lord in vain" refers not exclusively to speech; it's much bigger than that. We are not to *nasah*, or "carry," the name of the Lord as if it were nothing, as if it were empty. Rather, God intends for us to carry His name with all of its glory, weight, and substance.

Solomon and the Israelites take the name of the Lord in vain. They misrepresent Him among the nations. *The lights are going out.* A king gets kinged, a ruler gets ruled.

Solomon is known to Christians as a man who built the Temple of the Lord. But the reality is that Solomon built *many* temples to *many* gods,

Divided Kingdom

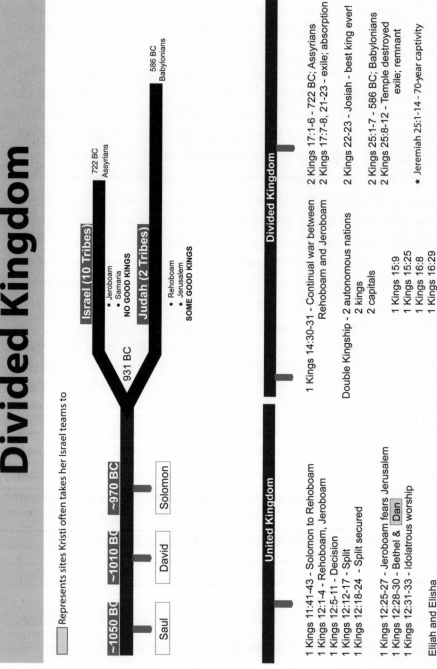

Represents sites Kristi often takes her Israel teams to

~1050 BC   ~1010 BC   ~970 BC

Saul   David   Solomon

931 BC

Israel (10 Tribes)
- Jeroboam
- Samaria
NO GOOD KINGS

Judah (2 Tribes)
- Rehoboam
- Jerusalem
SOME GOOD KINGS

722 BC
Assyrians

586 BC
Babylonians

United Kingdom

1 Kings 11:41-43 - Solomon to Rehoboam
1 Kings 12:1-4 - Rehoboam, Jeroboam
1 Kings 12:5-11 - Decision
1 Kings 12:12-17 - Split
1 Kings 12:18-24 - Split secured

1 Kings 12:25-27 - Jeroboam fears Jerusalem
1 Kings 12:28-30 - Bethel & Dan
1 Kings 12:31-33 - Idolatrous worship

Elijah and Elisha

Divided Kingdom

1 Kings 14:30-31 - Continual war between
Rehoboam and Jeroboam

Double Kingship - 2 autonomous nations
2 kings
2 capitals

1 Kings 15:9
1 Kings 15:25
1 Kings 16:8
1 Kings 16:29

2 Kings 17:1-6 - 722 BC; Assyrians
2 Kings 17:7-8, 21-23 - exile; absorption

2 Kings 22-23 - Josiah - best king ever!

2 Kings 25:1-7 - 586 BC; Babylonians
2 Kings 25:8-12 - Temple destroyed
exile; remnant

★ Jeremiah 25:1-14 - 70-year captivity

including high places or shrines of worship to Chemosh, Ashtoreth, and Molek, as well as the gods of all his foreign wives. Solomon is a temple-builder. Solomon is also a taker. He is the king described in 1 Samuel 8 who is going to take, and take, and take from the people. God gave Solomon wisdom, but the king didn't always live from that place.

When God Sees, God Acts

Another Jewish idiom applies here. When we read phrases such as "the eyes of the Lord," or so-and-so "did evil in the eyes of the Lord," or "the eyes of the Lord search throughout the earth," it alludes to the reality that when God sees, He acts. God's sight provokes His action. We see this all the way back in Genesis 22, when Avraham takes Isaac up on Mount Moriah and the living God provides a ram in the thicket rather than requiring Avraham to sacrifice his son. In English Bibles, when Isaac asks where the sacrifice is, Avraham replies by saying, "The Lord will provide." As mentioned previously, in Hebrew, that phrase is "the Lord will see (to it)." When God sees, He acts.

In this narrative with Solomon, God sees what is taking place. Through a Middle Eastern lens, we recognize that if Solomon builds temples all over Israel and leads the nation into immorality and pagan worship, God sees and responds accordingly. In essence, He tells Solomon, "Since this is your attitude, I am going to tear the kingdom from you—but not in your lifetime. It will happen during the lifetime of your son. For the sake of David and Jerusalem, I'm not going to tear all the kingdom from you; I will leave you one tribe."[4]

The Kingdom Divides

Solomon rules for forty years. He dies around 931–930 BC, and his son Rehoboam takes the throne. Rehoboam is a scoundrel. The people come to Rehoboam and ask him to lift the burdensome yoke his father Solomon placed on them. Remember, Solomon built his wealth by taxing the nations coming through the International Coastal Highway, while also implementing heavy internal taxation on the Israelites. In 1 Samuel 8, God, through the prophet Samuel, cautioned the Israelites that a human king would take and take and take from them. Solomon was the taker. He took the Israelites' money. He enacted forced labor, requiring some of the people to work for him for free. Now Rehoboam is king, and the people want a tax break. They want the heavy yoke lifted off.

We see what kind of man Rehoboam is by how he responds. Initially, he does well by consulting the elders who had served his father. They counsel Rehoboam to give a favorable reply to the people, thus ensuring the people's loyalty to the king. Unfortunately, Rehoboam rejects their advice and turns instead to his friends, the young men he grew up with, who are now serving him. They essentially tell him to make the tax burden worse, to increase it.

To be clear, if you were running for office, you would never run on this platform, right? Promising double taxation will not bode well for you at the voting precincts! But this is not a democracy, it's a monarchy—and Rehoboam is wearing the crown. He's on the throne; he has the power. The story line goes down quickly when Rehoboam rejects the wisdom of the elders and seeks out his friends.

The king refuses to listen to the elders and the people. The nation responds to Rehoboam's increased taxation by splitting. The United Kingdom becomes the Divided Kingdom, as detailed in 1 Kings 12. Rehoboam keeps the southern tribes, Judah and Benjamin, but loses the others. This split sends the Israelites down a dual trajectory. Under Saul, David, and Solomon, it is known as the United Kingdom. From Rehoboam's rule around 930 BC forward, it is known as the Divided Kingdom, with both kingdoms headed for exile in foreign countries. *The lights are going out.* Can God turn them back on? Have the Israelites gone so far that they can't come back?

Years ago, my mentor gave me a gift when she challenged me to always listen to the generations older than me. I am committed to this. Wisdom is found in the generations preceding us who have lived more life and are skilled in the art of living well.

Kingdom Rivalry

To be a nation, one needs a king and a capital. After the split, the northern tribes follow Jeroboam, one of Solomon's high-ranking administrators. He is crowned king of the Northern Kingdom of Israel. The tribes in the south become known as the Southern Kingdom of Judah.

Now there are two Jewish nations, with Rehoboam leading the Southern Kingdom of Judah and Jeroboam leading the Northern Kingdom of Israel. The issue of capital cities arises both for political and religious reasons. The south gets Jerusalem, which means they get God's house—the Temple. For the Jewish people, if they want to go see God, they go to Jerusalem! For the Northern Kingdom, Jeroboam makes the ancient city of Shechem the political capital.[5] From 930 BC on, two independent Israelite nations live side by side—Israel to the north, and Judah to the south. An ongoing animosity develops between Jeroboam and Rehoboam. It's like a sibling rivalry: north versus south.

If you have siblings, perhaps you have experienced how it is okay for you to antagonize and be annoyed by them, but if someone else messes with your brother or sister, loyalty outweighs familial differences, and you defend them. This is what the kings start to do. When there is no disruption from outside people groups, they fight with each other. But when external peoples try to invade, they band together against the other nations. They are living in a contractual relationship of hostility. But, as Jesus later says, "Every kingdom divided against itself…will not stand."[6] The Jews who hear Jesus say this are likely thinking about the country's division. They are a historical people; they remember.

More Golden Calves

Jeroboam has a problem. Though he rules over the Northern Kingdom of Israel, a significantly larger portion of the Israelite population and geography, the Southern Kingdom of Judah retains something irreplaceable: Jerusalem. Jeroboam fears that if the population of the Northern Kingdom goes down to Jerusalem multiple times a year to worship the living God at the Temple, they will stay and revert their allegiance to the house

Bull idol located in the Israel Museum in Jerusalem

of Rehoboam. Jeroboam knows he cannot compete with Jerusalem, or the house of God located there. From the ancient Israelite perspective, God is in the south.[7]

Jeroboam is about to logic himself into disaster. He operates without wisdom, failing in the art of living well. Rather, he trusts his own judgment. Have you ever thought up an elaborate plan that did not work out well for you? When we trust in our own knowledge, we can get ourselves in trouble. We logic ourselves into disaster. We are about to see this with Jeroboam.

Jeroboam does not want his people in the north going south to Jerusalem in order to worship. So, he comes up with a plan. Polytheism was strong in the ancient world; the Israelites couldn't seem to shake it. Remember, as God married Moses and the people by giving the tablets, the Israelites worshipped a golden calf at the base of Mount Sinai. Fast-forward to King Jeroboam, who decides to build two worship centers: one at Dan, located in northern Israel in a region known today as the Golan Heights, and the other at Bethel, in the southern portion of his kingdom just ten miles north of Jerusalem.

Jeroboam sets up a golden calf in each location, then tells his people, "These are your gods, who brought you out of Egypt." In doing this, Jeroboam takes the name of the Lord in vain. This setup becomes a sin to the Israelites because they stop going to Jerusalem. Instead, they go to Dan and Bethel to worship the golden calves. Second Kings 17:21 says, "Jeroboam enticed Israel away from following the LORD and caused them to commit a great sin." Once again, the Israelites look like all the other nations.

Now, when you imagine the golden calves, what do you think they look like? How big are they? Do you envision a life-sized, ferocious-looking Wall Street bull? Archaeological excavations have unearthed calves used in ancient worship. To date, the largest calf found in the land of Israel is only *seven inches by five inches!*[8] This reality has always hit me hard. The golden idols worshipped by the Israelites were likely the size of small stuffed animals!

When I take biblical studies teams to Dan, we go to the excavated worship center that Jeroboam built, including where the altar stood. We walk up large steps to a huge platform and can look out and see modern-day Lebanon. Standing in that place, we imagine the Israelites of the Northern Kingdom coming all the way to Dan. Upon arrival, they climb the steps with their sacrifices and lay prostrate to worship a surprisingly small idol. They take the name of the Lord in vain and misrepresent Him to the nations. *The lights are going out.* God sees, and when God sees, He acts! When He gets misrepresented, He shows up and rightly represents Himself.

We all have a version of this. When we get pressed, when we get scared, when we are not okay, we tend to reach for something or someone by habit or by history, as small as it may seem. We would do well not to judge the Israelites as though we don't have our own style of lying face down to an object or person.

Calamity Is Coming

For the prophets, the exile epoch serves as the center in the biblical narrative: pre-exilic, exilic, and post-exilic. Pre-exilic prophets such as Hosea and Amos prophesied before the exile. Exilic prophets such as Ezekiel and Daniel prophesied to the Israelites while they were in exile. Post-exilic prophets like Haggai, Zechariah, and Malachi prophesied after the exile. For the most part, the writing prophets of the Old Testament—including Isaiah, Jeremiah, and Amos—essentially deliver one message. They come on the scene and, in poetic language, issue a serious warning: "If you don't stop, calamity is coming. If you continue living like all the other nations, if you keep going to the Ashtoreth temples and throwing your children in the fire to Molek, calamity will come upon you. God will not allow you to live in the land and openly misrepresent Him in the eyes of the nations."

Do the Israelites listen?

I don't know about you, but I have had seasons in my life when I persisted in wrongdoing even though the Holy Spirit cautioned, "Turn—this isn't going to work out for you." But I wanted something. I was holding fast to it in love rather than loving the Lord. The longer I continued, the more it ate me alive. When I finally decided I'd had enough, God graciously restored and pieced me back together.

How does God respond when we allow—and even cause—the lights to go out?

The Lights Go Out in the North

The Northern Kingdom of Israel does not turn, and calamity comes. Around 722–721 BC, the Assyrians invade. The Assyrians were one of the most horrific people groups in history—think ISIS, which we previously mentioned in relation to Jonah. The Assyrians were not just conquerors, they were torturers. They invented crucifixion. The Romans would come along hundreds of years later and perfect that practice by the time of Jesus and the Gospel era. When the Assyrian war drum was heard, it would send waves of terror among people because they didn't just capture, they tormented.

The Assyrians invade the Northern Kingdom of Israel, carrying many of the Israelites back to Assyria and into exile. As for the Israelites that remain in the land, Assyria brings in five other people groups that intermarry with them.[9] We know them as the Samaritans, people who are ethnically half Jewish. Jesus sits with a Samaritan woman at a well more than 700 years later. The Israelites intermingled and intermarried so much that in historical and theological terms, we say the Northern Kingdom went into exile in Assyria and was absorbed, meaning they lost their distinctly Hebrew bloodline.[10] The Samaritan population emerges as ten Israelite tribes are immersed into Assyrian life, theology, and ethnicity. In essence, all but two of the tribes of Israel are lost. *The lights go out in the north.*

The Lights Go Out in the South

Regarding the kings of the north, the Bible repeatedly says so-and-so "did evil in the eyes of the LORD."[11] When the rule of one northern king ends, the next king comes along and does even more evil than his father before him, and the cycle continues. If you are an Israelite living in the Southern Kingdom and watching the lights go out on your brothers and sisters in the north, how do you feel?

The Southern Kingdom has some upright kings like Hezekiah and Josiah, who lead the people in renewal and revival. Because of this, Judah lasts a little longer than Israel. But ultimately, the people in Judah don't turn back to the Lord either. As we've observed over and over, when God sees, God acts. Two of the twelve tribes remain, but they are still misrepresenting the Lord and taking His name in vain.

In 586 BC, the Babylonians, under the kingship of Nebuchadnezzar, invade and conquer the Southern Kingdom of Judah. The Babylonian army breaks down the walls around Jerusalem. Nebuzaradan, commander of the imperial guard, enters Jerusalem and burns the Temple of the Lord to the ground, along with all the other important buildings. The people who remain in the city are taken into exile in Babylon.[12] Some of the poorest Israelites, like farmers, are left behind to work the land. *The lights have gone out in the south.*

Is All Hope Lost?

God's original vision was for the Israelites to fill the land and live like a tribe the world had never seen. He intended them to show what it was to walk in wisdom, to be skilled in the art of living well. The Assyrians captured the Northern Kingdom, taking those tribes into exile. They intermingled and intermarried to the point of being absorbed into the Assyrian way of life. The Babylonians conquered the tribes of the Southern Kingdom and took them to Babylon. At this point in the story, none of the twelve tribes have governance or autonomy in the land. They live in exile in other countries. Could they be any further from what God had originally planned?

The lights have gone out and the hope of Israel seems lost. If you are an Israelite who remains in the land, and you know the northern tribes have been absorbed in Assyria and the southern tribes have been exiled to Babylon—including men like Daniel, Shadrach, Meshach, and Abednego— how do you feel? Are you questioning whether your people have gone too far in misrepresenting the living God before the nations?

The Covenant Is on God

We are going to end this chapter on a hopeful note because we always end in hope. Let us ponder a few things that are beautiful. Jesus is of the tribe of Judah, which is in the south. The ancestors of Jesus go into Babylon. We hope His lineage continues because God still has one more promise to fulfill to Avraham. Here is where the gospel in its Old Testament beauty gets told because, if the promise depends on the Israelites or us, we are all in trouble. The Israelites have been absorbed in Assyria and exiled to Babylon.

Let's go back now to more ancient times. In Genesis 12, God comes to Avram and makes the promises. Then Genesis 15 provides one of the most watershed gospel passages in the entire Story of the Bible. Yet we often read it without understanding the cultural significance of what is taking place. The word of the Lord comes to Avram in a vision, instructing him to get a heifer, a goat, and a ram, as well as a dove and a young pigeon.

Now, if God came to you and told you to go get a bunch of animals and birds, how would you respond? "Why? What for? This is not one of our cultural practices!" Isn't it interesting that Avram knew precisely what was going on? God always meets His people exactly where they are, yet He never leaves them there. What God does with Avram in Genesis 15 is typical covenantal activity. This is gospel gorgeous.

In Avram's day, when you enter a covenant or contract with another party, you come together, bring animals, and cut them in half. You make a trench or pathway, then line up the animals along the pathway so their blood flows down into the trench. No covenant ever gets signed without blood; it's a requirement. In fact, in Hebrew, one does not "make" a covenant, one "cuts" a covenant. To ratify a covenant in Avram's day, both parties walk through the blood. In so doing, they communicate to each other, "If I break my end of the covenant, you can do this to me." It is a covenantal transaction.

To this day, more traditional Bedouin fathers and grandfathers do this to affirm the conditions of an engagement. The ceremony is not as elaborate, but they cut the throat of an animal, make a trail of blood, and the grandfather or father of the bride faces off with the grandfather or father of the groom. The patriarch from the bride's family walks through the blood, in essence saying, "If my daughter violates the marriage covenant, you can do this to me." Then the patriarch of the groom's family passes through, his actions communicating, "If my son violates the marriage covenant, you can do this to me." This echoes ancient covenantal activity.

The moment God instructs Avram to go get the animals and birds, Avram knows he is about to make a contract with God. If you're Avram in this moment, how do you feel? Scared? I would be thinking, *I can't keep this covenant. I'm going to mess up, and God will have to split me in half!*

Even if Avram can keep the covenant for five days, or seven months, or three years, he cannot do so forever. Avram isn't perfect. This is another one of those moments where God does something with Avram the world had never seen. Avram splits the animals, preparing for the covenantal ritual. Then something unusual and unexpected happens. God puts Avram to sleep—like the deep sleep He put Adam into before creating Eve. And then God, in the form of a smoking firepot, passes through the blood. The living God goes first! God is saying, "If I break this covenant that I am making with you, Avram, you can do this to Me."

In antiquity, covenants are always between two parties who pass through the blood. Both are accountable, and the greater party always goes first. So now it's Avram's turn! In Genesis 15, however, Avram never walks through the blood. He wakes up into a covenant that has been made and ratified by God alone. God does not let Avram walk through the blood because God has known from the very beginning that humanity cannot keep the covenant. If the covenant were left to us, we would break it!

God understands that He alone makes the covenant, and He alone upholds and keeps the covenant. By not allowing Avram to walk through the blood, God literally saves his life. God passes through a second time in place of Avram in the form of a blazing torch.

This is a tremor of the gospel because if the covenant hangs on the Israelite, we are in trouble. But if the covenant hangs on God alone, we have hope. When Avraham takes Isaac up the mountain in Genesis 22, the living God stays Avraham's hand. God's covenant with Avram is not bilateral; it is not on God *and* Avram. Rather, it is on God alone to make it, keep it, and uphold it. It is a unilateral covenant.

As we have journeyed through this narrative, we have seen the folly of the Israelites. They turn their hearts astray; they hold fast to other gods; they misrepresent the living God and take His name in vain. Those exiled from the Northern Kingdom intermingle and intermarry in Assyria to the point that they are absorbed. Those exiled from the Southern Kingdom have been carried off to Babylon, and the Babylonians burn the Temple of the Lord to the ground. At this point in the story, in every possible way, the Israelites have abdicated the original mandate given to them by the living God. The question is this: Is the covenant on the Israelites, or is it on God?

Genesis 15 answers in such an ancient and profound way. God knows from the very beginning that it is on Him to make, keep, and uphold the covenant. With Genesis 15 anchoring us, God unilaterally passes through the blood. He alone keeps this covenant from first to last. Genesis 15 is God saving Avram's life, as well as the lives of all Israelites and covenant breakers for all time. This is the reason we cannot die on the cross for our own sins—our blood can't cleanse us; it's not pure. Another had to shed His blood for us: the Son of God, Jesus Christ.

Hope in Exile

All twelve tribes are in exile, but the covenant is on God. There is hope. The Northern Kingdom never comes back; Assyria absorbs them. Through the prophet Jeremiah, God comes to the remnant of the Southern Kingdom in exile in Babylon, and He gives them a promise. Though they are going to be captives in Babylon for seventy years, at the end of the seventieth year, He will come get them from Babylon and bring them home to the Promised Land, where He will restore, renew, and reestablish them.

The exilic prophet Jeremiah receives words from God and gives them to the people. The Lord, through Jeremiah, tells the Southern Kingdom to build houses and settle down in Babylon, to plant gardens and enjoy the fruit, to marry and have children, to increase in number, and to seek the peace and prosperity of Babylon. This language does not sound exilic. Rather, it sounds hopeful.

Now we come to one of the most-quoted passages in Scripture, a verse anchored in exile. We often turn to this passage when we are in the midst of a difficult circumstance. Jeremiah 29:11 says, "'I know the plans I have for you,' declares the LORD, 'plans to prosper you and not to harm you, plans to give you hope and a future.'" Jeremiah delivers this word to a people living in exile in Babylon. This is hope when the lights have gone out!

The promise continues:

> "Then you will call on me and come and pray to me, and I will listen to you. You will seek me and find me when you seek me with all your heart. I will be found by you," declares the LORD,

"and will bring you back from captivity. I will gather you from all the nations and places where I have banished you," declares the LORD, "and will bring you back to the place from which I carried you into exile."[13]

If you are hearing this as an Israelite in Babylon, you're making a seventy-year calendar and starting to mark off the days. The countdown has begun! Year sixty-nine. Year fifty-two. Year nineteen. Year seven. Year five, two, one. About three months out, you start packing up—it's time to head home!

If the covenant rests on us, we are in trouble. If the covenant rests on God, we have hope. In the next chapter, we will pick up at the end of the seventy-year Babylonian exile. The kingdom has divided. The lights have gone out. Does the living God keep His word? We will find out soon!

Chapter 7

THE REMNANT RETURNS

We are headed into one of my favorite chapters in this entire book! The previous chapter covered a rough part of Israel's story. The lights went out as the Israelites did their worst and both kingdoms were taken into exile. But the narrative doesn't end there. We are about to see God do His best, and God's best is always stronger than our worst. The question we are going to answer is, When the lights go out, can God turn them back on? In the words of the prophet Isaiah, "Surely the arm of the LORD is not too short to save" (59:1).

God Will

While the Northern Kingdom goes into Assyria and is absorbed into the culture through intermingling and intermarrying, the Southern Kingdom receives a time-specific prophecy regarding the duration of its exile in Babylon. The prophet Jeremiah tells the people they are going to be exiles for seventy years, in what is often referred to as the seventy-year captivity.[1] When we know there is a definitive time frame for a difficult season, we can often find it easier to persevere. What is especially challenging is when pain is open-ended and seemingly unremitting.

In Jeremiah 25, God uses familiar language regarding the end of the seventy years. He essentially says, "I will punish the king of Babylon. I will repay the Babylonians for what they have done. I will gather you from the nations. I will bring you home." Doesn't that sound like the "I will, I will, I will" language used with Avram in Genesis 12? God is doing the work. God is going to get the Israelites, bring them home, and reestablish them in the land. The living God followed Israel into her self-imposed exile, just as He does for us today.

Promise Maker, Promise Keeper

Now we come to the end of the Old Testament. In the next chapter, we're going to dive into an era called the intertestamental period. Often in Bibles, a blank white page is present between Malachi, the last book of the Old Testament, and Matthew, the first book of the New Testament. It's a tricky page, because on the surface it appears as though nothing happened during that time span. But so much history went down during the 400 years between Malachi and Matthew! I like to say that God was preparing the nursery for baby Jesus during that time.

As Westerners, we are good at learning Bible stories isolated from others in the narrative as a whole. My passion is to help connect the dots. Each biblical story functions like a pearl that, when strung together with other pearls, creates a beautiful necklace.[2] We synthesize the Scriptures and practice biblical integration by connecting some familiar stories with others. Thus far in our journey, as we have traced the Scriptures chronologically, have you noticed that you are better understanding the Bible?

As we pick up the story line, the lights go out for the Northern Kingdom of Israel in 721 BC. Ten of the twelve tribes are absorbed in Assyria. In 587–586 BC, the Babylonians conquer Jerusalem and burn the Temple to the ground. The lights go out in the Southern Kingdom of Judah. From the Temple's destruction in 587–586 BC to it being rebuilt in 516–515 BC, approximately seventy years go by. Thus, in 516–515 BC, God keeps His promise and restores His presence in Jerusalem. The prophecy of a seventy-year captivity is proven true. God is a promise maker. God is also a promise keeper.

I don't know about you, but sometimes I want God to do a work all at once. I am an only child, and I can be a bit impatient. I want God to keep it moving! But as we will soon see, God doesn't turn the lights back on overnight. He does so methodically because He still has one promise to fulfill to Avram, a promise that will bless the nations: the coming of the long-awaited Messiah.

When we talk about the Israelites returning home, we call God's systematic work the three Remnant Returns. A remnant is a smaller portion of a greater whole. Two out of twelve tribes is a remnant, a smaller portion of the Israelite population. Three different groups of remnant Israelites will return to the land. God will gather them and bring them home, where He will renew, reestablish, and repurpose them. They are returning to their original mandate.

Overview of the Remnant Returns

Around 538 BC, Zerubbabel rises up and leads the first remnant return. Approximately 50,000 Israelites go back to the land with him. The purpose of this group is to rebuild the Temple of the Lord in Jerusalem. Zerubbabel, along with Joshua and the priests, prioritizes rebuilding the altar so the daily sacrifices can be reinstated. Then the Israelites get to work rebuilding God's house, or the Temple. This story is told in Ezra 1–6.

In the year 458 BC, Ezra, a priest well versed in the law and functioning like a pastor or seminary professor, leads the second remnant return. Ezra reinstates the constitution and teaches the Israelites the *mitzvot*—the laws or commands of the living God. Once more they can live under the Lord's rule and reign, anchored in abundance rather than scarcity. Ezra 7–10 details the second remnant return.

In 445 BC, Nehemiah leads the third remnant, who rebuild the wall around Jerusalem. Over time, God systematically turns the lights back on. The Israelites begin returning and filling the land once again. The Old

The Remnant Return

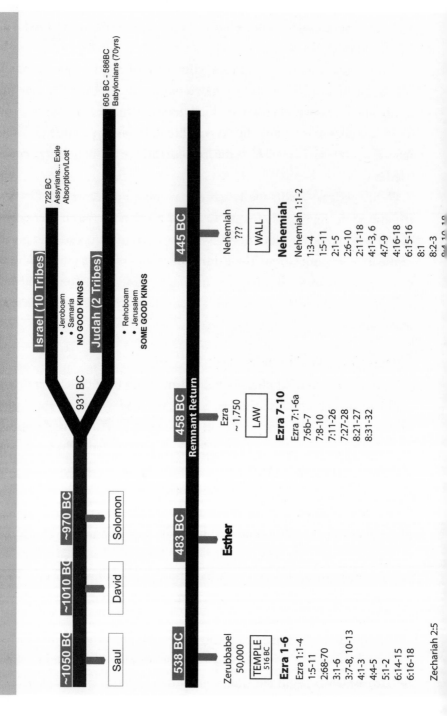

Israel (10 Tribes)
• Jeroboam
• Samaria
NO GOOD KINGS

722 BC
Assyrians... Exile
Absorption/Lost

605 BC - 586BC
Babylonians (70yrs)

Judah (2 Tribes)
• Rehoboam
• Jerusalem
SOME GOOD KINGS

931 BC

~1050 BC ~1010 BC ~970 BC

Saul   David   Solomon

538 BC   483 BC   458 BC   445 BC

Remnant Return

Esther

Ezra
~ 1,750

LAW

Nehemiah
???

WALL

Zerubbabel
50,000

TEMPLE
516 BC

Ezra 1-6
Ezra 1:1-4
1:5-11
2:68-70
3:1-6
3:7-8, 10-13
4:1-3
4:4-5
5:1-2
6:14-15
6:16-18

Zechariah 2:5

Ezra 7-10
Ezra 7:1-6a
7:6b-7
7:8-10
7:11-26
7:27-28
8:21-27
8:31-32

Nehemiah
Nehemiah 1:1-2
1:3-4
1:5-11
2:1-5
2:6-10
2:11-18
4:1-3, 6
4:7-9
4:16-18
6:15-16
8:1
8:2-3

Testament ends in approximately 430 BC with Malachi, the last writing prophet.

Hesed and Moreover

With our historical outline in place, now we start to string these pearls together and synthesize the biblical stories into a cohesive narrative viewed through a Middle Eastern eye. The Israelites do their worst and God responds by doing His best. *His best is always stronger than our worst.* This is gospel gorgeous, good news! As we eat the Scriptures and allow the Bible to tell the story, we are going to marry the books of Ezra and Nehemiah and enjoy watching God turn the lights back on.

One of my favorite Hebrew words is *hesed.* I have not yet braved getting a tattoo, but this beautiful word is a strong candidate if I ever decide to go for it! Hebrew is a word-poor language;[3] because of this, Hebrew words can have multiple meanings. Probably the best English equivalent for *hesed* is "steadfast love." *Hesed* relates to commitment or loyalty and is also understood to be merciful lovingkindness.[4] *Hesed* is kindness we do not deserve. When we expect judgment, *hesed* is God giving us mercy. *Hesed* is so good it hurts! God doesn't treat us as our sins deserve. He commits Himself to us. If one Hebrew word could capture what God does in the three remnant returns, it is *hesed.* When the Israelites do their worst, God responds with merciful lovingkindness.

The word "moreover" appears several times in English Bibles; it's a word we don't use often in our everyday vernacular. It carries the idea that God prepares to do something amazing, and then—moreover—He is going to do something even more amazing. This chapter is filled with "moreover" and *hesed.* When the lights go out, God is strong enough to turn them back on.

The First Remnant Return

Now we come to Ezra 1. There has been a change in kingdoms—the Babylonians who invaded Judah have been swallowed by the Persians. Cyrus, the Persian king, implements a practice that history shows was common for Persian monarchs. When the Persians conquered a people group, they allowed the subjugated group to return to their homeland. In this case, the Babylonians had plucked the Israelites out of their native lands and redistributed them throughout the empire.

After seventy years have passed, Cyrus allows the Israelites to begin returning home. The first remnant returns in 538 BC, led by Zerubbabel. Now, if you've been exiled in Babylon for seventy years, you're likely not thinking through the details of going home. Rather, you're grabbing a backpack and toothbrush, and leaving as quickly as possible! But let's take a look at how they prepare.

Ezra 1 describes the vast wealth the first remnant accumulates for their return journey, including 5,400 articles of gold and silver! This reminds us of another time in history when the Israelites came out of a wealthy land. They did not exit years and years of slavery in Egypt empty-handed; rather, they left with Egyptian gold, silver, and precious stones.[5] Now, as they leave Babylon, they travel caravan-style, returning with large amounts of gold and silver. The Israelites go back to their homeland with extravagant provision. *God is turning the lights back on.*

Some say the Babylonian captivity is when the Ark of the Covenant was lost, that perhaps the Babylonians melted it down and repurposed it. Every time I'm in Israel, I'm looking to the left and right, asking God that if the Ark of the Covenant is to be found, He let me be the one to find it!

At the end of Ezra 2, the generous hearts of the returning Israelites are illustrated by the freewill offerings they give for the rebuilding of the Temple. I love this passage; in view here are the descendants of Daniel, Shadrach, Meshach, and Abednego! When they come back to the land, there is deep gratitude in them, and they donate to the Temple treasury toward the rebuilding of God's house.

After the Israelites settle in their towns, their leaders get to work rebuilding the altar of the God of Israel. They are afraid of the surrounding people groups because Jerusalem does not have a wall; thus, they are vulnerable. Don't you love it that they build an altar in Jerusalem and start sacrificing on it before they rebuild God's house? These Israelites are eager to worship the living God in their homeland.

At this time in Israelite history, as at the time of Jesus, Jews[6] made two daily sacrifices—one in the morning and one in the evening.[7] By the first century, the morning sacrifice happened at 9:00 a.m., while the evening sacrifice took place at 3:00 p.m. In the account of Jesus' crucifixion, Jesus serves as the daily sacrifice. He is nailed to the cross at 9:00 a.m.,[8] thus fulfilling the morning sacrifice, and He gives up His spirit at 3:00 p.m.,[9] the time of the evening sacrifice. Jesus perfectly and completely fulfills Levitical law for the sacrificial lamb. God has known from the very beginning that the covenant is on Him. It is His faithfulness that will hold it.

Have you ever renewed your dedication to the Lord, only to have adversity come when you make your commitment? Similar to how your hot water heater goes out the very same month you get on a budget! The Israelites are about to experience this type of hardship.

As Zerubbabel and the first remnant rebuild the house of the Lord, their enemies catch wind of what is happening and approach the Israelites, saying, "We want to help you build a temple for your God." This sounds like intermingling, and intermingling leads to intermarriage—both of which God forbade the Israelites to do. This first remnant responds by holding the line. "No, thank you," they say. "We will do this on our own, without your help. We're not going to intermingle with you. We as Israelites are going to rebuild the house of the Lord."

As the Israelites stand firm, the true motive of these other people groups is revealed. They are troublemakers seeking to discourage the Israelites and hinder their progress in rebuilding the Temple. Keep in mind the context of what is taking place. This first remnant is courageously reconstructing the house of the Lord and is now in possession of 5,400 Temple articles of silver and gold—but the city has no wall. Envision that scenario. Imagine liquidating everything you own into cash. All your neighbors know your entire life savings is in an unlocked chest in a tent in your front yard. Are you sleeping well at night? This is the tension the Israelites are experiencing. Without a wall, they are unprotected and vulnerable. They are concerned not only about their safety and that of their families, but also the safety of the valuable artifacts they brought back.

This first remnant needs some support and reassurance. Haggai and Zechariah, post-exilic prophets who have Old Testament books bearing their names, come alongside and encourage Zerubbabel and the people to see this project through, to keep building God's house. Upon completion, the Temple is inaugurated in the year 516 BC. Jerusalem still has no wall, and the surrounding foreign people groups continue to stir up trouble, but the Israelites see it through. The house of the Lord once again stands in Jerusalem. God is turning the lights back on. The restoration is real.

A Wall of Fire

By way of brief reminder, of the three remnant returns, the first group rebuilds the Temple, the second group reinstates the constitution or law, and the third group rebuilds the wall. If we were planning the responsibilities of each remnant, would we have chosen this order? We likely would have had the first remnant *rebuild the wall* because that's practical and pragmatic; it makes sense. The second remnant would reestablish the law. Then when everything was safe and secure, the third remnant would rebuild the Temple and bring in the articles of gold and silver. We are seeing yet again that God does things well, and He often does them in ways we would not choose.

What gave the first remnant group the strength to see this project through? One of my favorite verses in the Old Testament offers insight as to what sustained them. As a reminder, the Hebrew term *davar* means "word." Throughout the Old Testament, the word—or *davar*—of the Lord comes to a person or group of people. At this point in the story, the Israelites have no wall. They are rebuilding the Temple, people groups are harassing them on all sides, and one sentence spoken through the prophet Zechariah holds them through this time. In Zechariah 2:5, God says this to the Israelites: "'I myself will be a wall of fire around it [Jerusalem],' declares the LORD, 'and I will be its glory within.'"

The Israelites don't have a wall they can see. They have a better, invisible wall. Through Zechariah, God tells them, "Stay at it. Keep building. I've got your back. I will be a wall of fire around you." I pray this language often. When I'm walking my dog, Chester, early in the morning, I ask God to be a wall of fire around me and my family. God does things in ways that may seem irregular. But I imagine most of us, if given the choice of a wall made of stone versus the living God of Israel being our wall of fire, are going to choose the latter! This word, this *davar* from the living God, holds them. I love this because I have experienced it in my own life. God is able to speak one word or phrase that sustains our spirit.

Imagine that you are an Israelite male, and every night you go to sleep with your wife, children, and maybe even grandchildren close by. You are aware of the hostile people groups all around, but even more so, you know who is going to protect you through the night and keep the enemies from coming in. You pray, "Lord, let that wall of fire hold tonight." If you're a wife, mother, daughter, or grandmother, you lay down at night knowing there's no city wall to offer protection from the harassing people groups. As you drift off to sleep, you pray, "Lord, thank You for being a wall fire around my family, around my children." Zechariah 2:5 is one of the most powerful lines in the Old Testament. The Israelites are back in the land, listening to and being sustained by this word from the Lord.

What words from the Lord are holding and carrying you? When you're uncertain, what *davar* do you cling to for comfort and guidance? Words from the living God help us hold our space and move forward step by step. God sometimes chooses methods and ways that seem unconventional at the time. But even in that, He does it better than we ever could!

The Book of Esther

The first remnant returns to Jerusalem, as detailed in Ezra 1–6. They complete the house of the Lord after a twenty-year rebuilding process. The very next passage, Ezra 7:1, begins, "After these things." It's natural to assume this is referring to all the happenings of the first remnant return. Yet there is another important book in the biblical narrative that occurs *between* Ezra 6 and Ezra 7—the entire book of Esther! To read the Bible chronologically through this portion of the story, you would read Ezra 1 through 6, followed by the book of Esther, then Ezra 7 through 10. After that comes the book of Nehemiah. The events of Esther happen between the first remnant return, led by Zerubbabel, and the second remnant return, led by Ezra.

The events detailed in the book of Esther begin around 483–482 BC. Xerxes I is on the throne as king of Persia. He throws a banquet, possibly a prewar practice for kings in antiquity prior to taking the soldiers away from their families. They would party and overdrink, then head off to fight a campaign. I often tell my college students, "There is no such thing as world history and biblical history; there's just history!" Perhaps the banquet in Esther 1 is part of Xerxes's prewar preparation as he readies his armies to invade Greece. For a point of modern cultural reference, the movie *300* portrays Xerxes as Esther's husband and the Battle of Thermopylae as one of the most infamous battles between the Persians and 300 Spartan soldiers.

This lavish banquet is set between Ezra 6 and 7. When the king requests that his wife, Queen Vashti, come be displayed before the people and nobles attending the banquet, she refuses. Xerxes reacts by deposing her as queen. Through a kingdom-wide search of beautiful virgins who come to the palace and join the king's harem, a young Jewish girl named Hadassah, meaning "myrtle," rises to the top and is chosen to replace Vashti as queen. Hadassah's Persian name is Esther, likely a derivative of the name of the Persian god Ishtar.

The story of Esther, her cousin Mordecai (who raised her after her parents died), and the evil Haman (who tries to destroy the Jewish people), all occurs between Ezra 6 and 7. We are going to come back to this, but for now, let's set this aside and move on to the second remnant return in Ezra 7. God is systematically turning the lights back on. The Israelites have done their worst, and we are seeing God do His best. He is returning, restoring, and reestablishing them. He is a wall of fire around Jerusalem. God is protecting His people!

The Second Remnant Return

In the year 458 BC, Ezra, a priest and teacher of the law, leads the second remnant return from Babylon back to the land. His story is detailed in Ezra 7–10. Ezra is a master of the Text; he reinstates the Torah and *mitzvot*, the instructions and laws from the living God. Ezra 7:1 begins, "After these things"—referring to the events of the book of Esther—"during the reign of Artaxerxes king of Persia." A quick tutorial on these names: Xerxes I is Esther's husband. After Xerxes dies, Artaxerxes assumes the throne. *Artaxerxes* means "whose reign is through truth." Artaxerxes is the son of Xerxes I and is historically known as Artaxerxes I. The second remnant return happens under his kingship.

Ezra and the Israelites, with a plethora of gold, silver, salt, provisions, and food in tow, return to the land caravan-style. In antiquity, you never traveled alone. If you chose to do so, you were likely to get robbed or assaulted. In Jesus' parable of the good Samaritan, we read about a man who was traveling alone when thieves attacked him. Traveling with a group or caravan of families helps prevent this from happening.

King Artaxerxes writes an imperial letter. This isn't a common practice for us today, but the Pope of the Catholic Church still utilizes it through something called a papal bull. In ancient times, when a king wrote a decree and sealed it with his signet ring, it was like his signature. It was an authoritative imperial proclamation. If you traveled with a letter from the king and someone tried to deter you, it was as though they were detaining the king. The king's people would deal with them accordingly. In antiquity, the safest way to travel was to have an imperial letter.

Artaxerxes I, son of Xerxes I, sends Ezra and the second remnant back to Jerusalem with an imperial letter. This letter, presented in Ezra 7, is not usually viewed as one of the more compelling portions of Scripture. We often miss the magnitude of this passage, yet it is so incredible that we are going to look at sections of it word for word! Through the letter, we see *hesed* and "moreover" in action.

Keep in mind a Persian monarch writes this letter for Ezra and the remnant returning. We pick it up in verses 12-13: "Artaxerxes, king of kings, to Ezra the priest, teacher of the Law of the God of heaven: Greetings. Now I decree that any of the Israelites in my kingdom, including priests and Levites, who volunteer to go to Jerusalem with you may go." Verses 15-16 continue: "Moreover, you are to take with you the silver and gold that the king and his advisors have freely given to the God of Israel, whose dwelling is in Jerusalem,"—did you catch the "moreover" and notice who is donating the silver and gold?—"together with all the silver and gold you may obtain from the province of Babylon, as well as the freewill offerings of the people and priests for the temple of their God in Jerusalem."

Read verse 17 mindful that a *Persian* king writes these words: "With this money be sure to buy bulls, rams and male lambs, together with their grain offerings and drink offerings, and sacrifice them on the altar of the temple of your God in Jerusalem." Does that strike you as an unusually specific list? King Artaxerxes knows Levitical law! The Persian king sounds more like an Israelite. He personally donates to the God of Israel. He understands the requirements of Levitical law and the worship system of the Israelites.

Let's look at the generosity demonstrated by the king as the letter continues in verse 18: "You and your fellow Israelites may then do whatever seems best with the rest of the silver and gold, in accordance with the will of your God." My goodness! The king is saying, "Use whatever is left however you see fit." This is *hesed*; this is "moreover." Artaxerxes feels more Israelite than Persian. He goes on: "Deliver to the God of Jerusalem all the articles entrusted to you for worship in the temple of your God. And anything else needed for the temple of your God that you are responsible to supply, you may provide them from the royal treasury" (vv. 19-20). If the letter had ended here, Artaxerxes's benevolence would have already been clearly evidenced. But he goes on to order the treasurers of the Trans-Euphrates to provide whatever Ezra asks for "up to a hundred talents of silver, a hundred cors of wheat, a hundred baths of wine, a hundred baths of olive oil, and salt without limit" (v. 22). He then declares the priests and Levites, the singers, gatekeepers, and temple servants to be exempt from paying taxes. This is some serious "moreover"!

At the end of the letter, Artaxerxes acknowledges Ezra's wisdom and then instructs him to teach the law of God to everyone. Again, the king sounds more Israelite than Persian. He finishes strong by saying in verse 26, "Whoever does not obey the law of your God and the law of the king must surely be punished by death, banishment, confiscation of property, or imprisonment." That's a lot! Artaxerxes writes this imperial letter loaded with benefits and provisions and sends Ezra and the second remnant back to the land. The hand of God is on them as they travel home. The Lord protects them and there is a wall of fire around them. Ezra reinstates the constitution. God has a house. The ways of the Lord are being taught. Do you see the lights coming back on?

The Third Remnant Return

Now we come to our third and final remnant return, led by Nehemiah and detailed in the book that bears his name. We are synthesizing the Scriptures, marrying, integrating, and stringing the pearls. God has been a wall of fire around Jerusalem, protecting the Temple, protecting the Israelites, protecting Ezra. Now it is time for the people to rebuild the wall around Jerusalem.

It is the year 445 BC. Nehemiah is in Persia, and some of his Jewish brothers who have been in Jerusalem come to him. Nehemiah knows his Israelite brothers have been home and inquires as to how it is going for those who have returned from exile. The men report that the remnant is in trouble and disgrace. Nehemiah learns that the wall of Jerusalem is still in shambles. If you recall, in antiquity, a city needed a wall for protection and as a sign of honor; the city it encircled was deemed to be powerful and structured. Jerusalem's wall is down, so she has a double dilemma: She remains unprotected, and she has lost her honor.

Nehemiah's response to this news is one of the most famous prayers in the Bible. He says, "When I heard these things, I sat down and wept. For some days I mourned and fasted and prayed before the God of heaven. Then I said: 'LORD, the God of heaven…let your ear be attentive and your eyes open to hear the prayer your servant is praying before you day and night for your servants, the people of Israel.'"[10] Nehemiah mourns for the condition of Jerusalem. This heartfelt, Jewish prayer includes Nehemiah's confession of his sins, as well as the sins of the Israelite people. In Nehemiah's mind, rebuilding Jerusalem's wall would restore her protection and honor.[11]

The Cupbearer and the Queen

As cupbearer to the king, Nehemiah is responsible for tasting all foods and beverages before Artaxerxes eats or drinks. That way, if someone tries to poison the king, it will be Nehemiah who dies. The cupbearer daily puts his life on the line for the preservation of Artaxerxes. Outside of this obvious risk, Nehemiah likely has a comfortable lifestyle in the imperial palace.

What we know from antiquity is that a common practice between servants and monarchy was for servants to mirror the expressions and emotions of the kings and their families when in their presence. It was expected that Nehemiah's highest fidelity, commitment, and faithfulness was to Artaxerxes. If the king was happy and Nehemiah was in his presence, then the cupbearer acted happy. If the king was sad while Nehemiah was in his presence, then he needed to act sad. To express a disposition other than that of the king was an indicator of divided loyalty.

In Nehemiah 2, the cupbearer takes wine to Artaxerxes. Up to this point, Nehemiah has not expressed sadness when with the king. In this moment, Artaxerxes notices a difference and asks, "Why does your face look so sad when you are not ill? This can be nothing but sadness of heart."[12] The question indicates that Artaxerxes is not feeling sad. Because Nehemiah is expressing sadness, he is not mirroring the king. Now he is afraid because it is clear the king has noticed. Nehemiah responds appropriately: "May the king live forever!"—as though he is reminding Artaxerxes, "I'm for you. I'm with you. I'm going to keep tasting your food and drinking your drink." Nehemiah goes on to explain that Jerusalem is in ruins and its gates have been destroyed by fire. The king asks what Nehemiah wants. Nehemiah prays, then asks the king for permission to return to Jerusalem and rebuild the wall.

Rebuilding the Wall

My college students often ask me, "How do I know what God's will is for my life? How can I know what my passion is, and how am I to direct my life accordingly?" I received some wisdom from my mentor years ago that has guided me in my own life. She said, "Kristi, pay attention to what makes you cry and what makes you mad. What is wrong with the world that makes you cry in such a way that you want to do something about it? And what is wrong with the world that makes you angry enough to do something about it?" The injustices and broken systems that make us cry and make us mad are often indicators of our passion points: areas we care enough about to seek change, issues that compel us to come off the bench and get in the game.

As Christians, so often we are told that being angry is bad. In his book *The Voice of the Heart*, Chip Dodd details eight emotions, including sadness and anger. I love how he describes anger as a passion. The Bible does not say, "Don't get angry." Rather, it says, "In your anger do not sin."[13] In my own life, there are issues and scenarios that make me angry because they are wrong. There are injustices that quicken me to the point that I feel angry enough to do something about them. Whether it's with your spouse, your friends, or your family, take some time to talk about what makes you cry and what makes you mad. This may be a revealing exercise!

One of Nehemiah's passion points is the wall of Jerusalem—so much so that he wants to go back, roll up his sleeves, and channel his emotion into a productive outcome. We are meant to be a feeling people! I was taught early on to "get over it" and stuff my feelings. It has taken years of therapy to help me learn to be connected to myself—to know what I feel and to be able to process it in healthy, wholesome ways. Nehemiah connects to himself, to the deep sadness he feels at the reality that God once again has a house, and the law has been reinstated, but Jerusalem still does not have a wall. This is not okay with Nehemiah.

The Israelites that return home with Nehemiah rebuild the wall in fifty-two days![14] Nehemiah 4:17 says that they held a tool in one hand for building, and a weapon in the other to fight off bandits. A remnant of that wall still stands in Jerusalem. Nehemiah knew his passion point; his passion spread to the third remnant, and they acted decisively to fix the problem.

Fidelity in a Foreign Land

Esther holds a role that in some ways is very difficult. From the time she becomes queen of Persia, she knows she will never get to go home. Esther dies in the imperial court of the Persians. Can you imagine watching your brothers and sisters return home, knowing you will never do likewise? Artaxerxes certainly seems more like an Israelite than a Persian, so we can see the strong potential that Esther influenced him in the ways of her Jewish people.

When I get to heaven, I want to ask what it was like for Esther to watch the remnants return, knowing she herself would never get to go home. We can often handle a challenging situation better when we know it has a definitive end. The Israelites are told that they will be in Babylon for seventy years. Esther, however, receives no such word. Her fidelity to the living God doesn't happen back in Jerusalem. It is worked out in the courts of the Persian monarchy from the moment she takes the crown until she dies.

Wouldn't it be incredible if, when we get to heaven, we find out that Esther played a significant role in the remnants being able to return? That she helped her brothers and sisters do something she knew she would never be able to experience for herself? I don't know if I could have done what she did.

The Joy of the Lord Is Your Strength

As we come to the end of the Old Testament, Zerubbabel, Ezra, Nehemiah, and thousands of Israelites have returned to the land while others have remained in Babylon—either by choice or necessity.

The Jewish people continue to wrestle with their identity. Rabbinic Judaism begins to form at this stage as they ask what it means to be a good Jew both *in* the land and *outside* of it. The people start to truly identify as monotheistic, living in a homeland and recognizing the importance of their Book. Those who return to Jerusalem and its environs recenter their lives around Torah and God's house in Jerusalem. Those who remain in Babylon recenter their lives around Torah and what it means to be a people of God outside of their homeland. The Jews who are living abroad are in a state of *diaspora* ("scattering"), and they must wrestle with questions such as, What should life look like for us who remain in Babylon? How do we worship without the Temple? How do we live out our faith in a foreign land?[15]

Meanwhile, the living God protects Jerusalem with its newly rebuilt wall; she has regained her honor. In Nehemiah 8, Ezra brings out the Book of the Law of Moses and opens it up. The people stand, because it is Jewish practice to stand for the reading of God's Word and sit for man's words. Ezra reads aloud from daybreak till noon as the people listen attentively. They begin to weep as they hear the law being read.

In verse 10, a familiar and oft-quoted passage, Nehemiah tells the people, "Go and enjoy choice food and sweet drinks, and send some to those who have nothing prepared. This day is holy to our Lord. Do not grieve, for the joy of the LORD is your strength." This day is not to be a day of mourning. Rather, it is a day set apart for celebration! The living God, promise maker and promise keeper, has *turned the lights back on*. He is faithful!

Chapter 8

THE INTERTESTAMENTAL PERIOD

The Bible is one Story, best read and understood from beginning to end. In this chapter, we are going to marry the Old and New Testaments by covering an era known as the intertestamental period. This window of time occurs between Malachi, the last book in the Old Testament, and Matthew, the first book of the New Testament. If you have a Bible close by, open it and see if it has a blank white page between the Old and New Testaments. This empty page is often how the intertestamental period is acknowledged. Among Christians, not much is known about this 400-year epoch. In this chapter, we are about to discover the pivotal shifts that occurred during this era.

The Timing of Jesus' Birth

First, let's look at a key passage of Scripture that provides context for where we are heading. Galatians 4:4-5 says, "When the set time had fully come, God sent his Son, born of a woman, born under the law, to redeem those under the law, that we might receive adoption to sonship." Have you ever wondered why Jesus was born *when* He was born? Why was He not born in the seventh century BC? Or in the modern day, with cell phones and airplanes that can make the spread of the gospel easier? We are about to gather clues that may shed some light on this.

Intertestamental Period

Represents sites Kristi often takes her Israel teams to

Old Testament	Intertestamental	New Testament

Malachi - 430 BC

400 Years
"Silent Years"
Galatians 4:4

Birth of Jesus - 6 BC

Persia (539 — 331 BC) Greece (331-63 BC) Rome — **Roman** →

Hebrew
Temple
Prophets

Alexander the Great and Greeks
- mentored by Aristotle
- conqueror, alcoholic

Greek
Synagogues
Pharisees
Sadducees
Essenes

Hellenism – Greek Culture...
1. Emphasis on education
2. Emphasis on individualism
3. Emphasis on Greek ideas...
   a. Health
   b. Wealth
   c. Competition

Rome prepares the way for the gospel...
1. Pax Romana
2. Common language (Greek)
3. Roads system (50,000 miles)

Zerubbabel, Ezra, Nehemiah

Jews in Palestine resisted Hellenism...
3 sects rose up to combat Hellenism...

Pharisee	Sadducee	Essene
Teacher of Law	Sanhedrin	Absolutist purist
Rabbi	70+1=71	Scribe/
Common	Wealthy aristocrat	Dead Sea Scrolls
People loved them	People hated them	Separatist...desert,
Oversaw synagogues	Oversaw Temple	communist
Hated Rome	Sympathetic to Rome	
~ 6,000	71	

Qumran Caves

© 2023 New Lens Biblical Studies

Through the previous chapters we have come to understand why Jesus was born *where* He was born. If you recall, God's original mandate for Israel was to occupy the land in proximity to the International Coastal Highway and rightly represent Him to the nations passing through. As we gain insight regarding the intertestamental period and the events surrounding the birth of Jesus, we will increase our understanding of the Gospels. This is the direction we are moving toward in the chapters to come.

Malachi, the last writing prophet of the Old Testament, lived and wrote around 430 BC. The men who came before him—Zerubbabel, Ezra, and Nehemiah—led the Israelites in the three remnant returns. The lights had gone out, but God systematically turned them back on. After the white page between the testaments, we come to the Gospel of Matthew, which details the birth of Jesus in chapters 1 and 2. Most scholars believe Jesus was born in either 6 or 5 BC—we will elaborate on those dates in the next chapter. This time frame, which I believe to be accurate, gives us about 400 years in between Malachi and Jesus, the era known as the intertestamental period.

Some commentaries refer to this period as "the silent years." This term seems a bit elusive, as it conveys the idea that God was silent for 400 years—that He wasn't moving, speaking, or acting in human history. What scholars actually mean by that terminology is not that God took a 400-year nap, got lost, checked out, or wasn't living in covenant faithfulness with His people. Rather, it indicates that there were no writing prophets of Israel during this time; Malachi was the last.

In John 5:17, Jesus makes the following statement to the Jewish leaders: "My Father is always at his work to this very day, and I too am working." God works throughout the intertestamental period. When I teach this at the college, I like to tell my students that God is preparing the nursery for baby Jesus. He is geopolitically, historically, and culturally laying the groundwork for the incarnation, for the birth of the Son of God upon the earth.

What Happens on the White Page?

When the Old Testament ends, Persia is the superpower of the world heading into the intertestamental period, after conquering the Babylonians in 539 BC. Scripture mentions several Persian kings, including Cyrus, Darius, Xerxes I, and Artaxerxes I. In 331 BC, the Greeks conquer the Persians and take over, which matters greatly for our narrative. The Greeks rule the Jews for much of the intertestamental period, up until approximately 160 BC, when a Jewish dynasty known as the Hasmoneans regain power over Jerusalem. Then, in 63 BC, the Romans conquer them. The Roman Empire controls much of the civilized world in Jesus' day, which frames the historical and cultural context of the New Testament. The transition of power moves from the Babylonians to the Persians to the Greeks to the Hasmoneans to the Romans. History sums up kingdoms conquering kingdoms.

Throughout the intertestamental period, the Jewish people continue to worship at God's house, located in Jerusalem—the same Temple Zerubbabel rebuilt with the first remnant return. When we flip the white page and head into the New Testament era, the Temple remains in Jerusalem, but synagogues show up throughout the land as well.

At the end of the Old Testament, the Jews speak Hebrew and Aramaic as they come out of exile. But when we turn the white page and move forward, much of the world speaks a specific kind of Greek known as *Koine* or "common" Greek, as well as Latin. The languages change between Malachi and Matthew.

As the Old Testament culminates, the prophets of Israel continue to speak to the leaders of Jerusalem. If you recall, Haggai and Zechariah minister and prophesy to those who take part in the three remnant returns. When we flip the white page between testaments, another shift occurs. Now Pharisees, Sadducees, and Essenes emerge as the Jewish leaders.

A lot happens on the white page between Malachi and Matthew! Sketching this out helps us string the pearls of the Old Testament with the pearls of the New Testament. *We are marrying them into one cohesive Story.*

Alexander the Great

As previously mentioned, the Greeks conquer the Persians in the year 331 BC and are the world superpower through the intertestamental period.

We can sum up this era in one name: Alexander the Great. This Macedonian king comes on the scene during the intertestamental period and, along with the Greeks, begins conquering the world. Alexander had incredible military prowess.

Alexander the Great was personally mentored by Aristotle, the famous Greek philosopher. As surprising as it may sound, Alexander was one of the most effective missionaries the world has ever seen. He embodied the Grecian way by conquering with the sword, while also recognizing the difficult, expensive, and bloody requirements to hold or subjugate with the sword. He opted to give the nations an ideal, a cultural norm that would make the world want to follow him, rather than despise him for conquering their land and subduing their people.

In a word, the effective missionary idea Alexander the Great propagated is called *Hellenism*. *Hellenic* means "Greek." Alexander spread the Greek culture, the Hellenistic way. Think Vegas. Hellenism can be considered one of the earliest forms of moral relativism. If it tastes good, eat it. If it feels good, do it. If you want to try it, knock yourself out. Nothing is off limits. Alexander conquers kingdoms with the sword, and then he gives them Vegas. He feeds the basest appetites of their flesh. And who doesn't want that? Who doesn't want to live in a world where if you want to try it, you can try it? If you want to eat it, you can eat it. If you want to do it, you can do it. The world embraces Hellenism. It gets to the point where Alexander comes calling and the nations don't even go to war against him. They just open their city gates and welcome him in.

Hellenism infects the world during the intertestamental period. Alexander goes about this by conquering a land, then planting a *polis*, which is Greek for "city." The plural is *poleis* or "cities." The Bible references a region known as the Decapolis. *Deca* means "ten." Think Decalogue or the Ten Commandments or Ten Words. The Decapolis is the region of the Ten Cities. Jesus goes to the Decapolis and faces a man so badly overcome that even the kingdom of darkness can't handle him. This demoniac who lives among tombs is described as being naked, chained, and cutting himself. Jesus frees

Ruins of the theater at Miletus

him by restoring him to his right mind. Jesus later returns to the region of the Decapolis and miraculously feeds 4,000.[1]

Americans have a saying: "What happens in Vegas, stays in Vegas." Vegas is where you go to lose yourself, to try the things you would never want anyone to know you are trying. Alexander comes in, conquers with the sword, and then sets up Vegas-like cities. Every polis Alexander establishes to infect the nations with Hellenism needs several components.

The Great Theater at Ephesus, on the western coast of Asia Minor (in modern-day Turkey)

The Greeks were all about the arts, so each polis needs a theater. They loved to write plays and music. They were eclectic as a culture and enjoyed entertaining in a theater.

Poleis must also have an arena or a hippodrome—an elongated track where chariot races take place. If you go to the hippodrome to watch the chariot races, the best seats are at the turn because that is where the crashes happen! This is antiquity's version of our NASCAR races.

A gymnasium served another fundamental part of a polis. *Gymnos* is Greek for "naked." Greek education was most often just men with men and sometimes women with women, and it happened in the nude. Today we go to the gym to work out, but for the Greeks, a gymnasium was their schooling or educational system. Alexander comes along and praises a very Greek idea, teaching that man is the measure of all things, a famous line given by a Greek philosopher.[2] Man is now preeminent.

Great Sphinx of Giza (Cairo, Egypt)

The gods of antiquity were capricious and scary looking. Recall the Egyptian sphynx or the four terrifying creatures in Daniel 7. After centuries and centuries of the gods looking like monsters, here come the Greeks, who believe there is nothing more important than humanity. Statues of Greek

Great Sphinx of Giza with Great Pyramid of Giza in background (Cairo, Egypt)

Corinth Museum – Goddess Aphrodite

Ephesus Museum – Goddess Artemis

gods and goddesses—Zeus, Aphrodite, Artemis, and Dionysus—look like humans and are often naked. The gods become like us, or we become like the gods. I once heard a religious teacher say, "When men became god,

Reconstructed Athenian Agora

Reconstructed Athenian Agora

Reconstructed Athenian Agora

God became a man." This is the world into which Jesus was born. To the Greek, nothing is more beautiful than the human body, so why cover it up? The Romans come along later and throw a toga on it. This gives us further insight regarding God's commandment to the Jewish people to not make any graven image of Him. The finite can never accurately portray the infinite. We will mistreat His name and take it in vain.

Next, to be a polis under Alexander and the Greeks, a city has to have an agora, or marketplace. This was a space primarily for city gatherings. The apostle Paul spent much time in the Athenian Agora interacting with people, listening to conversations, and considering how he could weave the gospel into their culture. This same agora was frequented by statesmen, poets, historians, artists, and philosophers—including Aristotle, Socrates, and Plato. Democracy is said to have been birthed in the Athenian Agora in the fifth and fourth centuries BC.

Finally, a polis under Alexander and the Greeks needs to have a temple, a place of worship.

At this point in history, the gods look like us. Naked man is the measure of all things. An early form

Reconstructed Athenian Agora

Ruins of the Temple of Apollo with the Corinthian Acropolis in background. The Temple of Aphrodite, goddess of love, was located at the pinnacle of the acropolis. It was so prominent sailors could see it from a distance. The Temple of Aphrodite was a primary reason Corinth was popular with sailors. The apostle Paul invited the Corinthian believers to embrace a different type of love, as detailed in 1 Corinthians 13.

of humanism and moral relativism has emerged, and the world eats it up. But a collision is coming as we marry the Old and New Testaments.

Hellenistic Culture

We can define the Greek culture by three areas of importance. At the top of the list, Hellenism values education. The Greeks prize knowledge, as personified by Aristotle, Socrates, and Plato. They love to learn. They are writers. According to rabbi and Jewish theologian Abraham Joshua Heschel, "The Greeks learned in order to comprehend. The Hebrews learned in order to revere. The modern man learns in order to use."[3]

Next, the Greeks are a culture of individualism. If humans are the measure of all things, then mankind's individual thought is the highest premium. Personal freedom and happiness are imperative. Living for self with less concern for others, looking out for number one, is the way of the Greeks.

Last, health and competition are core to the Grecian way of life. The Greeks gave us the Olympiad. Only men competed in the earliest Olympic games, and they did so naked. They would oil themselves so that they glistened in the sun because the Greeks apparently enjoyed watching naked men run around a track! If man is the measure of all things, and there is nothing more beautiful than the human body, why hide it? It was made to display and show off! This is the Alexandrian way, and the world bought into it. This is the cultural landscape of the intertestamental period.

Kingdoms Collide

Here's where we take a turn into the biblical world. The way of the Greek is about to collide with the way of the Jew. Hellenism promotes a culture of entertainment, as seen in the theaters, arenas, hippodromes, agoras, and gymnasiums. Entertainment encourages a passive stance. The Jewish people are a culture of celebration, which requires an active posture.[4] The Hebrew people learn the story, remember the story, and celebrate the story. They go to Jerusalem for the feasts and festivals. As a people of celebration, they want to actively participate with

Scythopolis (Beit She'an)

Scythopolis (Beit She'an) – Roman theater

God the Father to watch His kingdom come down to the ground. The moral relativism of the Greeks is about to collide with the pietism of the Jews. This happens on the white page between Malachi and Matthew, during the intertestamental period.

When I take teams to Israel, we visit the ruins of Scythopolis, one of the Decapolis cities. Josephus writes about this city, known today as *Beit She'an*,[5] in *The Jewish War*.[6] We walk through the ruins of the hippodrome, theater,

Scythopolis (Beit She'an) – Roman Palladius street

Scythopolis (Beit She'an) – public latrine

bathhouse, and agora. Though most of what we see today is from after the first century, it is an excellent example of what Hellenism was, and what the world was experiencing in growing fashion during the 400-year era between the testaments.

Alexander moves through the nations, conquering with the sword, and setting up poleis or Vegas-like cities that mirror the Greek way. The world loves it. Normally when one people group conquers another, the victors impose their cultural and religious norms, while the defeated acquiesce. The Greek way of feeding mankind the desires of the flesh is so effective that when the Romans conquer the Greeks militarily, the Greeks conquer the Romans culturally. This is the origin of Greco-Roman culture. The Greeks are supplanted militarily by the Romans, but the Romans love Vegas. So, they adopt the Greek gods and give them Roman names. Greek gives way to Latin, but the culture of Vegas, the moral relativism of the Greeks, is so powerful it even infects the Romans!

Does the Greek polis—with its theaters, arenas, hippodromes, agoras, and gymnasiums—remind you of American culture? As a Western people, we are much more Greco-Roman than we are Jewish. We are more Athens and Rome than we are Jerusalem. As a culture, we also value entertainment. Neil Postman, a former sociologist at New York University, wrote a book titled *Amusing Ourselves to Death*, which delves into the sweeping cultural impact of our addiction to entertainment. I require my college students to read this book as I read it alongside them.

Eventually, Alexander and the Greeks arrive in the land of Israel. Hellenism knocks on the door of the Jews. If you are Torah-loving, if you follow the laws of God—the 613 instructions given to Moses on Mount Sinai—if you value synagogue life, if you believe that living under the rule and reign of God is the greatest freedom, when Alexander comes calling, how do you respond? Many Jews tell him, "We don't want what you're offering. We don't choose Hellenism. We follow a different ethic. We are communal, not individualistic. Our two greatest commands are to love God and love our neighbor. The Greeks love themselves. We are a different kind of tribe. We leave the corners of our fields unharvested so the widow can find something to eat. We care about the poor. We don't mistreat the helpless. We care about justice and righteousness. We are a people of celebration; not entertainment."

The way of the Greeks is on a collision course with the way of the Jews.

Combating Hellenism

At the end of the Old Testament, the Jews listen to the voices of the prophets. By the time of the New Testament, Pharisees, Sadducees, and Essenes have entered the picture. Which begs the question: Where did they come from? The Pharisees, Sadducees, and Essenes originated during the intertestamental period. When Alexander seeks to infect the land of the Jewish people, pious, God-fearing, Torah-loving, synagogue-going, communal, way-of-the-Lord men stand shoulder to shoulder and form a wall to keep Hellenism out, while keeping the pure Jewish way in. The Pharisees,

Sadducees, Essenes, and eventually the Zealots rise up to preserve, protect, and honor the Jewish way of life as they see fit. Jewish people living in the intertestamental period are looking for a Pharisee or a Sadducee. Their origin in this time period is noble as they combat the incoming Hellenism. This is a great example of how a good thing can go wrong.

The Pharisees

The Pharisees teach the Mosaic law, the ways of God. They serve in a similar way that pastors, seminary professors, or Bible teachers function today. The Pharisees oversee the local synagogue. There's only one Temple, in Jerusalem, but synagogues are all over Israel, similar to how churches are widespread. Everywhere there's a synagogue, there's a Pharisee. They are governing, ruling over, and shepherding the people. This is true during the intertestamental period as well as in the New Testament.

Pharisees are blue-collar workers; they all have day jobs, as do rabbis. They are not allowed to be paid for teaching the Word of God. There is a law in the Mishnah that says you are not allowed to dig with the crown, which is a reference to the Word of God. In other words, one cannot profit from teaching the Scriptures.[7] Pharisees study and become masters of the law, but they also have income-producing professions, which is why the parables they share resonate with the working class.

At their origin, the Pharisees are the good guys. Josephus says that by the time of the New Testament, there are approximately 6,000 Pharisees overseeing synagogues.[8] Jesus often interacts with Pharisees, and they have rabbinic debates, dialoguing about the Text and its various interpretations. These are the Pharisees in the days of the intertestamental period. During this time, commoners love and follow their Pharisees; they are the rabbis and teachers of the law. They know what it means to love and follow God in their generation.

The Sadducees

Sadducees function differently than Pharisees. While there are thousands of Pharisees during the New Testament period, there are probably only hundreds of Sadducees. They are a contingent of priests, so Temple service in Jerusalem is the highest priority for them. They might have summer homes, too, because while Pharisees are blue collar, Sadducees are aristocratic. They are the white collar, wealthier, upper-echelon members of Jewish society. Many of them serve in an important court known as the Sanhedrin. Seventy-one members made up this court, with the high priest often serving as the president. In Jesus' day, the high priest was Caiaphas.[9]

By the time of the New Testament, the Romans are selling the high priest's office to the highest bidder. This is the world into which Jesus is born. Because the Sadducees are collaborators with the Romans, the common people hate them. They are seen as aristocratic and unrelatable. By the time of Jesus, the Sadducees are corrupt, but in the intertestamental period, they have a good origin, as do the Pharisees.

In contrast to Jesus' rabbinic dialogues with the Pharisees, He hardly ever interacts with the Sadducees. They are so far gone, and ultimately, are the ones who instigate Jesus' crucifixion. Jesus overturns tables in the Temple, a direct response to the injustices of the Temple courts and their practice of extorting money from the people by overcharging for the sacrificial animals and money-changing services.[10]

The Essenes

The third sect that rises up to preserve the Jewish way of life is the Essenes. They are the absolutists, the purest of the pure. Have you ever known someone so pure they're weird? To get away from Hellenism and the activities going on in the poleis, some of these purist men pack up their belongings and move to the Judean desert to a place called Qumran. These white-clad separatists become a colony known as the Essenes.

The Essenes go through *mikvah*, a baptismal pool, before eating their meals. My favorite thing about them—and my college students love this too—is that they are so concerned with not breaking the Sabbath that they refuse to relieve themselves on this set-apart day! After all, the Sabbath is about resting and ceasing from our work so we can celebrate God's work. The Essenes are so stringent that they do not allow their bodies to violate the Sabbath by working out waste. For a Jewish person, the Sabbath begins sundown Friday night and ends sundown Saturday night. Josephus tells us that at sundown Saturday night, the Essenes line up at the gate with their pails. When the gates are opened, they scatter throughout the desert to handle their business after holding it for twenty-four hours.[11] Do you better understand what I mean when I say they're so pure they're weird?

Something beautiful comes out of their piety. The Essenes rise up during the intertestamental period. A portion of them live in the Judean Desert taking baths before eating their communal meals. They're saying specific prayers. They're *not* relieving themselves on the Sabbath. You

Qumran Cave 4 in the Judean Desert

may be wondering how they spend their time! The Essenes at Qumran are devoted masters of the biblical text. They think constantly about the ways of the Lord. They are most well-known for the role many believe they played in scribing the Dead Sea Scrolls. During the Jewish revolt, the Essenes bury the scrolls in caves, to be found some 2,000 years later by Bedouin shepherds.

I take my Israel teams to Qumran. We walk through the ruins of this desert city built by the Essenes. Archaeologists believe they have located the scriptorium, including the inkwells used by these devout men. We take time to learn and study in the ruins of this room where the Dead Sea Scrolls were possibly scribed. The Essenes may have been weird, but we are grateful for them because they left what many describe as the greatest archaeological discovery of the twentieth century! John the Baptist comes out of the desert and is a master of the Text. Some scholars believe he may have been an Essene.

Entertainment or Celebration

These are the Jewish sects or groups who rise up to preserve the Jewish way of life and uphold the Scriptures when Hellenism is on the move. The Pharisees oversee the synagogues and teach the ways of God. The Sadducees oversee the Temple; they care for God's house. During the intertestamental period, both the Pharisees and the Sadducees are highly sought. The Essenes are in the desert as well as in cities, and they are scribing the Scriptures, unknowingly giving us a huge gift. These three sects originate during the intertestamental period, which explains why we don't see them mentioned in the Old Testament.

This brings us to some challenging questions for each of us to put before the Lord: Are we more of the kingdom of entertainment or the kingdom of celebration? Do we have a passive or active approach to life? Are we alive and awake, seeking to participate with God and seeing His kingdom come down to the ground? Like the Jews of the intertestamental period, we have the opportunity to live out the way of Jesus in a culture of entertainment. We grapple with some of the very same issues. We can locate ourselves in this part of the Story.

The Story of Hanukkah[12]

In the biblical book of Daniel, there is a prophecy about an event called the abomination of desolation.[13] Daniel predicts the occurrence of an event that is so dreadful, the result will be utter devastation. The Jewish people say this prophecy was first fulfilled during the intertestamental period. Because the Jews hold to a more cyclical view of time, prophecies have a way of repeating generationally. They say the second time this prophecy was fulfilled, the second abomination of desolation, occurred in AD 70, when Titus and the Romans sacked the Temple and burned it to the ground.

Let's now focus on the first abomination of desolation, which takes place during the intertestamental period. This atrocity propelled the events that result in the annual celebration of Hanukkah. Many Christians tend to think that Hanukkah is the Jewish version of Christmas, because both share the month of December and gifts are exchanged. But Hanukkah and Christmas are not related. Hanukkah is older than Christmas—it predates Jesus' birth! When Jesus lived upon and walked the earth 2,000 years ago, He celebrated Hanukkah. He knew this Jewish festival well.[14]

The story of Hanukkah, anchored in history, provides one of the most beautiful displays of the Jewish people as a culture of celebration. The Greeks conquer the world with the sword and then infect it with Hellenism through the establishment of poleis. The world bites down hard on this culture of entertainment. Alexander the Great dies during the intertestamental period. Because he has no heir, upon his death, the kingdom of Greece is handed down to four of his military generals, who are each given a portion.[15] Two of the four generals are significant to us here because they come to the lands of the biblical story.

One is a man named Ptolemy. A famous woman comes from the Ptolemies—we often think of her as an Egyptian because she ruled over Egypt, but she is actually Greek. Historically, she is known by her title, Cleopatra VII. This famous Cleopatra was a lover of Mark Antony, whom we will learn more about in the next chapter.

Our focus here will be on a general named Seleucus. He oversees what comes to be known as the Seleucid Empire, which is still Greek, though it is located across much of the Middle East. The Seleucids take control of the lands of the Jews from the Ptolemies and force the Jewish people to become Hellenized, whether they want to embrace the Grecian way of living or not. The Seleucids are opposed to the Jewish people keeping their national identity and religious autonomy or being a kingdom of celebration in the midst of the kingdom of entertainment.

The abomination of desolation occurs through a Seleucid king named Antiochus Epiphanes IV. Antiochus hates the Jews. From the moment he takes over, he aggravates, frustrates, and persecutes them, coercing them to abandon their Jewish ways and become Hellenistic.

Antiochus Epiphanes IV first forbids the Torah. To take out a people group, take away their sacred writings. Antiochus confiscates copies of the Torah and, when possible, burns them. Next, he outlaws the Jewish feasts. Antiochus prohibits the Jews from celebrating their annual rhythms and festivals. Then he bans the Sabbath, requiring the Jewish people to work on their day of rest. Circumcision of Jewish males is forbidden.[16] Antiochus Epiphanes IV is evil—so much so that he is nicknamed *Epimanes*, meaning "the mad one." Can you feel the collision of cultures?

Antiochus Epiphanes IV further provokes the Jewish people by dedicating the Temple in Jerusalem to a Greek god. The Jews are almost at their end, but the worst is still to come. The year 168 BC is important in history. Antiochus does the unthinkable and has a pig sacrificed on the altar in the Temple. For the Jew, God lives in His house, in Jerusalem. Pigs are unclean animals to the Jews, so now the Temple is unclean. This disgusting act by Antiochus is the abomination leading to desolation first prophesied by Daniel.

The Jewish people are so infuriated, they call an all-out revolt and go to war against the Seleucids. History records this as the Maccabean Revolt, initiated by a man named Mattathias. His third son was Judas Maccabee. *Maccabee* means "hammer"; Judas the hammer was a tough guy! The Maccabean Revolt is named after this family who rings the bell of insurrection. The Jewish people rise up and go to war to throw off the Seleucids. They've had it with Hellenistic rule and control. The Maccabean Revolt lasts seven years, from 167 BC to 160 BC.

The story of Hanukkah emerges in this uprising. God lives in Jerusalem in His house. There is an oil lamp in the Temple that burns continually, known as the menorah.[17] The priests attend to it all day, every day. It is known as the light or lamp of the Lord. For Jews, it signifies God's presence in the Temple. Think about it like this: If I were to pull up to your house and see that your lights are on, I would assume you are home. So it is with the lamp of the Lord. If it is lit, it is understood that God is in His house, in His Temple, with His people.

Within the Temple complex lay an oil storage area in which the light of the menorah—the seven-branched candelabrum—could remain lit. In Jewish understanding, if the light of the Lord goes out, God is no longer present; His glory has departed. The Maccabees and Jews need to rededicate the Temple that has been defiled under Seleucid leadership, but unfortunately, they only have enough oil for one night—and it takes seven days to make the appropriate oil for the lampstand. Talk about bad timing! Who has a week to wait for God's presence to reappear in the midst of war?

The miracle of Hanukkah is that the oil that was only enough for one night lasts for eight days and nights. The lamp of the Lord does not go out! The light of the Lord stays lit, kept aflame by the living God, who is with the Jews in their rebellion against the Seleucids.

The Seleucids are expected to win, but the miraculous presence of the Lord so impacts the outnumbered, outmanned, and out-armored Jewish men that they defy the odds and overcome Antiochus's regime. The Temple has been desecrated because "the mad one" has sacrificed a pig on the altar in the Holy of Holies. In the midst of the revolt, the Jewish people reclaim and rededicate the house of the Lord after being so moved and motivated by God's miraculous provision and presence.

Here is where we witness the Jewish people as a culture of celebration. When a major event like this goes down in their history, they make a holiday out of it and celebrate it annually. This is how Hannukah comes to be known as the Festival of Lights! The Jewish people remember this story for eight nights in December every year, setting aside consecrated time and space to commemorate that the lamp of the Lord did not go out in the Temple, invigorating them to overthrow the Seleucids.

At Hanukkah, a nine-branched candelabrum known as a hanukkiah is used. Eight candles represent each of the eight nights, and the middle candle, the *shamash* or "helper" candle, is used to light the others. Hanukkah is celebrated by retelling, remembering, and reimagining the story. Jewish parents tell this story to their children the way Christian par-

Lit hanukkiah

ents share the Christmas story with their children. Jewish people celebrate Hanukkah every year just as Christmas is celebrated every year. On night one, the Jews gather with family and friends and use the *shamash* to light the first candle. They tell the story of Hanukkah and eat good food, which is key to any quality celebration! They share their stories of how God's lamp has never gone out in their lives. Their story becomes our story in celebration. What God did for them He currently does for us.

On night two, the *shamash* is used to light the first and second candles, which provides double the light. They eat more good food. They tell and retell the story. They share stories of God's provision, of times when He came through. This ritual goes on through each of the eight nights, until all eight candles have been lit.

Several years ago, I hosted Hanukkah for eight straight nights. I had different groups of friends over, told the story, and lit the candles. We sat around, ate good food, and shared our God stories. It was one of the most powerful things I've ever done! The consecrated time in the middle of December impacted us all. Christmas is one of the busiest seasons of the year, but these eight nights afforded us time to pause and experience table fellowship together, while remembering and reimagining our God stories.

I am not suggesting we should become Jewish; that's not my point at all. I'm saying we as a Christian people need to come together and share a table and stories. I encourage you to consider hosting your own Hanukkah celebration. Invite your family and friends over to enjoy great food and experience the story of Hanukkah. Light your hanukkiah. Tell stories of when the light of the Lord did not go out in your lives, when you experienced the living God moving, breathing, and acting on your behalf. This is the story of Hanukkah, anchored in the intertestamental period.

People of Celebration

When God looks upon us, may He find us to be a people of celebration, a people who want to actively know Him and participate with Him in seeing His kingdom come. We don't want to follow the Greek way by living for ourselves. We believe that the highest ethic, the highest ideal, the way of Jesus, is anchored in giving our lives away because we know that God is giving them back to us in manifold fashion. We can afford to love God and love our neighbor because we are not orphans. We don't have to scrounge to provide, to strive and strain for ourselves. We're not just a saved people, we're a kept people. This is cause for celebration.

We want the Lord to be with us in the same way He was with the Jews during the intertestamental period. There has been a remnant in every generation who hold fast to the way of the Lord. When God looks upon us, may He see that we are part of that remnant.

Chapter 9

HEROD THE GREAT

In the previous chapter, we married the Old Testament with the New Testament as we discovered what happened during the intertestamental period. Now we come to the genesis of the New Testament, beginning with Matthew. We have already seen the living God fulfill two of the three promises He made to Avraham. In this chapter and the next, God fulfills the third promise, the incarnation, by taking on flesh and coming to live among humanity…and ultimately, dying in our place and resurrecting so that we might have the hope of eternal life.

Herod in History

Jesus is born into the world of Herod the Great, king of Judea. A key figure during the latter part of the intertestamental period, Herod the Great is born around 73–72 BC and dies in 4 BC. To help us better connect the timing of Jesus' birth with Herod, when the magi come to visit Jesus, He is a young child. Upon hearing that another king of Judea has been born, Herod is greatly disturbed and responds by having the infant and toddler boys of Bethlehem murdered.[1] Because Herod died in 4 BC, Jesus has to have been born before then, around 5 or 6 BC, as is believed by most scholars.

We tend to be familiar with Herod in connection to the genocide of baby boys in Bethlehem, but there is far more to his story. Herod was a strapping athlete and an outstanding hunter. The Jewish historian Josephus says Herod excelled at throwing the javelin and at archery.[2] He was far more Greek or Hellenistic than he was Jewish. As king of Judea, Herod was sandwiched between the Romans above him and the Jews below him. The pressure kept him in a state of paranoia. We are about to see that there is no difference in world history and biblical history. Let's walk through what this means.

Mark Antony of Rome and Cleopatra of Egypt are two famous historical figures. Cleopatra is not a name, it's a title. The Cleopatra being referred to here is Cleopatra VII, a Greek, who takes the throne in Egypt in 51 BC upon the death of her father, Ptolemy XII. Mark Antony, a Roman general and politician, Cleopatra VII, queen of Egypt, and Herod the Great, king of Judea, all know each other. They are contemporaries during the intertestamental period. Mark Antony the Roman nominates Herod to reign as king of Judea. Herod is known as a puppet king of the Roman Empire. He is like a marionette doll, moving at the discretion of the people controlling him.

Herod feels constant pressure to appease the Romans above him so they will leave him on the throne. Below him are his Jewish subjects, who hate him from the get-go because he is a collaborator with Rome and friends with Mark Antony. Herod is an Idumean, a descendant of Esau, of the ancient Edomite tribe. Because he is not purely Jewish, the people view him as an illegitimate authority on the throne.

With pressure from the Romans above and the Jews below, Herod continually tries to appease. Josephus tells us that Herod worries about Cleopatra VII as she ever attempts to get Mark Antony, her lover, to give the land of the Jews—the land Herod rules as king—to her.[3] And while Herod is Mark Antony's friend, Cleopatra is Mark Antony's lover. Herod fears she will convince Mark Antony to kill him and give her the land where the Jewish people live.

In this excerpt from *The Jewish War*, Josephus's description of Cleopatra makes it clear that Herod has good reason to fear her. Herod "turned all his personal treasures into cash and sent it to Antony and his staff."

Herod is trying to placate by bribing and giving them money. "Even so, he could not buy freedom from all trouble: Antony, ruled by his passion for Cleopatra, had become the complete slave of his desire, while Cleopatra had gone right through her own family till not one single relation was left alive," meaning she had them all killed. "And now thirsting for the blood of strangers, was slandering the authorities in Syria and urging Antony to have them executed, thinking that in this way she would easily become the mistress of all their possessions. She even extended her acquisitiveness to Jews and Arabs and worked in secret to get their kings, Herod and Malikus, put to death."[4]

Let's string a biblical pearl here. Cleopatra VII is queen of Egypt from 51 BC until her death in 30 BC. Her reign overlaps with Herod's when he takes the throne in 37 BC. Herod knows that Cleopatra wants to take his life and take over his land. If you are Herod the Great, as long as Cleopatra is alive, the one place on earth you are not going to is Egypt.

I find it interesting that when Jesus is born, an angel comes to Joseph, telling him to take Mary and baby Jesus to Egypt, where they stay until the death of Herod. The place of likely death for the illegitimate king of the Jews during Cleopatra's reign is a safe haven for the newborn legitimate King of the Jews. I can't help but wonder if even the memory of Cleopatra in Egypt would have thwarted Herod's pursuit of the holy family had he known they fled there.

Again, there is no such thing as world history and biblical history. There's just history!

Remez

There is a fascinating principle in Scripture known as *remez*, which is a Hebrew word meaning "hint."[5] A *remez* "hints" at something that happened previously, with the speaker/writer using only a few words to invite us into the past scenario or prior scripture.

Herod kills the two-and-under boys in Bethlehem while the rescuer of humanity escapes death by being taken from the Promised Land to Egypt. Matthew gives us a *remez* to Herod acting like Pharaoh, who slays the

Israelite boys in Egypt while the rescuer of the Israelites escapes right under his nose.[6] And, just as God delivers the Israelites from their Egyptian captors and takes them out of Egypt as they head toward the Promised Land, He does the same for His Son.[7] In other words, Matthew "hints" at Jesus serving as a second Moses figure who will redeem His people.

We can become so familiar with the individual stories of Scripture read and understood through our Western lens that we miss the fascinating pearls strung together throughout the Story of the biblical narrative.

Building to Appease

Paranoia causes Herod the Great, known as one of the greatest architects of the world, to build in order to appease both the Romans and the Jews who pressure him from all sides. A visionary builder, Herod's impressive construction projects can still be viewed and visited in the Promised Land today. He builds eight to ten palace fortresses, including the Herodium—the only one named after Herod, and the location where he is buried. There's also Machaerus, a hilltop stronghold along the edge of the Jordan Valley and Dead Sea, where Herod Antipas (Herod the Great's son) imprisons and beheads John the Baptist.[8] Herod often builds these palace fortresses, opulence married to security, in the middle of nowhere. He's Herod the Great, so they are, of course, luxurious. Herod likes to play god. He goes to the desert, where there is limited water, and builds lavish gardens and pools. He builds in the least likely of places just to prove he can.

Machaerus

If you recall, Alexander the Great infiltrates Judaism with Hellenism by planting poleis or Greek cities. We likened them to a city in America known as Vegas. Remember, to be a Hellenistic city, a polis must have an arena or hippodrome, a theater, an agora, a temple, and a gymnasium. To appease the Romans, Herod the Great builds a fully Hellenistic polis in the midst of the land of the Jews. It's located on the Mediterranean coast, a place called Caesarea. It's also known as Caesarea Maritima or Caesarea by the Sea. We see this city mentioned in the Bible. Herod builds it complete with a hippodrome, bath complexes, theaters, and temples. The king of Judea builds Vegas in the heart of the land. The Jews don't like it and respond, which means Herod also responds, because he builds to appease.

Herod turns his sights to Jerusalem, because for the Jews, the most important place in their entire faith is the Temple. Herod vastly expands the temple Zerubbabel rebuilds at the end of the Old Testament. By the time of its completion, Herod's Temple, also still known as the Second Temple, and the surrounding complex is the largest man-made platform in the world.[9] The Temple Mount complex Jesus walked on was approximately twenty-eight football fields in size, covering thirty-seven acres. I find it interesting that Jesus worshipped at the Temple refurbished and expanded by Herod the Great.

Masada

One of Herod's palace fortresses is Masada, the most excavated site in all of Israel. To date, Masada is more than 90 percent unearthed. (Archaeologists

Masada: Herod's clifftop palace fortress

always leave some ruins for future generations who will have better techniques and methodologies.) Masada carries great meaning for modern-day Israelis. They want the story told. They want their children to know it, and they want the world to know it. Before we get to the story of Masada, let's consider the enormity of the project Herod undertook.

The Hebrew word *masada* means "fortress,"[10] "strong place," or "stronghold." Located in the Judean desert near the Dead Sea, this aptly named cliff-top fortress serves not only as a palace, but also as a place of refuge. Remember, Herod hadn't inherited his crown, so his position as king is unstable. The Jewish people resent him because Rome gave him the throne. Masada offers a secure place Herod can go when he feels threatened. What Masada lacks in water or shade, it more than makes up for in stone. Herod's engineers use the available stone to build a nearly mile-long casemate wall that surrounds the entire plateau. Many of the troops assigned to Masada live within the casemate wall.

As one of the wealthiest men in the East, Herod has the means and power to fund anything he desires to build. This, combined with his need to demonstrate mastery over nature, leads him to build a lavish bath complex in the middle of the desert—water in the dry wilderness, an oasis in the barren and desolate wasteland. Herod combines luxury with security, a trademark of all his palace fortresses.

Herod the Great dies in 4 BC, but if we extend our timeline well into the New Testament, we come to a war that happened from AD 66 to 73 known as the First Jewish-Roman War. The story goes like this: Some Jewish extremists known as Sicarii, along with their wives and children, flee the Romans and come to Masada during this Jewish revolt. These rebels and their families live atop Masada for three years. It functions as its own city. The residents have cisterns and olive stores. They grow crops. They have pigeons and doves for meat and fertilizer, as well as other animals.

Eventually the Romans find these Jews at Masada. They build a wall around the fortress and start constructing a siege ramp in an effort to reach the top and seize the Jewish people. Keep in mind that the extremists have been killing Romans, so the last thing they want is for their wives and children to fall into Roman hands.

Murder is one of the most heinous crimes within Judaism. To take a life is profoundly serious. Josephus writes about the moment when the Sicarii are certain that the Romans will reach them atop Masada. The night before the Romans break through the casemate wall, the Sicarii men went home and "tenderly embraced their wives, and took their children into their arms, and gave the longest parting kisses to them, with tears in their eyes. Yet at the same time did they complete what they had resolved on; as if they had been executed by the hands of strangers."[11] This is a genteel way of saying they humanely killed their families rather than allow them to be captured by the Romans.

After most of the people had died, the few rebels left draw lots to determine who will put their brother down. Ten men remain, which dwindles to one man alive atop Masada. Suicide—taking one's own life—is one of the most egregious sins in Judaism. From a Jewish perspective, this last remaining rebel put his own soul in danger by taking the hit.

The Romans break through the casemate wall the next day, finding nearly 1,000 Jewish people dead. The Romans know they haven't starved the extremists, as there is plenty of water in the cisterns and food in the storage bays.[12] It is clear that the Jewish people have laid down their lives rather than be subservient to Rome.

Masada continues to be important to the Jewish people. Before many of the young men and women for the Israeli military are formally accepted, they are provided an opportunity to hike to the top of Masada at dawn. In the location where their Jewish ancestors laid down their lives, these young people may choose to pledge their fidelity to the State of Israel, reciting a creed that includes the phrase "Remember Masada, never again." Masada sits at the national conscience of the Israeli people in the same way Pearl Harbor or 9/11 sit in the conscience of the American people.

The Herodium

Herod lives in fear and rules through fear. He doesn't trust anyone, so he builds invincible palace fortresses like Masada and the Herodium, both of

Herodium from a distance

which are located in the Judean desert. Work on the Herodium begins in approximately 23 BC, halfway through Herod's reign, and he completes it in 15 BC in time for a special visit from none other than Emperor Augustus' son-in-law Marcus Vipsanius Agrippa. Herod takes a hill and transforms it into his own mountain, with a hard-to-miss cone-like shape of a volcano.

Like Herod's other palace fortresses, the Herodium contains an extravagant bath complex, including a domed ceiling in the tepidarium, thought to be the first of its kind in the land. Herod is ambitious and visionary. Driven by ego, Herod wants this palace fortress to be daunting and luxurious—and he succeeds in making it so.

The Herodium stands 400 feet above the surrounding territory. When I take teams to Israel, we stand at the top of the Herodium and, on a clear day, can see Bethlehem in the distance, as well as the Mount of Olives in Jerusalem.

At the base of the Herodium, Herod builds thirty-eight acres of lavish

Ruins of Herod's pool complex at the base of the Herodium in the Judean Desert

gardens and a massive, seventy-meter by forty-five-meter pool, complete with small boats and an island! This engineering feat proves again that Herod can dominate the barren desert.

Moving Mountains

Let's string some biblical pearls together. In Jesus' day, Herod was known as a man who could move mountains. He took the dirt from one hill and added it to another to build the Herodium.

In Matthew 21:21, Jesus says, "If you have faith and do not doubt…you can say to this mountain, 'Go, throw yourself into the sea,' and it will be done." Jesus is referring to a specific mountain and a specific sea. He is not a Greek philosopher; He is a Jewish rabbi.[13] The Jewish people dialogue around what's visible on the earth.

When I'm in Israel with teams, we go to the region where Jesus likely stood with His disciples when He made this statement. As we look out over the land, the only mountain that can be seen is the Herodium, and the only visible sea is the Dead Sea. Standing there allows us to tangibly perceive what Jesus is saying. In the context of Herod the Great, an illegitimate Idumean exalted to king by the Romans, if you have faith, you can tell the Herodium—which represents idolatry—to be thrown into the Dead Sea. Jesus believes that zeal for the Lord can overthrow kingdoms. In a holy invasion, the kingdom of light is constantly invading, conquering, and taking over the kingdom of darkness.

Herod's Death and Tomb

Herod the Great dies in New Testament Jericho, and servants carry his body twenty-four miles to the Herodium. Remember, he begins as a strapping athlete, but he lives an evil, selfish life, which has its consequences. In *The Jewish War*, Josephus details the pitiful end of Herod's life, including a broken spirit, difficulties with his children, and sickness throughout his body. His symptoms included "a slight fever, an unbearable itching all over his body, constant pains in the lower bowel, swellings on the feet as in dropsy, inflammation of the abdomen, and mortification of the genitals, producing worms as well as difficulty breathing…and spasms in all of his limbs."[14] That's a lot! Herod was in such a miserable state that he attempted to kill himself with a knife he often used to cut his apples; his cousin Achiabus stopped him just in time.[15]

When I first studied in Israel, we explored the top of the Herodium. I looked down the side of the rockface and noticed a small hole with yellow caution tape around it. Now, I am mischievous, so when I see a sign that says, "Do not enter," what do I want to do? Enter! Some of my classmates and I scurried down the side of the rockface. When we came to the hole, we looked inside and saw perfectly hewn steps—it was clear that something significant had been built into the side of the Herodium! The steps also said, "Do not enter," but we went in anyway! Inside were multiple chambers with flawlessly shaped rooms that were empty. We were excited, wondering what had once been in there.

Caesarea Maritima – theater

Caesarea Maritima – Herod's aqueduct

We hiked back to our bus and, as we were getting ready to drive off, I told our professor what we had done. When I asked him what we had seen, he said, "They have discovered Herod the Great's tomb here, in the side of the hill. They've already removed his sarcophagus and all that he was buried with, which is why it is empty." This is one of my most favorite Indiana Jones-like experiences!

Caesarea Maritima

Herod the Great was also known as an inventor. He

built things that had never been built before. This was demonstrated in the polis Herod began building around 22 BC to appease the Romans. I like to think of Caesarea, also known as Caesarea Maritima or Caesarea on the Sea, as a little Rome away from Rome, in Judea. It had a bath complex and theater, as well as a hippodrome for chariot racing that was able to seat thousands. In Caesarea, Herod built the largest artificial or man-made harbor of his day. To deliver water to Caesarea, Herod built the largest aqueduct in Israel, supplied by springs near Mount Carmel.

Let's string together a few pearls. Caesarea serves as a key location throughout the book of Acts; it is a very biblical city. In Acts 8, after Philip ministers to the Ethiopian eunuch along the side of the road, the Spirit of the Lord takes Philip away and he eventually ends up in Caesarea. Acts 10 details

Caesarea Maritima – hippodrome

Caesarea Maritima – ruins of Herod's Promontory Palace

Peter going into the house of a Roman centurion named Cornelius, who lives in Caesarea. Peter talks with him, as well as his family and friends who are gathered there. Cornelius and those who are present with him receive the Holy Spirit at Caesarea.

In Acts 12, Herod the Great's grandson, Herod Agrippa, is living in Caesarea. This Herod likes Vegas as well. One day as Herod addresses the people, they start worshipping him, saying, "This is the voice of a god, not of a man."[16] Josephus explains their praise in this way: As Herod Agrippa stands up in the theater, the sun shines on him and the silver metallic threads sewn into his robe make him glisten like a god. The people worship him as such, and rather than giving glory to the living God, Herod takes the glory for himself. An angel of the Lord strikes him down and he dies.[17]

Acts 23–26 also take place at Caesarea. Paul spends two years under house arrest there and stands before the Roman governors Felix and Festus, as well as King Agrippa II. He gives a defense of the Christian faith in the promontory palace at Caesarea.

It's important for us to synthesize these biblical stories and understand contextually that the power of God through the apostles was at work in the polis of Caesarea. The kingdom of light was invading the kingdom of darkness. Jewish people did not go into Roman homes; they were considered unclean. Yet Peter, a clean Jew, goes into the home of Cornelius, an unclean Roman. Through table fellowship, Cornelius and his family and friends receive the gift of the Holy Spirit and are baptized.

Caesarea Maritima looked like a Greek city. It was a city of entertainment. Pontius Pilate lived there, as did Herod the Great and the Roman governors Felix and Festus. Herod built an entire polis on Judea's Mediterranean coast. It housed one of the first amphitheaters in Judea. The acoustics of the amphitheater are phenomenal! When I take biblical studies teams to Caesarea, I have them sit at the top while I go down on the stage. Then, in my everyday conversational voice I teach, and they are able to hear me perfectly. There is a unique excellence in the way that Herod carried out his building projects.

Temple Mount – Eastern Wall of the Old City, Jerusalem

Temple Mount – Dome of the Rock

The Temple Mount

Understandably, the construction of a Roman city in the heart of Judean country angered the Jews. Thus, in the same way that Herod built Caesarea to appease the Romans, he undertook another massive building project in Jerusalem to appease the Jews and retain their loyalty.

Herod recognized that the Jews valued cleanliness and purification. He used this to his advantage by expanding the Pool of Siloam, the largest public pool in Jerusalem. Thousands of Jewish pilgrims came to visit the Temple annually, which required cleansing in a *mikvah*, or ritual purification bath, before entering. In John 9, this pool is where Jesus sent the blind man to wash his eyes and be healed. The Pool of Bethesda, which is north of the Temple Mount, was central to Jesus' healing of the invalid man in John 5.

Jesus was born into a Herodian world. He performed miracles in a pool

Western Wall: men's side

Western Wall: women's side

built by Herod the Great. The Temple where Jesus worshipped was constructed through the genius, wealth, and ambition of Herod the Great. By the time Herod was finished expanding the Temple Mount, it was the largest temple platform on earth at that time, covering nearly thirty-seven acres. To put that size into perspective, about twenty-eight football fields could fit on the complex. By making such grandiose improvements to the Temple, considered by Jews to be the holiest place on earth, Herod kept himself in better standing with the Jewish people and succeeded in his intent to outdo the First Temple built by King Solomon.

Legacy of Stone

The influence of Herod the Great as a master architect and builder outlived his life. His legacy of stone can still be viewed and touched today throughout the land of Israel, perhaps overshadowing his legacy as an evil dictator.

And while the stone remnants of the Herodian world Jesus was born into are indeed impressive, Jesus' "legacy of stone" is living and unending. According to 1 Peter 2:4-5, "As you come to him, the living Stone—rejected by humans but chosen by God and precious to him—you also, like living stones, are being built into a spiritual house." We are invited to participate in the living legacy of Jesus, the *legitimate* King of the Jews. And that is what we'll explore in the upcoming chapters.

Chapter 10

THE GOSPELS: PART 1

So far in our journey through the biblical narrative, God has fulfilled the promise of Avram's descendants becoming a nation. This happened at the base of Mount Sinai when God gave the Torah, or instructions for how to live in true shalom. And God wasn't done; He also fulfilled the promise of land. Over and over, the living God proves to be both a promise maker and a promise keeper. From Genesis 12 to the end of the Bible, God keeps His promises not only to Avram, but to the whole world.

Keep in mind God's original mandate that the Israelites would fill the Promised Land because the International Coastal Highway went right through it. Rather than sending Avram to the nations, God plants Avram and his descendants along the highway so that, as the nations come through, they bear witness to a new tribe—something the world had never seen. This tribe would leave the corners of their fields unharvested so widows could find something to eat. They would welcome the *ger*, the stranger among them, as they remembered what it was like to be strangers and slaves in Egypt. They would be a people living under the one true God, who does not require sacrifice upon sacrifice, all the way up to your children. This was the original plan.

Now we are about to see God bring the remaining promise to pass: that through Avram's seed, all the nations will be blessed.

Preparation for Baby Jesus

Previously, as we learned about the rise of the Pharisees, Sadducees, Essenes, and Herod the Great during the intertestamental period, we referenced Galatians 4:4 with regard to the *timing* of Jesus' birth. When the time had fully come, when circumstances were as they needed to be, God sent His Son to rescue the world.

How did God prepare the world for the arrival of Jesus? Four influential scenarios were developing as the Romans took power over this land in 63 BC.

First was the *Pax Romana*, or Roman Peace. Beginning around 27 BC, the Pax Romana provided approximately 200 years of peace for the Roman Empire. Jesus was birthed into a relatively quiet period in history when Caesar Augustus was on the throne.

Next, *Koine*, the common Greek language, permeated the Roman Empire, thus making communication between people groups easier. Whether aristocratic, plebian, or slave, most people spoke *Koine* Greek.

Third was the establishment of more than 50,000 miles of Roman roads. The Romans unknowingly created pathways that would be used for transmitting the message of a coming rescuer. During this era of peaceful Roman rule, the geopolitical world was connected.

Last was the emergence of synagogues, which served as local worship centers throughout the Roman Empire. When the apostle Paul visited cities and towns, he typically visited the local synagogues first.[1] As the message of the gospel was being transmitted, synagogues provided places where it could take root. When travelers arrived in a town, they would often go to the synagogue, where the message was being taught.

The combination of Roman peace, a shared language, Roman roads, and synagogues set the stage for the arrival of the promised rescuer. God readied the nursery for baby Jesus. This deliberate preparation yielded a convergence of circumstances resulting in the most ideal opportunity in human history up to this time for Jesus to come into the world and the message of the gospel to spread quickly.

Retreat or Engage

Let's consider this question as we continue stringing the pearls of Scripture: Throughout the Gospels, does Jesus encourage His people to *retreat from* or *engage with* the world? In other words, are we to withdraw from the world, or is God inviting us to join Him in engaging it? In this chapter and the next, the Bible will answer this question for us.

God Versus Satan?

At the beginning of the biblical narrative in Genesis 3:15, God says this to the serpent: "I will put enmity between you and the woman, and between your offspring and hers; he will crush your head, and you will strike his heel." This may very well be the first messianic promise given in Scripture. In this passage, the living God explains the ramifications of shalom disrupted. A son will come from a woman. And this son will crush the head of the serpent as the serpent strikes the son's heel.

Now, let's take another look at Galatians 4:4: "When the set time had fully come"—we've already noted how God prepared the moment historically—"God sent his Son, born of a woman." This rings back to Genesis 3:15. As God prepares the world for Jesus' birth and begins a fresh chapter in the Story, let's establish a thesis that is going to help us greatly.

Did you grow up with or know some version of an understanding that the world is in a cosmic battle of God versus Satan? This is awful theology! Satan does exist and is indeed evil. Satan tries to get you off the path of shalom. But Satan is not the opposite of God. God and Satan are not equals! They are on completely different playing fields.[2] The Story of the Bible is not God versus Satan.

I want to contend for a perspective that we are about to see play out in Scripture: *Jesus did not come to save you from the devil; He came to save you from you.* He came to change your life in such a way that you become a worthy offering to the world, so that the world will bear witness to Him.

The Birth of Jesus

As we make our way through the book of Matthew, keep this question in mind: Are we a people of retreat or engagement?

Matthew 1:18-21 is a familiar passage that details the birth of Jesus. In it, Matthew describes an angel appearing to Joseph in a dream. The angel tells Joseph that Mary is going to give birth to a son, whom Joseph is to name Jesus, because He will save His people from their sins. My thesis for the Gospels and the rest of the New Testament is that *Jesus came to save us from our sins in order to send us into the world.* Jesus did not come to save us from the world. He saves us from our sins and sends us into the world to be ambassadors of engagement.

We've already discussed the time in history when the Greeks came on the scene and began worshipping the human body. When men became gods, God became a man. The one true God took on flesh and came to live among us. This gift of Jesus was a direct result of God's great love for the world, as noted in John 3:16—one of the most well-known verses in the Bible.

The movement of Scripture is the living God coming closer and closer to us. In Genesis 1, we see the Spirit of God hovering. In the desert, the living God comes down and tabernacles with and among His people. In the New Testament, God comes toward us through Jesus—God made flesh, living among us. From Pentecost onward, the Holy Spirit lives inside of us. Throughout the Story of the Bible, the living God comes closer. Hovering. Down. Toward. In.

Immanuel means "God with us."[3] Shalom has arrived, such as the world had not known since the garden of Eden. A new Adam is here.[4] These are the signs of spring. The third promise to Avram is being fulfilled.

Jesus came to save us from our sins in order to send us into the world.

The Response to Jesus' Birth

Herod hears about the birth of Jesus and is greatly disturbed.[5] Augustus was said to have made a play on words in Greek when he said that it is safer being one of Herod's swine (in Greek, *hus*) than his son (in Greek, *huios*).[6]

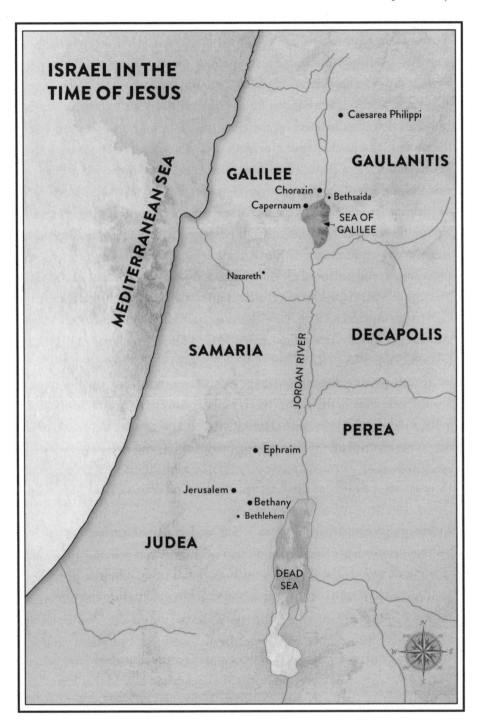

ISRAEL IN THE
TIME OF JESUS

• Caesarea Philippi

GAULANITIS

GALILEE

Chorazin •
Capernaum • • Bethsaida

SEA OF
GALILEE

MEDITERRANEAN SEA

Nazareth •

SAMARIA

JORDAN RIVER

DECAPOLIS

PEREA

• Ephraim

Jerusalem •
•Bethany
• Bethlehem

JUDEA

DEAD
SEA

(Remember, Herod, as a Jew, didn't eat pork, so his pigs escaped death!) Herod killed his own sons. He killed one of his wives. He was ruthless.

Jesus is born in the town of Bethlehem. Throughout the Old Testament, the land was known as Canaan when inhabited by the Canaanites and Israel when inhabited by the Israelites. When we come to the New Testament, the land has been broken up into different districts. In the north is the Sea of Galilee. The lower Jordan River comes out of this sea and empties into a much larger body of water known as the Dead Sea. To the left (west) of these water markers are three districts. To the north, by the Sea of Galilee, is the district of the Galilee. In the middle is the district known as Samaria. Further south is the district of Judea. Both Jerusalem and Bethlehem are down south in Judea. To the east of the seas and the Jordan is the district of Gaulinitis. Right below Gaulinitis is the district known as the Decapolis—the Vegas-like cities, and below the Decapolis is Perea. The western side is predominantly Jewish, while the eastern side leans strongly toward the Gentiles, or the kingdoms of darkness.

Just three miles from Bethlehem is the Herodium, one of Herod's palace fortresses. From the top of the Herodium you can see Bethlehem. Jesus is born right under the nose of Herod! We don't know historically if Herod was at the Herodium the day of Jesus' birth in Bethlehem, but he very well could have been. We would have written this story differently, having Jesus born far away from crazy Herod! The Story of the Bible is not God versus Satan. The living God is sovereign above all. Jesus is born in Bethlehem, fulfilling messianic prophecy.

Herod tries to kill baby Jesus and the family flees to Egypt, but they don't stay there. After Herod the Great dies, the family doesn't return to Bethlehem because one of Herod's sons, Herod Archelaus, is now ruling in Judea. So, the family goes farther north, to the region of the Galilee, and settles in the country village of Nazareth, where Jesus grows up.[7] In the first century, Bethlehem and Nazareth were not the modern large cities we see today; they were villages with likely just a few hundred residents.

Twelve-Year-Old Jesus

When we were getting our new frames in chapter 2, we talked about how the Bible is like God's photo album. It contains the best of who He is and what He wants us to know about Him. We see this "snapshot" idea in the biblical accounts of the life of Jesus, as there are considerable gaps between the details of His birth, escape to Egypt, relocation to Nazareth, and the next mention of Him as a twelve-year-old. After this glimpse of Jesus, the next time we encounter Him in the biblical narrative is when He is about thirty years old. This should pique our curiosity. Why was this snapshot of twelve-year-old Jesus included in God's photo album when there would otherwise be a lengthy gap between Him as a young boy and Him as a thirty-year-old man?

In keeping with Jewish tradition, every year Jesus' parents went to the Temple in Jerusalem to celebrate the feast of the Passover.[8] Here, we see the fidelity of Mary and Joseph, traveling from Nazareth in the region of the Galilee through Samaria to Jerusalem for this annual pilgrimage.

Luke 2:42 says, "When [Jesus] was twelve years old, they went *up to* the festival" (emphasis added). Remember, you always go "up" to Jerusalem, even though from a map, it looks like they are traveling down to the south. We notice these details when reading the Bible through the Middle Eastern lens in which it was written.

After the feast, Jesus stays in Jerusalem, but His parents think He is in the midst of the caravan of Galilean families traveling home together. After a day of travel, they look for Him among the group, only to discover He is not with them.

Have you ever lost your child in a grocery store or elsewhere? It happens! With our Western lens on, it can be easy to question Mary and Joseph. How could Jesus' parents leave the city without knowing where He was? But when we look through our Middle Eastern lens, we recognize that in antiquity, those who are part of a communal culture never travel alone; they always travel with a group for safety and shared provisions. This helps us better understand why Mary and Joseph didn't realize Jesus wasn't with them. They would have assumed He was elsewhere in the caravan, playing with cousins and friends, or hanging out with other relatives.

Upon returning to Jerusalem, Mary and Joseph search for three days. I don't know about you, but I would have been panicking. After all, they had lost the Son of God! Eventually, Mary and Joseph find twelve-year-old Jesus interacting with the Temple teachers, listening and asking questions. *Jesus is engaging rather than retreating.* He is dialoguing with the religious leaders in Jerusalem at the Temple. These are learned, well-studied men—Pharisees and rabbis, masters of the Text. Jesus is holding His own. All who hear Him are astonished at His answers and degree of understanding.[9]

In this scenario, Jesus is showing aptitude to become a rabbi. In the first-century world, Judaism had various stages of educational formation for both boys and girls. Around the age of twelve or thirteen, the highly gifted boys would move on into further study. The not-so-gifted would take up apprenticeship with their fathers to learn a trade. We previously talked about how you can't "dig with the crown," meaning you cannot be paid to teach the Scriptures. Thus, young men showing aptitude for rabbinic study would do both. They would apprentice with their fathers, learning the family trade, while also studying Scripture for hours a day.

This gives us insight as to what Jesus has been doing in Nazareth. He is learning to be a carpenter, as English Bibles often translate it. Perhaps more accurately, Jesus was a *tekton*, Greek for "artisan" or "builder." Remember all the fortresses Herod the Great constructed? Stone was the primary resource used for building in that world. Jesus is practicing being a *tekton* while also showing aptitude as a twelve-year-old who can craftily debate the Pharisees of Israel.

If you have ever envisioned baby Jesus, in the manger, already knowing Hebrew and having Torah fully memorized, Scripture paints a different picture! Jesus emptied Himself and became a man.[10] Luke 2:52 says, "Jesus *grew* in wisdom and stature and favor with God and man" (emphasis added). Scripture contends that Jesus put time and effort into learning the Text.

Sea of Galilee

Jesus Engaging the World

The next time we see Jesus in the Story, He is thirty years old. I believe that historically and culturally, we have a good idea of what Jesus was doing from twelve to thirty. He was living in Nazareth, learning to be a *tekton* alongside Joseph. He was also studying Torah for hours a day, preparing to be a rabbi.

Here is where we return to retreating or engaging.

With Nazareth being a village of only a few hundred residents, there likely wasn't enough work for Jesus and Joseph in this town alone. So where did they go to work? Four miles away from Nazareth was a Vegas-like, Hellenistic, Greco-Roman city called Sepphoris, the capitol of Herod Antipas's Galilee until AD 19 or 20. An average workday likely included Jesus and Joseph walking to Sepphoris to build with stone, earn their wages, then return home to Jewish Nazareth in the evening. Have you ever considered that Jesus may have worked in a place with pagan elements?

Jesus was daily experiencing the very world He came to save. He was in

Sunset on the Galilee with the lights of Tiberias on the opposite shore

the midst of both Jews and Gentiles. Geographically and biblically speaking, other than Jesus' visits to Tyre and Sidon, for the vast majority of His life, He did not travel outside a 100-mile radius from where He was born. Yet His disciples would take the gospel to the ends of the earth, beyond the Galilee, Samaria, and Judea. Jesus is intentionally with and among the world He came to save.

We can only imagine what young Jesus may have seen in Sepphoris—such as passing by a theater with plays given to the honor of Dionysius, the god of entertainment and wine. The theater is first century; Jesus *may* have helped build it. Even as a young boy, Jesus is engaging with the very world He came to save.

It is striking to me that the living God allowed Jesus to be born in Bethlehem, in direct proximity to the Herodium, while also letting Jesus live in Nazareth and work as a *tekton* in a place like Sepphoris. We are getting to know Jesus in His cultural, historic, geographic world.

Capernaum Synagogue from the fourth/fifth century AD—the white stones were most likely built on the original black basalt synagogue in which Jesus attended, taught, and healed

Capernaum Synagogue

Capernaum Synagogue

Jesus came to save you from your sins in order to send you into the world, just as He modeled.

Jesus' Baptism

The next snapshot the biblical narrative provides from the life of Jesus comes when He is thirty years old. Luke 3:21-23 details Jesus' baptism. It also states that Jesus was about thirty when He began His ministry. Have you ever wondered why the Bible gives this specific age? In this era of Judaism, thirty appears to be the age of rabbinic authority.[11] Jesus fits in His world.

Today, we have a seemingly endless number of denominations—whether that be Methodist, Episcopalian, Lutheran, Pentecostal, Presbyterian, or Baptist—all with preferences regarding baptism. But what was baptism in Jesus' first-century Jewish world, before any of our denominations existed? Why did people get baptized?

Mikvah is the Hebrew word for a ritual purification bath. First-century *mikva'ot* (the plural of *mikvah*) can still be seen throughout the land of Israel.

Kristi teaching at Arbel, with the Sea of Galilee and the region of the Evangelical Triangle (Chorazin, Capernaum, and Bethsaida) in the background

These baptisms were done in living water, such as rivers, well water, or springs, because people wanted the water to be pure, coming from natural sources.

There seem to be four primary reasons people would go through *mikvah* or living water in the first-century world.

First and primary, it served as ritual purification, done anytime a person had become unclean. Mary would have been ritually purified forty days after having Jesus. This was a rhythm of their life and culture.

Second, a person was being baptized into or under a doctrinal affiliation. John the Baptist came out of the wilderness preaching a message of baptism and repentance for the forgiveness of sins.[12]

Third, upon choosing your rabbi, you would be baptized into the name of that rabbi. This indicated taking on that rabbi's yoke (teaching) and coming under their authority. Similarly, followers of Jesus today are baptized in the name of the Father, Son, and Holy Spirit.

The fourth reason a person would be baptized was ordination into ministry.

I believe this is the reason for Jesus' baptism in the Gospels. It marked the genesis of His formal rabbinic ministry. Jesus was not baptized for the repentance of His sins. Nor was He baptized into a certain doctrinal affiliation or theology. Jesus was not baptized upon choosing a rabbi to follow. Rather, Jesus emerges from the waters of the Jordan River as a rabbi of Israel. Immediately after He is baptized, He goes into the desert for forty days and nights. After that, His ministry takes off. Remember, Jesus cannot get paid for teaching the Scriptures, so He keeps His day job as a *tekton* to earn income.

Now we better understand the living God's presence at Jesus' baptism. Jesus emerges as a rabbi of Israel, teaching differently than the other rabbis and Pharisees. The living God speaks and endorses Jesus: "This is my Son, whom I love; with him I am well pleased."[13] Jesus demonstrates what it looks like when God becomes a man.

The Evangelical Triangle

Jesus was born in Bethlehem. He was raised in Nazareth with His family. As a fully grown man, a rabbi of Israel, He lived in Capernaum, on the northwest shore of the Sea of Galilee.[14] Jesus was a traveling teacher. He was a man of the Galilee, known as a Galilean rabbi or a rabbi of the north.

Why does Jesus move to Capernaum on the shore of the Sea of Galilee, in a region known as Galilee of the Gentiles? Speaking of Jesus, Matthew provides the answer:

> Leaving Nazareth, he went and lived in Capernaum, which was by the lake in the area of Zebulun and Naphtali—*to fulfill what was said through the prophet Isaiah*: "Land of Zebulun and land of Naphtali, the Way of the Sea, beyond the Jordan, Galilee of the Gentiles—the people living in darkness have seen a great light; on those living in the land of the shadow of death a light has dawned."[15]

The prophet Isaiah continued: "For to us a child is born, to us a son is given, and the government will be on his shoulders. And he will be called

Wonderful Counselor, Mighty God, Everlasting Father, Prince of Peace. Of the greatness of his government and peace there will be no end."[16] This passage gets me so fired up! By now you may be hearing "O Holy Night" in your head!

What does Jesus' life look like? He lives as a rabbi of Israel in the city of Capernaum, Galilee of the Gentiles. He cannot be paid to teach the Word, so He earns income as a *tekton*. From time to time, He goes out for rabbinic ministering. Scholar, professor, and author Shmuel Safrai held that in the first-century Jewish world, a man could not be away from his family for more than thirty days without getting his wife's permission. Peter does not abandon his wife and family to follow Jesus. They have a work-rest rhythm of ministering then returning home. Jesus experiences *Shabbat*, or Sabbath, with His family. He spends a lot of time at the synagogue in Capernaum.

The vast majority of Jesus' earthly ministry took place in a relatively small area known as the "evangelical triangle" or the "triangle of ministry." This triangle is made up of three villages just north of the Sea of Galilee (refer back to the map on page 189). We've already mentioned one, Capernaum. The others are Chorazin and Bethsaida—where Peter and Andrew are from—a distance of only a few miles. Perhaps you have envisioned Jesus ministering in a much larger area. Why on the entire map of Israel is Jesus focused on this region? What is going on here?

This triangle was in direct proximity to the International Coastal Highway, which ran through Capernaum. Jesus lives and ministers here as the nations are coming through, seeing what it looks like when God becomes man and lives out the way of shalom. Remember, God's purpose from the beginning was to reach the nations and bring all people to Himself. His heart is for the entire world.

Matthew 4:17 says, "From that time on Jesus began to preach, 'Repent for the kingdom of heaven'—the way of shalom—'has come near.'" Jesus is bringing heaven to earth, the inauguration of the kingdom of God. The government will be on His shoulders, and it will not end. This is some of the most beautiful language in the entire Bible.

Is Jesus withdrawing or engaging? Jesus is not just engaging the Jews; He

Sunset on the Sea of Galilee

is engaging the nations. The light of the world is engaging the darkness. This is good news!

The Greater Reaching for the Lesser

In the first-century world, people chose their rabbi. The lesser reached for the greater. After listening to various rabbis teach, you would approach the rabbi you wanted to follow and request to be his *talmid*, or disciple. If the rabbi said yes, you would be baptized into his name and under his yoke. Jesus is highly irregular when He comes on the scene. He starts doing the choosing. The greater reaches for the lesser and says, "Come, follow Me."

In Jesus' first-century Jewish world, you don't just want to know what your rabbi knows, you want to be just like him—an embodied icon of his teachings, an ambassador of him in the world. Jesus is countercultural, choosing His disciples and saying, "I think you can be just like Me."

This helps us understand why the two sets of brothers Jesus approaches around the Galilee drop their nets to follow Him.[17] Are they abandoning their families? No, but they are coming under His authority and yoke.

We often think of Jesus as only having twelve disciples, but He actually had many more! While He does choose only twelve *apostles* or *missionaries*,[18] He surrounds Himself with far more people than that. For example, in Luke 10, Jesus sends out seventy-two; and that number very likely included women! In fact, Acts 1 records 120 disciples gathered in one place—both men *and* women. Luke 24 details two disciples walking and talking on the road to Emmaus. One is named Cleopas. They invite Jesus to come stay with them, indicating the two disciples could very well have been related, making them brother and sister or Mr. *and Mrs.* Cleopas!

Jesus the greater is calling people considered the lesser, inviting those disciples to be just like Him.

Following Your Rabbi

Let's string some biblical pearls together.

What does it look like when God becomes a human?

Matthew 4:23-25 details Jesus' ministry throughout the Galilee region as He teaches, preaches, and heals—drawing large crowds wherever He goes. Jesus offers wellness, restoration, resurrection, and renewal. He reestablishes the way of Eden, showing the world what that looks and feels like.

When we read about the disciples in the book of Acts, they are traveling around, preaching the good news of the kingdom, going to synagogues, healing people, casting out demons—they are doing the very acts they watched their rabbi do!

What does it look like for you to engage your world? How will you show up in such a way that people bear witness and see evidence of what it looks like when God becomes a man and takes up residence in your life? *This* is why we are here.

Jesus came to save you from your sin and send you into the world—engaging it as He did.

Calming the Chaos, Walking on the Abyss

As a reminder, the ancient Israelites were primarily a land or desert people. Their nemesis, the Philistines, were a water or maritime people. Oftentimes in Jewish literature, water represents chaos. It's the abyss, the unknown.

In Genesis 1 at creation, the Spirit of God hovered over the waters—over the chaos or unformed. This creation account reveals the living God bringing order to chaos. Light here, land there. Birds in the air. Fish in the sea. God orders the chaos, the formless gains form. The early chapters of the Bible answer who authorizes dominion over the chaos, who will bring shalom to the disruption.

Amazingly, Jesus as a Galilean rabbi lives close to the sea. Figuratively speaking, He lives by the chaos.

Let's get into the skin of Jesus' Jewish disciples. In Matthew 8:23-27, they take a boat out on the water, and Jesus falls asleep as a storm erupts on the chaos. The last time in their story someone exercised dominion over the chaos to bring it to calm was the living God bringing order to chaos at creation. The disciples bear witness to God made flesh. Jesus' ministry is all about Him bringing calm to chaos, shalom to that which is disruptive, and light to darkness.

We find in John 6:16-21 yet another water story. The disciples are out on a boat headed back to Capernaum. A strong wind suddenly blows in, causing the waters to grow rough. Much to their astonishment, they see Jesus walking on the water toward their boat. I don't know about you, but I would have been totally freaked out if I saw that! Imagine these Jewish disciples watching their rabbi walking on the chaos—they were terrified as they bore witness to what it looks like when God truly becomes man.

This God-made-man is saying, "Come follow Me. Come be My disciple.

I think you can be just like Me." Jesus continues to say this to us today, inviting us to move from chaos to calm.

No More Chaos

Let's close out with a beautiful passage from Isaiah 40: "A voice of one"— this is a prophetic reference to John the Baptist—"calling: 'In the wilderness prepare the way for the Lord; make straight in the desert a highway for our God. Every valley shall be raised up, every mountain and hill made low; the rough ground shall become level, the rugged places a plain. And the glory of the Lord will be revealed, and all people will see it together. For the mouth of the Lord has spoken'" (vv. 3-5).

You and I are here as the current living generations of followers of Jesus. God invites us to engage the world in such a way that we create a highway in the desert of this world for people to bear witness to Jesus as the living water the earth craves. His transformation in our own lives levels mountains, raises valleys, straightens crooked places, and smooths rugged areas.

This, then, begs the question: Can people tell you belong to Jesus? If someone interacts with you for any length of time, will they recognize you as a follower of Jesus? The ministry Jesus does for us makes us harbingers of it in our modern-day world. We are not here to retreat; we are here to engage.

In Revelation 21, the living God pulls back the curtain, giving Jewish John a vision of heaven, or the world to come, as the Jews call it. John opens the chapter saying, "Then I saw 'a new heaven and a new earth,' for the first heaven and the first earth had passed away, and there was no longer any sea." God isn't saying there will be no beaches in heaven; His vision is that there will be no more chaos!

We are being pulled and invited into a Story that had a very good beginning, Genesis 1–2. We are also being pulled and invited into a Story that has a very good ending, Revelation 21–22. Hang on. Don't give up. Don't give in. The living God is still moving in your life. We are headed to a place where there will be no more chaos.

Chapter 11

THE GOSPELS: PART 2

Through the pages of this book, I have repeatedly stated that the Bible is one Story, best read and understood from beginning to end. In this chapter, we will continue working our way through the Gospels. So far, Jesus has been baptized and received His rabbinic authority. He lives in Capernaum, working as a *tekton*. As a rabbi, He models the greater choosing the lesser, a highly unusual practice in the first-century world—and our own. The adversary tested Him in the wilderness. Jesus has begun His ministry of preaching and healing. He teaches what we know as the Sermon on the Mount, His *halakha*, or way of walking and living.

During the vast majority of His life and ministry, Jesus travels around the northern district or region of the Galilee. In the pages to come, we will string together some familiar biblical stories and accounts of Jesus' ministry. As we look at them through a Middle Eastern lens, we will better understand what the biblical authors intended to communicate. These stories center on biblical sites where I take my Israel teams. We experience in embodied form that the Bible is not only the best Story that's ever been written, it's also the truest; these things happened.

When we think about Jesus' journey to the cross, we often do so from

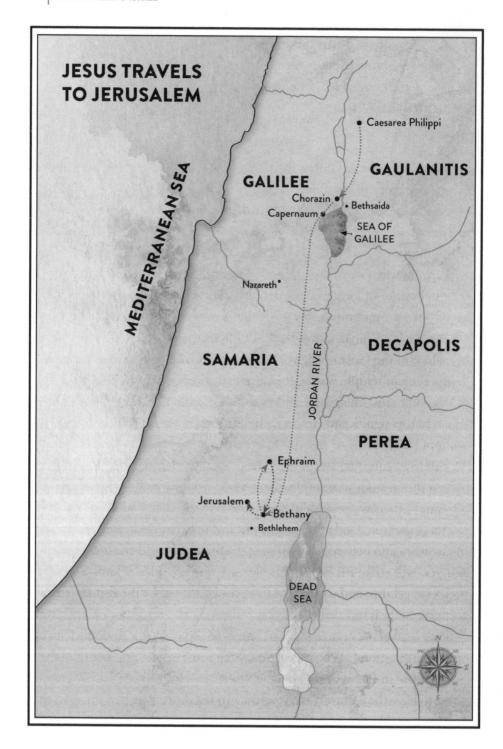

JESUS TRAVELS
TO JERUSALEM

MEDITERRANEAN SEA

GALILEE

GAULANITIS

Caesarea Philippi

Chorazin
Capernaum
Bethsaida

SEA OF
GALILEE

Nazareth

JORDAN RIVER

SAMARIA

DECAPOLIS

PEREA

Ephraim

Jerusalem
Bethany
Bethlehem

JUDEA

DEAD
SEA

the vantage point of events and actions *happening to* Jesus. But we are about to explore the same pathway through the lens of *Jesus happening to* the crucifixion. Jesus knows He is headed to Jerusalem, and He begins a methodical march that direction.

Caesarea Philippi

We now come to a famous moment that we want to understand within the greater Story of the Bible. It centers on a Vegas-like Hellenistic place called Caesarea Philippi. Rabbi Jesus brings His disciples here—a seemingly unusual choice. But as we will soon see, this is a hinge moment in the rest of the Story.

Early on when we were getting our Middle Eastern lens, we talked about the importance of location, location, location. Geography—where events occur—has great significance throughout the biblical narrative.

The ancient Roman city of Caesarea Philippi is located north of the Sea of Galilee in the Golan Heights, at the base of Mount Hermon. In antiquity, a Roman temple was built in front of an enormous hole in the side of the mountain. The people believed this hole was the entrance to Hades, which factors significantly into why Jesus brought His disciples to Caesarea Philippi.

Before we continue, let's string some biblical pearls by taking a quick look back at the creation accounts in Genesis 1–2. The Spirit of God hovers over the waters, then systematically brings order to the chaos. After Adam and Eve eat of the fruit, God tells the serpent, "I will put enmity between you and the woman, and between your offspring and hers; he will crush your head, and you will strike his heel." This passage, Genesis 3:15, is known as the protoevangelium, and some scholars consider this to be the first time the gospel message is revealed in Scripture.

Let's return to Caesarea Philippi, where Jesus brings His disciples to ask an eternal question: "'Who do people say the Son of Man is?'"[1] "Son of Man," or *ben adam* in Hebrew, is a *remez* or "hint" back to Genesis 3:15. Who is going to have the authority to crush the head of the serpent?

The disciples offer some responses: John the Baptist. Elijah. Jeremiah, or one of the other prophets. Jesus then asks who *they* think *He* is. Simon Peter answers rightly: "You are the Messiah, the Son of the living God."[2]

As we look at Jesus' reply to Peter through the cultural framework in which He speaks, the significance of this location becomes clearer. In Matthew 16:18, Jesus says, "I tell you that you are Peter, and on this rock I will build my church"—this is the first time Jesus mentions the church—"and the gates of Hades will not overcome it." Contrary to popular interpretation, when Jesus says, "On this rock I will build my church," He is *not* referring to Peter, even though Peter's name, *Petros* in Greek, means "rock." Rather, Jesus likely refers to *the rock He is standing on.* Remember, rabbinic teaching is visual. A rabbi will not typically use an illustration unless it can be readily seen by his disciples. The rock Jesus stands on represents the powerful dominion of darkness. It is positioned across from a Roman temple covering the hole believed by the ancients to be the gates of Hades—all at a site where the Greek idol Pan is being worshipped.[3] Here, Jesus addresses the spiritual forces of evil and idolatry while declaring Himself to be the head of the church. As He stands on the rock, He may even be pointing to the supposed gates of Hades.

If the "rock" being referred to is not Peter, then why does Jesus specifically address Peter? In verse 19, Jesus says, "I will give you the keys of the kingdom of heaven; whatever you bind on earth will be bound in heaven, and whatever you loose on earth will be loosed in heaven." With these words, Jesus gives Peter rabbinic authority. In antiquity, rabbis had the authority to bind and loose. When a disciple brought a question or concern to their rabbi, the rabbi rendered a binding or loosing that the disciple was then obligated to carry out. From Caesarea Philippi forward, Peter walks in this rabbinic authority.

It is important to note that when people build gates, they do so to keep others out. At Caesarea Philippi, Jesus is saying, "You will storm the gates of Hades; they will not be able to keep you out." Jesus exhorts His disciples to engage, not retreat. This location is the last place the disciples expect Jesus to build His church. He is expanding their vision.

I was raised with the understanding that holiness is about abstaining from a list of sins to avoid the gates of Hades at all costs. Jesus embodies a different way: Holiness is engaging in actions that bring the kingdom of God in our midst. *Holiness is not just the absence of something, it is also the presence of something.*

After addressing Peter, Jesus orders His disciples not to tell anyone that He is the Messiah. His time has not yet come. At Caesarea Philippi, Jesus begins revealing to His disciples what is about to happen to Him—"that he must go to Jerusalem and suffer many things at the hands of the elders, the chief priests and the teachers of the law"—the Pharisees and Sadducees— "and that he must be killed and on the third day be raised to life."[4] As Jesus deliberately heads toward Jerusalem, He performs miracles that are precursors of what is on the horizon through His crucifixion and resurrection— hints that He is the one who will crush the enemy's head.

Remember, Jesus is known as a rabbi of the north. The majority of His ministry takes place in the cities of Capernaum, Chorazin, and Bethsaida. This northern rabbi now heads "up to" Jerusalem, with some strategic stops along the way. John 1:5 says, "The light shines in the darkness, and the darkness has not overcome it." Jesus is a man on a mission.

When we view the conversation Jesus has with Peter and the other disciples at Caesarea Philippi through the lens of analysis and as an individual story, we miss that it is intricately connected to the cross and what Jesus was preparing to do in Jerusalem. This is the beauty of synthesis, of reading the Bible from 35,000 feet as a comprehensive narrative.

Bethany

As Jesus journeys southward to Jerusalem, He comes to the town of Bethany. Bethany lies approximately two miles—or a thirty-minute walk—from Jerusalem. This is not Jesus' first time in Bethany. When He made the annual

Lazarus Tomb sign in Bethany

pilgrimage to Jerusalem, He would likely have stayed here. This time, Jesus comes with a different purpose than before.

John 11 details the story of Jesus and His friends Mary, Martha, and Lazarus—siblings who live in Bethany. Jesus receives a message from the sisters that Lazarus is sick. Upon hearing the news, Jesus says in verse 4, "This sickness will not end in death. No, it is for God's glory so that God's Son may be glorified through it." Scripture states that Jesus loves Mary, Martha, and Lazarus, yet He doesn't immediately set out to heal Lazarus. Rather, Jesus stays in His current location two more days—and Lazarus dies.

Later, upon arriving in Bethany, Jesus comes to the tomb of Lazarus and asks that the stone be removed. Martha questions the wisdom in this, reiterating that Lazarus has been there for four days. Jesus prays to His Father, then in a loud voice, commands, "Lazarus, come out!" The dead man walks out of the grave, still wrapped in linen and cloth. Jesus instructs those around him to remove his grave clothes.

Something about Jesus raising Lazarus from the dead in Bethany causes the religious leaders to react so strongly that they start plotting to take His

Lazarus Tomb in Bethany

life. Why is raising Lazarus such a big deal? Location, location, location. *Where* things happen in Scripture matters as much as what happens. Many of Jesus' miracles occur in the region of the Galilee. When He comes close to Jerusalem, He brings the messianic reality to the doorsteps of the Phari-sees and Sadducees. As long as Jesus is up north in the Galilee, the religious leaders don't have to deal with Him, for He does not threaten their dealings in the house of God. Now that Jesus is in Bethany, a couple miles from Jerusalem and the Temple, a reckoning is about to take place.

Historically, the common people seem to embrace Jesus as Messiah. It's the religious leaders who refuse to proclaim Him as Messiah; they'll lose their jobs if they do.[5]

Ephraim

In response to this miracle, many of the Jews put their faith in Jesus, while others go tell the Pharisees about what happened. The religious leaders—including the chief priests, Pharisees, and Sadducees—meet and discuss how to handle the threat Jesus presents to them. Their stated concern is that more and more people will follow Jesus, resulting in the Romans coming and taking their Temple and nation. Ultimately, this meeting is about how to preserve the power of the religious elite, who are nervous and scrambling.

Caiaphas, the high priest, speaks up during the meeting and unknowingly prophesies Jesus' death. He says, "It is better for you that one man die for the people than that the whole nation perish."[6] From this point on, the religious leaders begin scheming how to kill Jesus. Because of this, Jesus no longer makes public appearances in the region of Judea. He, along with His disciples, retreats to a village called Ephraim, near the wilderness, around nine-and-a-half miles from Jerusalem.

In the first century, Ephraim was known as a place where bandits and outlaws would hide out. I love it that Jesus spends His days prior to the crucifixion hanging out with criminals and convicts, people on the run! Jesus understands that holiness is not the absence of something; rather, holiness is the presence of something. Jesus was not afraid to be around sinners. *His cleanness could make unclean clean.*

I often wonder: If Jesus came back today, would we miss seeing Him because we don't go to the places He goes?

When I take teams to Israel, we go to Ephraim, known today as Taybeh (pronounced Tie-Bay). This is one of the few predominately Christian villages in the West Bank and is unique in that it doesn't have any mosques or synagogues. We go to Taybeh to study in a fully intact first-century style home such as the kind in which Jesus would have been born. A fascinating feature of some of the homes in this village is that they often had a concealed hole in the wall connecting the homes. This provided an avenue of escape for those running from the authorities.

Back to Bethany

Jesus cannot stay hidden for long. Six days before Passover, He returns to Bethany and attends a dinner hosted in His honor by Mary and Martha. The Bible casually mentions that Lazarus was sitting there![7] How would you feel if someone you knew died, and a few weeks later, you walked in their house and saw them sitting at a table eating?

A sizable group of Jews realize Jesus is back in town and come to see Him, as well as Lazarus. News travels fast when a man who died and lay in a tomb for four days shows up alive again! A living Lazarus is very bad news if you don't want to acknowledge Jesus as Messiah. People see and converse with him. I like to envision Jesus grinning at people's reactions to Lazarus!

Lazarus is now on the radar of the religious leaders, and they scheme to kill him as well. His embodiment of the resurrection power of the living God is causing Jews to believe in Jesus, so he too poses a threat to the power of the religious leaders. They are angry, scared, and conspiring. It's laughable that the religious leaders' best plan was to kill a man Jesus had just raised from the dead! Did they not consider that if they succeeded in killing Lazarus, Jesus could raise him from the dead a second time? In that moment, holiness is the presence of resurrection power at a dinner in Bethany, in close proximity to Jerusalem.

As we continue the story, we see the prominence of women as well as the poor choices of some men. At this particular dinner, Mary anoints Jesus, while Judas is described as a thief. One gets it right; the other gets it

Gethsemane

wrong. Both are sitting at the table with Jesus, but they relate to Him quite differently.

Jerusalem

John 12:12-19 describes Jesus' triumphal entry from Bethany into Jerusalem. The throng of people present to celebrate Passover take palm branches and go out to meet Jesus, shouting "Hosanna!" as He rides in from the east on a donkey. How does this crowd in Jerusalem know who this Galilean rabbi is? These people witnessed Jesus summoning Lazarus from the tomb! This is the power of the witness of one life, one dead man walking. The crowd continues to talk about the miracle, causing an uproar in the city.

In your story, is holiness the *absence* of or the *presence* of something?

Gethsemane

As Jesus makes His way to the cross, He arrives at Gethsemane with His disciples. *Gat* refers to a grape or wine press, and *shemen* means "oil."

Gethsemane combines two farming products (grapes and olives) into one word, likely hinting at the large-scale production of both wine and oil on the Mount of Olives. It is a place of pressing.

Throughout the feast of Passover, thousands of people gather in this grove on the Mount of Olives. Jesus leaves His disciples and begins passionately praying to His Father, three times asking that "this cup"—death by crucifixion—pass from Him. His emotions are so strong He begins to sweat drops of blood, a condition known as *hematohidrosis*. Jesus is pressed in the place of pressing.[8]

Each time Jesus returns to His disciples, He finds them sleeping rather than praying for Him. The third time, Jesus identifies Himself as the Son of Man,[9] *ben adam*. As Jesus announces His betrayal to the disciples, Judas approaches with a large group of armed men sent by the religious leaders determined to keep their power. Though this scenario looks like the betrayal is happening to Jesus, in reality, Jesus is happening to Jerusalem. Jesus does not fall to the cross, He sets His face to it…beginning at His march to Jerusalem from Caesarea Philippi.

As the men arrest Jesus, Peter cuts off the ear of Malchus, the high priest's servant. We often imagine Peter pulling out a huge sword in defense of Jesus. But is that what really happens? Jews have come to Jerusalem from all over, making the Romans edgy. They live in Jerusalem to keep the peace. It is unlikely that the Romans allow Jewish men to walk around carrying large swords if they can prevent it. Remember, Peter is a fisherman by profession, so he more likely has a small dagger.

Malchus is a servant or representative of Caiaphas, the high priest. According to Levitical law, a priest was not allowed to have any kind of visible, physical deformity.[10] This would render them unable to serve as priest, a regulation that applied to all priests, and most likely the high priest's servant. This context helps us better understand Peter's actions as he pulls out his knife and grabs Malchus' ear, cutting it. Though at face value we may read this as a violent act, it is not intended as such. By disfiguring Caiaphas's servant, Peter communicates that neither this man nor his master, the high priest, belong in the Temple; Caiaphas is an illegitimate priest.

The Jewish historian Josephus provides an example of this happening. He writes: "But being afraid that Hyrcanus, who was under the guard of the Parthians, might have his Kingdom restored to him by the multitude, he cut off his ears; and thereby took care that the High Priesthood should never come to him any more: because he was maimed: while the law required that his dignity should belong to none but such as had all their members intire [sic]."[11]

Elsewhere, Josephus says, "Antigonus himself also bit off Hyrcanus's ears with his own teeth, as he fell down upon his knees to him, that so he might never be able upon any mutation of affairs to take the high priesthood again, for the high priests that officiated were to be complete, and without blemish."[12]

In that day and time, you could lose your ears if someone felt you were not fit to serve in the high priesthood!

We see the heart of God through Jesus' response. In the midst of being betrayed, seized, and arrested, the Son of Man touches the ear of the high priest's servant and heals him.[13] It's a good thing that wasn't me—I would have put his ear on backward, or on top of his head! In Gethsemane, holiness is the presence of good returned for evil.

Golgotha: The Crucifixion

Jesus is brought to the home of Caiaphas, the high priest, where the religious leaders are gathered. They bring false witnesses to testify against Jesus, and He is condemned to die. He is also taken before Pilate, the Roman governor, where the religious leaders again accuse Him. Pilate acquiesces to the demands of the people to release Barabbas and crucify Jesus.

The Romans did not crucify people up on hills. They preferred to crucify their victims along a main road, naked and exposed for all to see at eye level. Guards created a gap between the loved one and the crucified. Imagine someone you love hanging from a cross ten feet away from you, but you are unable to reach out to or comfort them.

As mentioned earlier, in Jewish tradition, 9:00 a.m. and 3:00 p.m. marked the times of the *tamid*—or daily—perpetual sacrifices. According to Mark 15, Jesus is placed on the cross at 9:00 a.m. He hangs between life and death for six hours, including three hours of darkness beginning at noon. At 3:00 p.m., Jesus cries out and gives up His spirit. The perfect Son of God, the Lamb of God, fulfills the sacrificial requirement for all time.

In the West, we often consider Jesus' words "My God, my God, why have you forsaken me?" to be a prayer of deliverance. But is this really what He is doing?

Jesus has been serving as a rabbi. In His first-century world, how does a rabbi orient his followers to a certain place in the Text? He has no way to cite the Text as we do today with chapters and verses. As a people of the Text, when a rabbi starts reciting the Text, the people know exactly where he is, and ideally can pick up where he leaves off.

I want to offer the perspective that Jesus' statement is not a prayer to God for deliverance from the cross; rather, Jesus is talking to the people who are witnessing this horrific crucifixion. Even as He is distraught on the cross, He continues shepherding His followers, comforting them, reminding them that the Scriptures foretold all that is taking place.

Jesus orients the people to the words of Psalm 22:

> My God, my God, why have you forsaken me?
>> Why are you so far from saving me,
>> so far from my cries of anguish?...
> But I am a worm and not a man,
>> scorned by everyone, despised by the people.
> All who see me mock me;
>> they hurl insults, shaking their heads...
> Many bulls surround me;
>> strong bulls of Bashan encircle me.
> Roaring lions that tear their prey
>> open their mouths wide against me.
> I am poured out like water,
>> and all my bones are out of joint.

My heart has turned to wax;
it has melted within me.
My mouth is dried up like a potsherd,
and my tongue sticks to the roof of my mouth;
you lay me in the dust of death…
For he has not despised or scorned
the suffering of the afflicted one;
he has not hidden his face from him
but has listened to his cry for help.[14]

I do not believe the living God forsook Jesus on the cross. The apostle Paul said God was, in Jesus, reconciling the world back to Himself.[15] If the living God cannot bear witness to the suffering of Jesus, you and I don't have a prayer. If He can't look at our sin, how does He forgive us of it? The living God does not turn His face on His Son. On the cross, Jesus is being a rabbi and Messiah shepherd.

At the very moment Jesus gives up His spirit, the curtain of the Temple is torn in two from top to bottom. In Jewish and Middle Eastern tradition, a grieving father would rip his robe from top to bottom. The Temple curtain ripping in this way signifies the Father grieving, tearing His robe from top to bottom as His Son dies.

The earth shakes. Rocks split. Tombs break open and once-dead saints walk out of their graves and into the city.[16] The Lazarus story has multiplied many times over. The resurrection power of the living God is on display, walking around Jerusalem.

Through it all, many women are watching from a distance. They bravely stomach the crucifixion. They do not run away or avert their gaze.

The Tomb: Resurrection

According to John 20, Mary Magdalene goes to Jesus' tomb only to discover the stone had been rolled away. She hurries back to Peter and John to tell them Jesus' body is missing.

Peter and John run to the tomb, seeing the empty linen and graveclothes. Interestingly, Jesus doesn't choose to reveal His resurrected self to these men—some of His most intimate disciples. This is significant. In a culture where women could not even testify in court, and important messages were typically entrusted to men, Jesus once again chooses those perceived as lesser to carry the most important message ever given. We learn much about the heart of Jesus in whom He chooses to reveal Himself.

Instead of giving this moment to Peter and John, Jesus gives it to Mary Magdalene. To many, she is known as the apostle to the apostles. Jesus does something else here that is gospel gorgeous! He interacts with Mary *in the garden*. She doesn't recognize Jesus; she thinks He is the gardener. John incorporates a *remez* or "hinting" back to the garden of Eden. Magdalene is the new Eve. Eve bit the fruit, and her eyes were opened to shame. Magdalene's eyes are opened to the resurrected Jesus. The living God speaks yet again with a woman in a garden.

Tabgha

What does Jesus do after raising Lazarus from the dead, marching into Jerusalem, suffering crucifixion, and rising from the dead?

Remember, holiness is presence, not just absence. Jesus meets His disciples in the normal and ordinary circumstances of life.

John 21 details a beautiful redemption. The disciples are probably near Tabgha, an area on the western shore of the Sea of Galilee. Simon Peter goes out to fish, and the others join him. They catch nothing all night, an unusual predicament for professional fishermen. Jesus shows up on the shore and instructs them to throw their net on the right side, a beautiful allusion to the region of the Decapolis. Jesus makes sure that all—even the Gentiles— are reached; in essence, He says, "I'm making you fishers of men in *that* world also."

From where the disciples are on the water, they can't tell it is Jesus, but they do as He suggests. So many fish fill their net that they can hardly haul it in! When John recognizes that it is Jesus, Peter jumps into the water and heads to the shore. The other disciples follow, bringing in the boat loaded down with fish. Upon their arrival, Jesus has prepared a breakfast of fish and bread for them.

This is no ordinary meal. Jesus sets a table of reconciliation. In Jewish culture, who you eat with signifies welcoming and embracing them. These are the same men who ran from Jesus in the hours when He needed them most. Jesus is offering restoration.

Three times Jesus addresses Peter, asking him, "Do you love me?" Remember, it was just days prior that Peter had three times denied knowing His Lord. Now, Jesus instructs Peter three times to feed and take care of His sheep. Through table fellowship on the shores of the Sea of Galilee, Jesus reinstates Peter to a place of leadership, reinforcing confidence in him. Fast-forward to the day of Pentecost, after tongues of fire fall on the God-fearing Jews in Jerusalem and they speak in other languages, Peter addresses the crowd, and 3,000 are added to the community of believers. Peter gives us hope that Jesus knows how to redeem and restore us when we fail.

Holiness Coming

As we conclude our journey through the Gospels, let's do so with the words of John 21:25: "Jesus did many other things as well. If every one of them were written down, I suppose that even the whole world would not have room for the books that would be written." The Gospels provide us with snapshots, but Jesus did so much more than what was recorded! The Gospels are not accounts of things that Jesus did *not* do…all that He abstained from. Rather, the Gospels account for what Jesus *did* do: holiness coming to the ground, the kingdom of heaven invading earth, light coming into darkness.

Chapter 12

TIKKUN OLAM

An ancient African proverb says, "If you want to go fast, go alone. If you want to go far, go together." As the people of God, we take a long view. The New Testament church has existed for more than 2,000 years and counting. We depend on the faithfulness of the living God to walk with us to the new heaven and earth, until we reach the shores of the new Jerusalem.

Setting Upon the Heart

When the living God opened the door for me to go study the Bible in Egypt and Israel back in 2007, I learned a Hebrew phrase that stays with me to this day. I often think about it when I open my Bible. It is the phrase *sim lev*. *Lev* is Hebrew for "heart," and *sim* is Hebrew for "set" or "set upon." *Sim lev* means "to set upon the heart." In the rabbinic Jewish tradition of Jesus, this is the purpose of reading the Scriptures over and over again. We want to set the Word of God upon our hearts.

There was a Middle Eastern student who asked his rabbi, "Why do you say that we want to set the Word upon our hearts? Why don't we want to hide the Word in our hearts?" His question reminds us of the words of the psalmist, who said, "I have hidden your word in my heart that I might not sin against you."[1] The rabbi responded, "My son, the human heart tends to be hard. We set the Word upon our hearts so that, as life breaks our hearts, the words can fall right in."[2]

What breaks your heart at this moment, in this season of life? What part of the Word of God do you need to fall into your heart? We want to be people of God who *sim lev*—who set the Scriptures upon our hearts. *We want to be people informed by the Word of God, empowered by the Spirit of God, to walk the way of God in the earth.*

Matthew's Jewish Context

The first narrative of the gospel in the New Testament is the Gospel of Matthew, though it was not the first Gospel written. Most scholars believe the Gospel of Mark was penned first, and both Matthew and Luke appear to borrow a significant amount of content from the Gospel of Mark. Some decades after Matthew, Mark, and Luke were already in circulation, John writes the fourth and final Gospel in our Bibles. Matthew, Mark, and Luke, the first three, are known as the Synoptic Gospels because they tend to see the story very similarly,[3] and of those three, the Gospel of Matthew is the most Jewish.

For instance, notice how Matthew 1 begins with the genealogy of Jesus, tracing His lineage back to father Abraham, showing that He qualifies to be the Messiah, the Son of God, the Savior of the world. Jewish Matthew, one of the original twelve disciples, walks with Jewish Jesus in their Jewish world 2,000 years ago. With that overview, let's look at our key passage.

Believing Versus Following

According to Matthew 10:1-4,

> Jesus called his twelve disciples to him and gave them authority to drive out impure spirits and to heal every disease and sickness. These are the names of the twelve apostles: first, Simon (who is called Peter) and his brother, Andrew; James son of Zebedee, and his brother John; Philip and Bartholomew; Thomas and Matthew the tax collector; James son of Alphaeus, and Thaddaeus; Simon the Zealot and Judas Iscariot, who betrayed him.

Sea of Galilee with mustard seed/plant in the foreground

That may seem like only a list of names, but we are about to discover who and what some of these names represent.

There is a world of difference between being a *believer in* Jesus and a *follower of* Jesus. Being a believer in Jesus is actually a passive posture. You can sit on your couch and believe. In contrast, being a follower of Jesus is an active posture. It stirs up different feelings and promptings inside you. It sets you in motion; it sets you on fire—holy fire. Being a follower of Jesus invites you to walk with Jesus, as opposed to merely knowing about Jesus.

When you think about the word *discipleship*, what comes to your mind? What image do you see? If we could go back 2,000 years to the Jewish world of Jesus with His disciples, discipleship would look like walking with friends around your rabbi. In Jesus' world, it is very much a relationship on the move. You want to walk so closely to your rabbi that the dust of his sandals gets all over you; you don't want to miss any of his words.

In the first century, rabbis liked to move. They did not teach behind a lectern with a dry-erase board or a screen. No, Rabbi Jesus walks through a field of mustard plants or seeds with His disciples. All of a sudden, He pauses and says, "The kingdom of heaven is like a mustard seed, which a man took and planted in his field."[4] If you want to walk with Jesus, you have to be ready to *walk*. Jesus is on the move. And He is doing things here on earth to this very day.

Jewish discipleship happens not only in one relationship with the rabbi, but also in multiple relationships within the community. We often think of discipleship as one-on-one mentorship, which is much more the Greek world of Socrates, Plato, and Aristotle. Jesus and His followers engaged in ongoing discussion, including rich disagreement.

What is your honest assessment of your relationship with Jesus right now? Have you been living more like a *believer in* Jesus or a *follower of* Jesus?

Tikkun Olam

The interesting thing about the rabbi-*talmid* ("disciple") relationship in Jesus' Jewish world 2,000 years ago is that you don't just want to know what your rabbi knows, you want to be just like him. You want to embody him. When someone tastes your life, they should taste your rabbi. When people listen to you, they should hear the teachings of your rabbi. Spending time with a disciple is one way to know that disciple's rabbi. This achieves a much stronger relationship than just believing or knowing the way of your rabbi. Faith is expressed in who we are and how we live. When we practice the way of Jesus—when we walk with Jesus—we partner with Jesus.

If we truly embody and partner with Jesus in our lives, what exactly are we participating in? What does Jesus want to achieve in this world? The Jewish people call it the *tikkun olam*, which means "the repair of the world." Jesus invites us to partner with Him in repairing this world He created. In what Christians often refer to as the Lord's Prayer, Jesus prays, "Your kingdom come...on earth as it is in heaven."[5] Jewish people rarely talk about heaven. Rather, they talk about bringing heaven to earth. We don't have to wait to experience eternal life...the good (*tov*) life. We can experience the fullness of walking with Jesus now in this life. This is promised to us as a people who practice the way of Jesus, who follow and walk with Him rather than simply believing in Him. Remember what Jesus said in John 17:3: "Now this is eternal life: that they know you, the only true God, and Jesus Christ, whom you have sent." That does not begin later in heaven; it begins now on earth.

When I think about partnering with Jesus and the *tikkun olam*, I am reminded of a story I heard about ten years ago while in Israel with a team. Part of what I have so enjoyed in taking teams to Israel—aside from studying the Bible in the land where it happened—are mealtimes when group members share their stories. One night in Israel as we were having dinner, a grandmother on our team started telling us this story. She and four of her friends, all grandmothers, all seasoned women, had been getting together on Friday nights for a few years to study the Bible. Don't you love that you live in a world where grandmothers meet on Friday nights to study the Bible? There is something beautiful about that!

During their Friday evenings together, they realized that as retirees, their time was more or less their own. As they continued studying the Bible, it seemed to invite them out into the world to act on what they were learning. These five grandmothers began praying about what to do. They decided to take two of the four Friday nights each month to put care packages together. Then they visited local strip clubs, met with the girls working there, and gave them the care packages. They prayed with and loved on those girls. They chose to *be* the love of Jesus—to *embody* Him.

Understand, we now live in a world where grandmothers storm strip clubs! I love this so much! This is what *tikkun olam* looks like; it is partnering with Jesus in the repair of the world. The grandmother on our Israel team talked about getting to know the club bouncers over the years. I can imagine them saying, "Hey Frank! Hey Fred! Your mama raised you better than this! God has a better plan for your life!" After a few years, as these grandmothers ministered to the girls, two left the profession, started coming to church with the grandmothers, and began a relationship with Jesus. Neither of them had a college education, though they both wanted to go to college. What is so beautiful to me is that it was the grandmothers who assisted these women in getting enrolled in college and helped fund their tuition. That's accepting the invitation to partner with Jesus in the repair of the world—and it will cost you.

The Lesser Reaching for the Greater

If you lived in Jesus' first-century world, you chose your rabbi. The lesser reached for the greater. You would listen to different rabbis communicate their yoke—or body of teachings. Eventually, you would choose the rabbi whose teachings demonstrated that he had a handle on who the living God is, what He is like, and what it means to walk with Him. You would approach that rabbi and ask him for permission to become a follower, a disciple. It was a big deal for a rabbi to accept you as one of his *talmidim* or disciples.

Jesus comes onto the scene and does the exact opposite. Rather than waiting for the lesser to reach for Him, a holy rabbi of Israel, Jesus walks around choosing His disciples. The greater reaches for the lesser. Doesn't this make you love Jesus even more? He's a chooser! In our world, this would be like you shooting free throws in your driveway and Michael Jordan, in his prime, driving down your street, seeing you, pulling over and saying, "You've got a really nice shot. I think you can be just as good as me at basketball. Would you like to come shoot baskets with me?" Or it would be like Tiger Woods, in his prime, admiring your golf stroke and declaring he can help you reach his level of prowess. Or the late Aretha Franklin pulling up next to you at a stoplight as you are singing at the top of your lungs with your windows down. She looks over at you and says, "You have an incredible voice! Do you want to go on tour with me?" To be clear, none of us will ever sing like Aretha Franklin; she'll always be the queen!

These analogies help provide a sense of what it meant, in the first-century world, for a holy rabbi of Israel to find you and say, "You right there, come follow me. I think you can be like me." Imagine the new life breathed into the followers of Jesus! This is who He is and what He is like. Now we better understand Jesus' words in John 15:16, when He said to His disciples, "You did not choose me, but I chose you and appointed you so that you might go and bear fruit—fruit that will last." He did not say, "I chose you to *believe* in me." He said, "I chose you to *go* and bear lasting fruit." Jesus invited His disciples to partner with Him in the repair of the world. To follow Him. To walk with Him. To be like Him. Practicing the way of Jesus means partnering with Him.

Jesus rebels against cultural norms when He chooses His disciples. Consider the twelve. With the *tikkun olam*—the repair of the world—on the line, surely Jesus picks the strongest, the smartest, the fastest. Surely He picks people who have already managed to get their lives together so they can be more effective at partnering with Him.

I would contend that this mindset is actually the way of empire ideology and not the way of the kingdom—meaning an empire likes to swallow up all that is strong and mighty. God's kingdom functions differently. If you want to know who Jesus is and what He is like, look at who He chose to partner with in repairing the world. If He was willing to choose them then, He is willing to choose you and me today. The repair of the world has been under way for 2,000 years, and it carries on. It is our turn, as the current living generations, to practice the way of Jesus.

Sons of Thunder

Mark 3 repeats the list of names given in Matthew 10. In Mark, we learn that "James son of Zebedee and his brother John" are the "sons of thunder."[6] That's quite a nickname! In Jesus' world 2,000 years ago, what gets you called a "son of thunder"?

Jesus and His disciples, including James and John, live up north in the region of the Galilee. They want to travel south to Jerusalem, but there is a problem. They have to go through a region called Samaria. At the time of this story, the Jews and the Samaritans have had an approximately 700-year feud. Can you imagine being mad at someone for 700 years? Talk about an intense multigenerational disagreement. History tells us that during the trip from Galilee to Jerusalem, from northern to southern Israel, fights would break out between the Jews and the Samaritans. During one of these trips, James and John earn their nickname "sons of thunder."

According to Luke 9, Jesus knows His time is limited and decisively sets out for Jerusalem. He sends messengers to a Samaritan village to prepare for His arrival. Because His destination is Jerusalem, the people in the village do not welcome Jesus—they do not extend hospitality. Let's pause here. In the Middle Eastern world—then and now—hospitality is one of the highest virtues of honor. If you refuse hospitality to a stranger, it is not merely like a slap in the face; it is more like a throat punch—a severe insult. James and John—two of the original twelve called by Jesus—have some violent thoughts about the Samaritans disrespecting them. They ask Jesus, "Lord, do you want us to call fire down from heaven to destroy them?"[7]

This story amazes me! By asking Jesus that question, they appear to think they really can call down fire from heaven. Have they actually tried this before? Their response to the slight by the Samaritans seems…extreme! Have you ever *not* been invited to a birthday party? Was your response to gather your friends and go burn the party host's house to the ground? Likely not!

These are two of the twelve Jesus chose. In response, Jesus rebukes James and John. I wonder what He said. "Guys, we're not here to burn villages to the ground. That's not part of the *tikkun olam*. That's not repairing the world. We love the Samaritans."

If you want to know who Jesus is and what He is like, He calls sons of thunder to follow Him. Sons of thunder find seats at His table because Jesus knows it is less their work and more His work.

A Tax Collector and Zealot

Let's continue in Matthew 10: "Philip and Bartholomew; Thomas and Matthew the tax collector; James son of Alphaeus, and Thaddaeus; Simon the Zealot and Judas Iscariot, who betrayed him." I want to highlight that a tax collector and a Zealot were two of the twelve because in Jesus' world 2,000 years ago, tax collectors and Zealots did not get along. They were on opposite ends of the spectrum. Tax collectors collaborated with the Roman Empire. Rome would overtake a region and appoint indigenous people in that area to serve as their middlemen, to collect taxes, and give the money to Rome. Oftentimes, these tax collectors became dishonest. For example, if Rome required 10 percent, they would charge 12 percent, sending 10 percent to Rome while pocketing the other 2 percent. This is why the people despised them.

The Zealots envisioned a world on the opposite end of the spectrum. They could not stand the Roman Empire. They believed that the kingdom of God was going to come with a sword. The Zealots wanted to fight the Romans and overthrow their power in order to reestablish Jewish independence.

There was a certain sect of Zealots known as the Sicarii. The Sicarii were assassins who carried a hooked knife and concealed it as they walked around the marketplace or forum. When they found a collaborator with Rome or one whom they felt was not helping them overthrow Rome, they pulled out the knife and stabbed the person in their sternum, then turned up the knife to puncture the heart. Then they would pull out the knife and conceal it again as they stealthily made their escape through the crowd.

What did it look like to have a tax collector and a Zealot together on a day-in, day-out basis? Did Matthew and Simon get along? Can you envision Matthew sleeping with one eye open every night, making sure to always know where Simon was? I wonder if Simon punched Matthew in the back of his head while they walked down the street…and how many times Jesus had to separate them! "Simon, you go to that corner. Matthew, you go to that corner." Normally these two do not agree with each other, yet they attempt to remain in agreement under their rabbi.

If you want to know who Jesus is and what He is like, He calls sons of thunder, tax collectors, and Zealots to follow Him because He knows that in close proximity to Him comes real-life change and transformation. He chooses them just as they are; and He chooses us in like manner.

Naming Shame

Matthew 11:19 is another passage that very much interests me in connection with how Jesus impacts others. Matthew writes, "The Son of Man"— meaning Jesus—"came eating and drinking, and they say, 'Here is a glutton and a drunkard, a friend of tax collectors and sinners.'" Matthew intrigues me in both chapters 10 and 11 of the Gospel that bears his name because he mentions being a tax collector. Notice that Matthew names his *shame*, not his strength. He doesn't say, "Matthew, the son of Alphaeus," or "Matthew, the good sibling to his brothers and sisters," or "Matthew, the good neighbor." No, Matthew learned something about what it means to walk with Jesus. In Matthew 10:3, when he lists the apostles and writes about himself, he scribes, "Matthew the tax collector."

When you meet someone for the first time, do you name the worst thing about yourself? Who does that? Matthew shows vulnerability. He doesn't name his strengths; he names his shame.

As we mature from being *believers in* Jesus to *followers of* Jesus, as we move from being passive to more active—actually walking around with Jesus, partnering with Him in the repair of the world—we start to notice the differences in our orthodoxy and orthopraxy. Orthodoxy is right thinking or doctrine; orthopraxy is right living. In other words, we begin to recognize the things we say we believe but are failing to live out.

As we read the Gospel stories, we experience a deeper invitation into our own stories. This is what Matthew 10 is showing us with the sons of thunder, tax collectors, and Zealots. We could also dig into Judas Iscariot, another questionable character Jesus included in His original twelve.

What if the seed of the kingdom lies in your wound, not in your strength?

When Matthew was called by Jesus, he was sitting at the tax collector's booth.[8] Matthew was engaging in the very profession that brought him a sense of cultural exclusion and shame. Yet Jesus invited him to follow. Jesus chose this tax collector and others.

If you want to know who Jesus is and what He is like, He comes for you in your place of shame. He meets you in that space because in close proximity to Him comes transformation. We need to bite down on this: Jesus is not afraid of you. Jesus is not afraid of the absolute most shameful part of your story—that chapter you don't read out loud. Jesus already knows it. What if it's true that He comes to meet you in that shameful place? Matthew was in the midst of collecting taxes when Jesus approached him and said, "Hey, you right there, I think you can be like Me. Come follow Me." Matthew got up and followed his new rabbi.

The Cave You Fear to Enter

From October 2019 to March 2022, with all the COVID disruptions and cancellations, two-and-a-half years went by before I returned to Israel. While my address is in Tennessee, Israel and Jerusalem feel more like home to me. During those two-and-a-half years of not being in the land, I felt like I was living in a type of exile. In that time, I came across this quote by Joseph Campbell: "The cave you fear to enter holds the treasure you seek."

During this era, I returned to therapy—my fourth season of it—and I am doing a deeper work than I have ever done in my own story. For years, I have walked my puppy son, Chester, multiple times a day through my neighborhood. Occasionally, we encounter a lady who stops to chat and often says, "Kristi, I'm praying for you. Keep going. I'm praying for you."

One morning as I was walking Chester, she was walking toward us and paused to ask, "Oh, Kristi, how are you doing? How can I pray for you?" I was feeling open and safe that morning, so I decided to go there a little bit. I said, "Well, you can pray for me because I am back in therapy. I feel like God wants to repair some things in me."

I had come to the realization that I keep trying to repair the world without letting Jesus repair me, and God showed me that I cannot go any further until we do some deeper work. As scary as that has been, I'm going for it! So, I told the neighbor lady, "I'm back in therapy. It's my fourth round." She looked right at me and said, "Oh honey, what's so wrong with you that it's taking four times?"

Do you know the shame I felt in that moment? I have a hundred versions of that same question in my own narrative of self-judgment. I've often wondered, *What is so wrong with me that it has taken multiple seasons of therapy—and will likely take more?* With God's grace, I am walking into the cave that I fear to enter and discovering that it does indeed hold the treasure I seek. I am learning that I don't go into it alone. The living God goes with me. He is repairing my soul and my life. He is equipping me to partner with Him in repairing the world.

None of us can give what we do not have. What cave do you fear to enter? The living God meets us right where we are, but He never leaves us there. Where are you today? God invites you to courage up and lean in. You are going to feel the invitation to go deeper in your own story, to receive the repair of the Lord, that you might partner with Him in the *tikkun olam*, the repair of the world.

When You Were Called

As we head into Acts through Revelation, let's look at these words from the apostle Paul:

> Brothers and sisters, think of what you were when you were called. Not many of you were wise by human standards; not many were influential; not many were of noble birth. But God chose the foolish things of the world to shame the wise; God chose the weak things of the world to shame the strong. God chose the lowly things of this world and the despised things—and the things that are not—to nullify the things that are, so that no one may boast before him. It is because of him that you are in Christ Jesus, who has become for us wisdom from God—that is, our righteousness, holiness and redemption.[9]

These words comfort me. I may be a mess, but I am His mess, and my life is in His hands. The living God will do me no harm.

We mature from being believers to followers. We don't want to merely know about Jesus, we want to walk with Him. We want to receive His repair and be part of the agency of it in our day and time. We practice the way of Jesus in order to partner with Him in the *tikkun olam*, the repair of the world. Our best days lie before us.

As we move forward, take some time to consider what the living God is saying to you. What is He asking you to do? Who will you share this with, and when? Remember, the cave you fear to enter holds the treasure you seek. Let's be people of the Word. Let's build these rhythms into our lives and allow the Word of God to renew our minds. Let's be serious about it.

Like Father, Like Son

As Jesus chooses His disciples, He chooses like His Father, the living God, does.

In antiquity, the firstborn son had preeminence, receiving a double portion of the inheritance.[10] And it was the fertile, fruitful woman who held value.

But as you recall the Story we have explored together, who does the living God choose to partner with Him? It's not Cain, it's Abel. It's not Ishmael, it's Isaac. It's not Esau, it's Jacob. It's David, the youngest of eight boys.

Isaac and Jacob were second-born sons married to barren women. The living God doesn't choose who we would choose.

Empowered by the Spirit

In the Gospels, the disciples learn Jesus' way, His *halakha*. Now, at the beginning of Acts, they know His way and need the power to live it out. Acts to Revelation tells the story of the followers of Jesus seeking to be just like Him in the world.

After the resurrection, Jesus walks around for forty days, speaking about the kingdom of God. On one occasion while eating with His disciples, He instructs them not to leave Jerusalem, but to wait for the gift His Father promised them. The gift was the infilling of the Holy Spirit, which happens on what is known as Pentecost. Remember, God's original plan was to plant Avraham and the Israelites in the Promised Land in proximity to the International Coastal Highway; this resulted in the nations *coming to* them. At Pentecost, this gets reversed. Jesus tells His followers that when they receive the gift of the Spirit, they will be His witnesses in Jerusalem, Judea and Samaria, and all the way to the ends of the earth. They will *go to* the nations.

Acts 1 happens in Jerusalem. By the end of Acts, the gospel has reached Rome.

As it was with the early followers of Jesus, we too are meant to be a people informed by the Word of God and empowered by the Spirt of God to bring heaven to earth.

We live between the two comings or visitations of Jesus. The plan wasn't for Him to come just once; He is going to come again. We live with the hopefulness of His second coming.

Remember, the Story of the Bible is of the living God coming closer and closer. *Hovering* at creation. *Down* in the desert. *Toward* through Jesus. *In* at Pentecost. The Spirit within us empowers us to walk out the way of Jesus.

Three Snapshots

Acts through Revelation contain story after story of Jesus' followers being like Him as best as they can, partnering with Him to take the gospel to the ends of the earth, to places like Corinth and Thessaloniki. We will now look at three snapshots that illustrate the disciples walking out what it means to be followers of Jesus.

Rise Up and Walk!

Our first snapshot comes from Acts 3. Peter and John, two of the original twelve apostles, go up to the Temple in Jerusalem at 3:00 p.m., the time of the evening *tamid* sacrifice. Their actions here remind us that the earliest followers of Jesus remained Jewish after Jesus' resurrection; they continued with Jewish liturgy and practice. A man lame from birth asks them for money. Keep in mind that for years they watched Rabbi Jesus go through the Galilee teaching and healing. Pentecost happened shortly before this scene in the Temple. As this lame man requests Peter and John give him money, I like to imagine them saying, "This is our opportunity to do what Jesus did!" I'll be honest, I might have requested to practice on a guy at home, just to make sure this new power from on high worked! After all, everybody lives in Jerusalem; this was an extremely public moment. Peter and John choose to act like Jesus, commanding the man to walk. Peter takes him by the hand, and he begins walking, leaping, and praising God. In our first snapshot, all who see are amazed!

Riot in Ephesus

The next snapshot comes from Acts 19 and takes place in Ephesus, one of the largest and most important cities in the Roman Empire. To understand the magnitude and wealth of Ephesus, the Great Theater at Ephesus was built to hold nearly 25,000 people. Often, the theater in a city could hold approximately 10

The Great Theater at Ephesus

The Colosseum in Rome, Italy, is the largest ancient amphitheater ever built

percent of the city's population. If that was true for Ephesus, the city had around 250,000 residents.

Greco-Roman cities typically had a god or patron deity believed to give them power, provide sun and rain, etc. The patron deity of Ephesus was the goddess Artemis. The Temple of Artemis at Ephesus, with its 127 columns, was known as one of

Hellenistic theater at Pergamum, built during the third century BC

All that remains of the once-spectacular Temple of Artemis at Ephesus

the Seven Wonders of the Ancient World. The wealth of Ephesus allowed the city to be one of only a handful that were lit at night.

The apostle Paul, whose Hebrew name is Saul, makes his way to Ephesus. He is of the tribe of Benjamin. This may sound familiar, as we have previously seen a Saul of the tribe of Benjamin in the Old Testament.

Jewish Paul speaks boldly about the kingdom of God in the Vegas-like city of Ephesus. Through the power of the Holy Spirit, he performs many miracles. Some of the people who believe Paul's message stop worshipping Artemis, and this proves problematic for the economy, as it interrupts the sale of Artemis shrines and other goddess-related trinkets. When the silversmith Demetrius explains this predicament to fellow craftsmen and trade

Library of Celsus at Ephesus, built in the second century AD

Ruins of ancient streets at Ephesus

Temple of Artemis model at the Ephesus Museum

workers, warning that the temple and glory of Artemis will be discredited, the people angrily shout, "Great is Artemis of the Ephesians!"[11] Paul has caused what I like to call a gospel ruckus. The people rush into the theater. Again, they shout, "Great is Artemis of the Ephesians!"—for nearly two hours.[12] One of the largest Greco-Roman cities in the ancient world has been turned upside down because of Paul's willingness to be a follower of Jesus, not just a believer.

Raised to Life

The third snapshot comes from the next chapter, Acts 20. Paul is preaching in a home as the followers gather to break bread. He preaches so long that

Eutychus, who sits in the window listening, sinks into a deep sleep, falls out the third-story window, and dies. What I love about Paul in this moment is that he so understands the *tikkun olam* that he goes downstairs, raises Eutychus from the dead, and returns upstairs to eat and continue teaching! As if everything that had just happened was perfectly normal!

Interestingly, *Eutychus* means "happy" or "fortunate." His name certainly describes his destiny in this story. Eutychus is another Lazarus. Everyone who sees him bears witness to the miracle.

Paul embodies the reality that we don't just want to know what Jesus knows, we want to be like Him as we engage the world.

Take the Adventure

One of my favorite quotes comes from a character in C.S. Lewis's *The Lion, the Witch and the Wardrobe*, who says, "Let us go on and take the adventure that shall fall to us."[13] The Bible is filled with stories of those who took their adventures. It's our time to take ours.

When I was sixteen, an adventure found me. I learned about a world-famous archaeologist in Israel named Dr. Gabriel Barkay. For some reason, I really honed in on him. I read about him in *Biblical Archaeology Review* and any other resources I could find. Dr. Gabi discovered the silver scroll amulets that contain the priestly benediction[14] and are the oldest portion of Scripture ever found, predating the Dead Sea Scrolls by 400 years.

Many years later, in the fall of 2007, I was on a flight headed to Cairo to study in Egypt and Israel for the first time. I remember thinking, *I'm going to Jerusalem—that's where Dr. Gabi Barkay lives. Wouldn't it be wild if I was walking down the street one day and saw him?*

After our time in Egypt, we arrived in Israel and were in Jerusalem for study. I was a nerd then, too, so wherever my profs were, I was right by them, taking notes and asking questions. My prof was speaking with someone on the phone and told the person we would see them that afternoon. I assumed we were going to hear someone give a lecture later that day.

We continued on to the site and waited for our speaker to show up. The next moments were like something from the movies. I looked up, and there he was: Dr. Gabi Barkay! I could not believe it! I had about twenty seconds to figure out what I was going to do before he walked on by. Should I sit back and take a picture? Or act crazy and make a fool of myself? Maybe both? I reached down in my bag to get my camera and when I looked back up, Dr. Barkay was talking to my prof. It was then that I realized *he* was who we were there to hear!

This was my first time in Israel, so I didn't recognize we were at Ketef Hinnom, the famous site where Dr. Barkay discovered the silver amulet scrolls. As we sat listening and taking notes, he gave an hour-long lecture, pointing out landmarks and telling the story.

I was freaking out the entire time! This man whom I had followed from the time I was a young girl stood thirty feet from me. The reality that I, who had been grown up in a Southern culture that did not embrace women studying theology or archaeology, or teaching Bible, was in Jerusalem with a world-famous archaeologist, at the very site that made him legendary, was mind-blowing.

This is who the living God is; this is what He is like.

Dr. Gabi finished his lecture and, once again, I had some decisions to make. Should I go straight to "May I have your autograph?" Or "May I have your autograph *and* a picture?" I decided to somewhat play it

Dr. Gabi Barkay lecturing at Ketef Hinnom, March 2018

Dr. Gabi Barkay and Kristi at Ketef Hinnom, March 2018

Dr. Gabi Barkay lecturing at Ketef Hinnom, March 2019

cool. I walked up to him and said, "Dr. Barkay, I've followed your work since I was sixteen years old. I'm from Mississippi back in the States." He looked at me thoughtfully. We started talking, and I was trying not to make a fool of myself. He asked me what I liked to read; I told him the Mishnah and Talmud—which totally shocked him!

He asked if I planned to come back to the land; I told him I certainly hoped to. Dr. Gabi then handed me his number, saying, "If you come back, please call me. I give lectures here." On the inside, I was going nuts! But I was still playing it cool on the outside. I asked if I could give him my number too, so that if I called him, he would know it was me and answer. After we exchanged numbers, I forgot to ask for my autograph, but I did get a picture!

One day after I had been home from studying in Egypt and Israel for a few months, I was sitting with my friends and my phone rang. I looked down, and the screen flashed, "Dr. Gabi Barkay." I couldn't believe it! My friends said, "Answer the phone!" Again, I was totally freaking out. I let it ring five or so times before calmly answering, "Hello, this is Kristi." Dr. Gabi said he and his wife, Esther, had been talking about me, and he wanted to call and see how I had been doing.

I began taking teams to Israel in 2008. From that first team on, Dr. Barkay has come to the Begin Center in Jerusalem and given that one-hour lecture to our teams! Several years ago, after one of the lectures, I asked Dr. Gabi if he would ever come to Tennessee and do a symposium. He thought for a moment and said, "I've always wanted to stay at the Opryland Hotel." To date, we have brought him to Tennessee three times. We treated him and Esther to a unique Opryland Hotel experience, with a room overlooking the waterfalls! I've taken him to an orthodox synagogue in Nashville and experienced his faith in that context.

Once when in Tennessee Dr. Gabi said, "Kristi, I've always wanted to visit a…" but he couldn't quite come up with the word. I thought he might say the replica of the Parthenon in Nashville, but much to my surprise, he eventually said, "I've always wanted to go to a honky-tonk." That was the last place I expected him to say! To be clear, I had never been to a honky-tonk either. On a weekday afternoon, I took this world-famous archaeologist to a honky-tonk in Nashville! Only the living God could have written this script.

Nashville billboard advertising "Jerusalem Uncovered" with Dr. Gabi Barkay, February 2019

Where do you take a renowned Israeli archaeologist when he comes to visit Nashville, Tennessee?
To Cracker Barrel, of course!

Fast-forward to 2020 when COVID hit, and I couldn't go to Israel for two-and-a-half years. During that time, Dr. Gabi developed an auto-immune disease and couldn't speak for six months. When I heard that he had improved enough to be able to speak again, I called to check on him. In the course of that conversation, he said, "Kristi, I'm not the man I used to be." I told him he was still every bit of the man I had known and loved since I was sixteen. It was a moment where I got to share my soul with him and express gratitude at being able to meet and learn from him, to walk with him for years and bring him to Tennessee.

In March 2022, I was finally able to take a team back to Israel. For the first time in fourteen years, Dr. Gabi was not able to meet with us at the Begin Center and give his lecture. I share that story because so much has been gained and so much has been lost through that experience. An era is over, but I will continue to go on and take the adventures that come to me.

You never know where the adventure is going to take you. Be a person who says yes when it comes, no matter what it is going to cost you, regardless of what you may gain or lose. Be a person who *follows* Jesus, not just believes in Him.

A New Heaven and Earth

As we close out this journey together, let's look at Revelation 21–22. I cannot imagine the Bible without these passages. The living God, in His faithfulness, gives a vision of what the Jews call the world to come, what Christians refer to as heaven.

As mentioned earlier, Jewish people don't tend to talk about heaven or the afterlife. They are very much focused on the here and now, bringing heaven to earth, cleansing and repairing the world. We are invited to take Jesus at His words from the Sermon on the Mount: "Your kingdom come… on earth as it is in heaven."[15]

Revelation 21–22 gives us hopeful expectation of the world to come, the heaven that, according to the Bible, comes down to us:

> I saw "a new heaven and a new earth," for the first heaven and the first earth had passed away, and there was no longer any sea. I saw the Holy City, the new Jerusalem, coming down out of heaven from God, prepared as a bride beautifully dressed for her husband. And I heard a loud voice from the throne saying, "Look! God's dwelling place is now among the people, and he will dwell with them. They will be his people, and God himself will be with them and be their God. He will wipe every tear from their eyes. There will be no more death or mourning or crying or pain, for the old order of things has passed away." He who was seated on the throne said, "I am making everything new!" Then he said, "Write this down, for these words are trustworthy and true." He said to me: "It is done. I am the Alpha and the Omega, the Beginning and the End."[16]

We are headed here. We must go on and take the adventures that will fall to us. We are not here to simply believe in Jesus; we are here to follow Him—to actively participate in heaven coming to earth, the *tikkun olam*, the repair of the world. The goodness of heaven will be brought to earth through you and me—all because of Him.

RECOMMENDED RESOURCES

Bailey, Kenneth E. *Jesus Through Middle Eastern Eyes: Cultural Studies in the Gospels*. Westmont: IVP Academic, 2008.

Burge, Gary M. *The New Testament in Antiquity: A Survey of the New Testament Within Its Cultural Context*. Grand Rapids: Zondervan Academic, 2009.

Hoffman, Alice. *The Dovekeepers*. New York: Scribner, 2011.

Joy, Rebekah. *Wealth of the Wilderness: A Middle Eastern Pathway for Transformation Through Difficult Seasons*. Nashville: Midbar Press, 2020.

Maier, Paul L. *Pontius Pilate*. Grand Rapids: Kregel Publications, 2014.

NIV Archaeological Study Bible: An Illustrated Walk Through Biblical History and Culture. Grand Rapids: Zondervan, 2006.

NIV Cultural Backgrounds Study Bible: Bringing to Life the Ancient World of Scripture. Grand Rapids: Zondervan, 2016.

NIV First-Century Study Bible: Explore Scripture in Its Jewish and Early Christian Context. Grand Rapids: Zondervan, 2014.

Richter, Sandra L. *The Epic of Eden: A Christian Entry into the Old Testament*. Westmont: IVP Academic, 2008.

Tverberg, Lois. *Reading the Bible with Rabbi Jesus: How a Jewish Perspective Can Transform Your Understanding*. Grand Rapids: Baker Books, 2017.

Wright, N.T. and Michael F. Bird. *The New Testament in Its World: An Introduction to the History, Literature, and Theology of the First Christians*. Grand Rapids: Zondervan Academic, 2019.

NOTES

An Invitation to Feast on the Best and Truest Story Ever Told

1. Gary M. Burge, *Jesus and the Jewish Festivals* (Grand Rapids, MI: Zondervan Academic, 2012), 11.

Chapter 1: Israel: Name. Nation. Place.

1. They do so based on Deuteronomy 8:10: "When you have eaten and are satisfied, praise the LORD your God for the good land he has given you."

2. The beginning of nearly every blessing in modern Judaism is "Blessed are you, Oh Lord our God, King of the Universe…," signifying that God is the one receiving the blessing, not the item.

3. Today, *Middle East* serves as a political term, while scholarship uses *Ancient Near East* (*ANE*) to differentiate a similar geographical area. I have chosen to use the more familiar term *Middle East* throughout this book.

4. Psalm 19:7-8, 10, emphasis added.

5. In Hebrew, this word can also mean "fool," "naïve," or "lacking wisdom," depending on the context. The Hebrew Lexicon of Brown, Driver, Briggs says "simple, possibly as open-minded."

6. Psalm 19:10.

7. The tradition of using honey started in the Middle Ages. The teacher would make use of a board with the Hebrew alphabet on it and cover it with honey, which served as a reminder of the sweetness of learning. From Marvin Wilson: "Rabbinic tradition informs us that it was the Jewish practice to use honey in a special ceremony on the first day of school. The young child was shown a slate which had written on it the letters of the alphabet, two verses of Scripture (Lev. 1:1, Deut. 33:4), and one other sentence: 'The Torah will be my calling.' The teacher next read these words to the child, and the child repeated them back. Then his slate was coated with honey, which he promptly licked off, being reminded of Ezekiel, who said after eating the scroll, 'I ate it; and it tasted as sweet as honey in my mouth' (Ezek. 3:3). After this ceremony, the child was given sweet cakes to eat with Bible verses from the Torah written on them" (Marvin Wilson, "The Sweetness of Learning," *Jerusalem Perspective*, January 1, 1992, https://www.jerusalemperspective.com/2634/#note-2634-6).

8. For an excellent resource on this concept, I highly recommend Eugene Peterson's *Eat This Book* (Grand Rapids, MI: Wm. B. Eerdmans, 2009).

9. Walter Brueggemann has much to say on the topic of abundance and scarcity in his article "The Liturgy of Abundance, the Myth of Scarcity: Consumerism and Religious Life." In it, he states: "We say it takes money to make money; Paul says it takes poverty to produce abundance. Jesus gave himself to enrich others, and we should do the same." https://sanantonioreport.org/wp-content/uploads/2016/09/the_liturgy_of_abundance.pdf, accessed June 19, 2022.

10. Jesus uses the metaphor of a foundation in His conclusion of the Sermon on the Mount (Matthew 7:24-27).

11. "Canaan and Ancient Israel," *University of Pennsylvania Museum*, https://www.penn.museum/sites/canaan/Home%26Family.html, accessed June 19, 2022.

12. See 1 Samuel 8:5.

13. When traveling in the Middle East today, if I approach a person and ask them their name, they will typically reply with their name *and* its meaning. Middle Easterners take great pride in their name.

14. In fact, we see this from the very beginning in Genesis 3:8-9, when God asks, "Where are you?" God is a seeker.

15. Genesis 18:19.

16. Leviticus 19:9-10; 23:22; Deuteronomy 24:19-21; Ruth 2:1-3.

17. Exodus 22:21; 23:9; Leviticus 19:34.

18. Genesis 12:3: "...and all peoples on earth will be blessed through you."

19. Genesis 1:2.

20. Exodus 40:34-38.

21. John 1:14.

22. Acts 2:4.

23. There are differing rules regarding the naming of a girl. It could be the next time Torah is read in synagogue (Monday, Thursday, Saturday), or the third day, fifth day, etc. It depends on the traditions of the family/community.

24. Exodus 3:6.

25. For example, Exodus 3:6, 15, 16; 4:5; Acts 3:13; 7:32.

26. Genesis 17:5.

27. Genesis 21:3, 6.

28. Genesis 25:26.

29. Genesis 27:1-29.

30. Genesis 32:26.

31. Genesis 27.

32. Genesis 22:11-13; 46:1-4; Exodus 3:1-10; 1 Samuel 3:9-10; Luke 10:38-42; 22:31-34; Acts 9:1-6.

33. John 4.

Chapter 2: Middle Eastern Lens

1. Psalm 3:3.

2. Genesis 2:7; John 20:22.

3. *Song of Songs Rabbah* 1:10—"Another matter, 'your cheeks are lovely with ornaments,' when they explore the *halakha* with each other, like Rabbi Abba bar Mimi and his colleagues. 'Your neck with beads,' when they would string together matters of Torah, from Torah to Prophets, and from Prophets to Writings, and fire is ignited around them, and the matters were as joyful as when they were given from Sinai. At their primary giving from Mount Sinai, were they not given in fire, as it is stated: 'The mountain was burning with fire to the heart of the heavens' (Deuteronomy 4:11)?"

4. Matthew 16:13.

5. Ruled by Phillip the Tetrarch from 4 BC to AD 34, Caesarea Philippi followed closely the Imperial and Pan cults. In fact, Philip was the first "Jewish" ruler of the area to issue human portraits on coins, considered by Jews of the day as a form of idolatry and extremely offensive (see Exodus 20:4).

6. For example, Matthew 8:13; Mark 1:30-34; Luke 8:43-48; John 5:8-9.

7. John 11:53.

8. See Luke 8:54-55.

9. Bethany lay as close to Jerusalem as one could get without being in the city limits.

10. Matthew 8:2-4.

11. David Bivin, *New Light on the Difficult Words of Jesus* (Holland, MI: En-Gedi Resource Center, 2005), 93-94.

12. See Exodus 3:2-3.

13. In fact, in biblical Hebrew, all words are formed by verbs; the language centers on action—what someone or something is doing. This is also why Hebrew sentences in the Bible almost always begin with the verb, and then the subject follows.

14. Exodus 3:7.

15. We also see this in the life of Jesus. In John 11:35, Jesus weeps with and for Lazarus's family. He does the same for us.

16. Protagoras: "Of all things the measure is Man, of the things that are, that they are, and of the things that are not, that they are not" (DK80b1).

17. Genesis 15:6; Romans 4:3; Galatians 3:6; James 2:23.

18. Jonah 1:2.

19. F.P. Retief and L. Cilliers, "The history and pathology of crucifixion," *PubMed.gov*, https://pubmed.ncbi .nlm.nih.gov/14750495/; accessed June 24, 2022.

20. As evidenced in reliefs and hinted at in 2 Kings 19:28.

21. See Jonah 4:2.

22. Jonah 4:11.

23. Genesis 15:1; 1 Samuel 15:10; 1 Kings 17:2; Isaiah 38:4.

Chapter 3: Genesis—Deuteronomy

1. Remember, through *Rediscovering Israel*, you are being invited to see Scripture through a different cultural lens...a Middle Eastern lens.

   You have already been invited to take a fresh look at the book of Jonah, a story that has very little to do with Jonah or a whale!

   Here is an invitation to perhaps rediscover Genesis 3 and 4, recognizing that "sin" is not mentioned in Genesis 3 as is so often taught or assumed through a Western lens. Rather, it is used for the first time in the Bible in Genesis 4:7 when the Lord is cautioning Cain: "But if you do not do what is right, sin is crouching at your door; it desires to have you, but you must rule over it."

   Shortly before Adam and Eve eat the fruit, Genesis 2 ends with: "Adam and his wife were both naked, and they felt no shame" (v. 25). What is implied in Genesis 3 through Adam and Eve covering their nakedness after eating the fruit is that *shame* first enters the story here.

   How various translations title Genesis 3 is intriguing. For example, the NIV and KJV call it "The Fall"; the NASB "The Fall of Mankind," and the NLT "The Man and Woman Sin." In contrast, the Tree of Life Version titles Genesis 2:25 through Genesis 3 "From Innocence to Shame," hearkening back to a Middle Eastern world of honor/shame.

2. *Canaan* means "trader/merchant," but can also mean "humble." Also, Canaan was the son of Ham and grandson of Noah, and his descendants resided in the Promised Land.

3. As illustrated by the prophets of Baal and Asherah in the showdown with Elijah on Mount Carmel in 1 Kings 18.

4. This heinous act was probably quite rare. We see glimpses of it in the Bible (Genesis 22; Judges 11; Ezekiel 16:20). We also read of how *not* to be like the other people (see Leviticus 18:21; 20:1-3; Deuteronomy 12:31; 18:10).

5. See Ellen F. Davis's *Getting Involved with God: Rediscovering the Old Testament*, as well as this article /sermon: https://faithandleadership.com/ellen-f-davis-radical-trust.

6. This is attested in numerous biblical passages (for example, Genesis 34:20; Ruth 4:1-2; Proverbs 31:23).

7. Genesis 23:9-11.

8. Genesis 23:14-15.

9. 2 Samuel 24:21-24; 2 Chronicles 3:1.

10. Exodus 15:22-26.

11. Exodus 16.

12. Exodus 16:31.

13. Deuteronomy 25:18.

14. Exodus 17:8-16.

15. Exodus 19:1-2.

16. Genesis 22:17.

17. Hosea 2:14-20.

18. In fact, they recite these verses from Hosea when they wrap the tefillin (phylacteries—prayer boxes) around their fingers and arms.

19. See Exodus 32.

20. Exodus 32:26-28.

21. Acts 2:41.

22. Rabbi Jonathan Sacks, "From slavery to freedom: Rediscovering the meaning of Passover," *ABC*, updated September 24, 2020, https://www.abc.net.au/religion/rediscovering-the-meaning-of-pass over/11029104, accessed June 19, 2022.

23. See Numbers 14:34.

Chapter 4: Joshua—Ruth

1. Joshua 3:10.

2. See Joshua 1:13.

3. This phrase occurs an astounding four times in the first chapter of Joshua and three times in Deuteronomy 31!

4. Joshua 1:9.

5. *Theos* is Greek for "God," and *krateo* is Greek for "to rule."

6. Exodus 14:21.

7. Though we do not know the exact location of Adam, it likely stood where the Jabbok meets the Jordan River, within a range of 17-30 miles!

8. Joshua 5:12.

9. Many consider Jericho to be one of the oldest fortified cities in the world, testifying to its strength in location and resources. See Kathleen Kenyon, "Excavations at Jericho," *JSTOR*, Vol. 84, No. 1/2 (Jan. - Dec. 1954), 103-110, and Bryan Windle, "Biblical Sites: Three Discoveries at Jericho, *Bible Archaeology Report*, May 25, 2019, https://biblearchaeologyreport.com/2019/05/25/biblical-sites-three-discoveries-at-jericho/, accessed July 4, 2022.

10. A *tell* or *tel* is an artificial hill made of strata and layers of civilizations built upon one another.

11. Joshua 8:30-35.

12. Genesis 12:6-7.

13. *Babylonian Talmud* 23b, 18.

14. Joshua 8:34.

15. *Daily Press*, Newport News, VA, March 18, 1962, 24.

16. Joshua 23:14.

17. Joshua 23:10.

18. Judges 17:6; 18:1; 19:1; 21:25.

19. See Judges 2:7-13.

20. *Shimshon* comes from the Hebrew word for "sun," *shemesh*.

21. We know, for example, that both Samuel and John the Baptist appear to submit to lifelong Nazirite vows in 1 Samuel 1:11 and Luke 1:15 respectively, as do Samson's parents, inferred from Judges 13:7. In Acts 18:18, the apostle Paul appears to take a Nazirite vow for a season. He also pays for the sacrifices of four others appearing to take Nazirite vows in Acts 21:23-24.

22. The Hebrew word translated "feast" also means "drinking bout." And, let's face it, he kills the lion in a vineyard.

23. See John 2:1-12.

24. Judges 16:1-22.

25. Matthew 6:22.

26. Judges 16:23-30.

27. Hebrews 11:32.

28. Ruth 1:1-5.

29. Ruth 1:16.

30. See Deuteronomy 25:5-10.

31. See Ruth 4:9-10.

Chapter 5: 1 Samuel—1 Kings

1. It could also mean "his name is God (*El*)."

2. 1 Samuel 3:3.

3. 1 Samuel 3:7.

4. 1 Samuel 3:9.

5. 1 Samuel 3:19-21.

6. See Genesis 1:2.

7. Though difficult to narrow down Philistine history, they likely come from the Aegean Sea region and should be associated with the "Sea Peoples" who fought the Egyptians. For further reading, see *Anchor Yale Bible Dictionary*, "Philistines" by H.J. Katzenstein and Trude Dothan.

8. See Joshua 3.

9. Exodus 20:7 (NKJV).

10. 1 Samuel 6:17.

11. We see this several times between the Philistines and Israelites (I Samuel 17:51; 31:9), and throughout the Bible and Ancient Near East as attested in several reliefs.

12. 1 Samuel 5:6-7, emphasis added.

13. Exodus 15 marks the first time the metaphor of kingship is used for God.

14. See 1 Samuel 8:10-18.

15. Saul means "asked [for]"—as in, "You asked for it!" God has a sense of humor. Note that Saul's name means "question," and he questions *everything*!

16. 1 Samuel 16:1-13.

17. We see examples of this in the *Iliad* with Achilles defeating Hector and the fight between Menelaus and Paris. In Egyptian lore, *The Tale of Sinuhe* features a similar scene between Sinuhe and an enemy.

18. 1 Samuel 17:39b.

19. See 1 Samuel 17:46.

20. 2 Samuel 8.

21. 1 Kings 9:15.

22. 2 Samuel 7.

23. Mark 3:24.

Chapter 6: The Divided Kingdom

1. 1 Kings 4:25.

2. Deuteronomy 10:20; 11:22; 13:4.

3. See Leviticus 18:21; 20:1-5; 2 Kings 23:10; Jeremiah 32:35.

4. See 1 Kings 11:13

5. 1 Kings 12:25

6. Matthew 12:25.

7. See 1 Kings 12:26-33.

8. "Bull statuette," *The Israel Museum*, https://www.imj.org.il/en/collections/371859, accessed July 18, 2022.

9. 2 Kings 17:24.

10. Some of the northern tribes kept their tribal identification. In the New Testament, Anna was from the tribe of Asher (see Luke 2:36). Barnabas (Joseph) was from the tribe of Levi (see Acts 4:36).

11. See 1 Kings 16:25; 2 Kings 8:18; 13:2.

12. 2 Kings 25:1-21.

13. Jeremiah 29:12-14.

Chapter 7: The Remnant Returns

1. Jeremiah 25:11-12.

2. Recall our discussion of this in chapter 2.

3. "Biblical Hebrew includes only about 8,000 words, far fewer than the 400,000 or more we have in English. Paradoxically, the richness of Hebrew comes from its poverty. Because this ancient language has so few words, each one is like an overstuffed suitcase, bulging with extra meanings that it must carry in order for the language to fully describe reality." Lois Tverberg, *Walking in the Dust of Rabbi Jesus: How the Jewish Words of Jesus Can Change Your Life* (Grand Rapids, MI: Zondervan, 2012), Kindle edition.

4. The book of Ruth prominently exemplifies what *hesed* (also spelled *chesed*) looks like with skin on. We also see it in Hosea 6:6—"I desire *hesed*, not sacrifice"—and translators most often use the English term "mercy," from the Greek word *eleos*, when Jesus quotes this passage in Matthew 9:13 and 12:7.

5. See Exodus 12:36.

6. The term *Israelite*, though still attested during this period of history, begins to shift to *Jew*, from the

Persian name of the province of the conquered kingdom of Judah, *Jehud*. People from Judah become Jews. This term appears predominantly in Ezra, Nehemiah, and Esther.

7. See Exodus 29:38-39.

8. See Mark 15:25.

9. Mark 15:33-37.

10. Nehemiah 1:4-6.

11. The prophets speak primarily against walls—see Isaiah 22:8-11 (written while Hezekiah builds a wall around Jerusalem) and Zechariah 2:3-5. In their view, God serves as the protection or "wall" around a city. Kings and priests desire them as practical protection against invasion.

12. Nehemiah 2:2.

13. Ephesians 4:26.

14. Nehemiah 6:15.

15. This rethinking of life outside of a homeland by the Jews in Babylon aids the Jewish people significantly when, from AD 70 onward, they find themselves once again without God's house and outside of Jerusalem.

Chapter 8: The Intertestamental Period

1. See Mark 5:1-20 and 8:1-13.

2. Protagoras of Abdera (c. 485–415 BC) is credited with the line from two different sources. See Plato's *Theaetetus* 160d.

3. Abraham Joshua Heschel, *God in Search of Man* (New York: Farrar, Straus and Giroux, 1983), 34.

4. For more, check out Kristi's *Gospel on the Ground* Bible study (Nashville, TN: Lifeway, 2022).

5. Spelled *Beth Shan* in most English translations.

6. See Josephus, *The Jewish War*, 2.466-471.

7. "Make them [the words of the Law (Torah)] not a crown wherewith to magnify thyself or a spade wherewith to dig. And thus used Hillel to say: He that makes worldly use of the crown shall perish. Thus thou mayest learn that he that makes a profit out of the words of the Law removes his life from the world" (Mishnah, Aboth 4:5, Danby translation).

8. See Josephus, *Antiquities*, 17.42.

9. See John 11:49.

10. In fact, archaeologists have discovered weights that prove inaccurate in their measurements.

11. Josephus, *The Jewish War*, 2.147-149.

12. For a fascinating look at this story, read 1 Maccabees 1–4.

13. First mentioned in Daniel 9:27.

14. See John 10:22-23.

15. This division among generals is known as the *Diadochi*, "Successors."

16. See 1 Maccabees 1:48.

17. See Exodus 25:31-40 for a description of this lampstand.

Chapter 9: Herod the Great

1. See Matthew 2:1-18.

2. Josephus, *The Jewish War*, 1.21.13.

3. Josephus, *Antiquities*, 15.3.8.

4. Josephus, *The Jewish War*, 1.18.4.

5. Scholars call these "allusions."

6. See Exodus 1:15–2:10.

7. Notice Matthew's use of Hosea 11:1 in Matthew 2:15.

8. See Josephus, *Antiquities*, 18.5.2.

9. Even though Herod's Temple far exceeds Zerubbabel's in expanse and grandeur, people continue to call it the Second Temple because sacrifices never ceased on the altar in the midst of rebuilding. See Leen Ritmeyer, "Locating the Original Temple Mount," *BAS Library*, March/April 1992.

10. As used in 2 Samuel 22:2; Psalm 18:2; 31:3; 71:3; 91:2; and 144:2.

11. Josephus, *The Jewish War*, 7.9.1.

12. See Josephus, *The Jewish War*, 7.8.6.

13. While it is accurate to refer to Jesus as a rabbi, *rabbi* wasn't an official title until post AD 70. *Sage* would be the more academically accepted term.

14. Josephus, *The Jewish War*, I.33.5.

15. Josephus, *The Jewish War*, I.33.7.

16. Acts 12:22.

17. Josephus, *The Jewish War*, XIX.8.2.

Chapter 10: The Gospels: Part 1

1. Compare Paul and Barnabas's words in Acts 13:46 to their actions in Acts 14:1. Paul always went to the Jew first and then to the Gentile.

2. Dualism/ditheism, the idea that God and Satan are equal and opposite, is poor theology.

3. See Matthew 1:23.

4. See Romans 5:12-21 and 1 Corinthians 15:45-49.

5. See Matthew 2:1-3.

6. *Saturnalia* 2:4, 11.

7. See Matthew 2:19-23.

8. See Luke 2:41.

9. See Luke 2:47.

10. See Philippians 2:6-7.

11. Mishnah, *Avot* 5:21.

12. See Matthew 3:1-6 and Mark 1:4-5.

13. Matthew 3:17.

14. See Matthew 4:12-17.

15. Matthew 4:13-16, emphasis added.

16. Isaiah 9:6-7a.

17. See Matthew 4:18–22.

18. The Greek word for "apostle" is the Latin word for "missionary." Both simply mean "sent ones."

Chapter 11: The Gospels: Part 2

1. Matthew 16:13.
2. Matthew 16:16.
3. Because of the worship of Pan at this location, Caesarea Philippi was also known as Panias.
4. Matthew 16:21.
5. There are a few exceptions, but even they function more as "closet disciples," hiding under the cover of darkness or showing up at the last minute (for example, Joseph of Arimathea and Nicodemus).
6. John 11:50.
7. See John 12:2.
8. See Luke 22:39-44.
9. See Matthew 26:45.
10. See Leviticus 21:16-21.
11. Josephus, *Antiquities*, 14.13.10.
12. Josephus, *The Jewish War*, 1.270 (13.10).
13. See Luke 22:51.
14. Verses 1, 6-7, 12-15, 24.
15. See 2 Corinthians 5:17-21.
16. See Matthew 27:51-53.

Chapter 12: *Tikkun Olam*

1. Psalm 119:11.
2. The story as quoted by Sharon Hersh goes like this: "A disciple asks the rebbe, 'Why does Torah tell us to "place these words *upon* your hearts"? Why does it not tell us to place these holy words *in* our hearts?' The rebbe answers, 'It is because as we are, our hearts are closed, and we cannot place the holy words in our hearts. So we place them on top of our hearts. And there they stay until, one day, the heart breaks and the words fall in'" (*The Last Addiction: Own Your Desire, Live Beyond Recovery, Find Lasting Freedom* [Colorado Springs, CO: WaterBrook, 2010], 161).
3. The word *synoptic* comes from the Greek word meaning "seen together."
4. Matthew 13:31.
5. Matthew 6:10.
6. Verse 17.
7. Verse 54.
8. See Mark 2:13-15.
9. 1 Corinthians 1:26-30.
10. Deuteronomy 21:15-17.
11. Acts 19:28.
12. Acts 19:34.
13. C.S. Lewis, *The Lion, the Witch and the Wardrobe* (New York: Scholastic, 1950), 184.
14. See Numbers 6:24-26.
15. See Matthew 6:10.
16. Revelation 21:1-6.

To learn more about Harvest House books and
to read sample chapters, visit our website:

www.HarvestHousePublishers.com

HARVEST HOUSE PUBLISHERS
EUGENE, OREGON